THE GUIDE TO TRAUMA-INFORMED AND EMOTIONALLY MINDFUL CONFLICT PRACTICE

THE GUIDE TO TRAUMA-INFORMED AND EMOTIONALLY MINDFUL CONFLICT PRACTICE

Jeremy A. Rinker

Co-published with the Association for Conflict Resolution

ROWMAN & LITTLEFIELD
LANHAM · BOULDER · NEW YORK · LONDON

Published by Rowman & Littlefield
An imprint of The Rowman & Littlefield Publishing Group, Inc.
4501 Forbes Boulevard, Suite 200, Lanham, Maryland 20706
www.rowman.com

86-90 Paul Street, London EC2A 4NE

British Library Cataloguing in Publication Information available

Library of Congress Cataloging-in-Publication Data Available

ISBN 978-1-5381-6859-2 (cloth)
ISBN 978-1-5381-6860-8 (paper)
ISBN 978-1-5381-6861-5 (electronic)

∞™ The paper used in this publication meets the minimum requirements of American National Standard for Information Sciences—Permanence of Paper for Printed Library Materials, ANSI/NISO Z39.48-1992.

CONTENTS

ACKNOWLEDGMENTS   vii

INTRODUCTION Trauma-Informed Response to Community
Legacies of Violence: Refocusing Peace
Work on Trauma and Emotions to Level
Social Disparity   1

1 PROBLEM SETTING TRAUMA AND EMOTIONS
IN CONFLICT TRANSFORMATION PROCESSES
Trauma, Identity, and Victimhood   29

2 DEVELOPING A TRAUMA-INFORMED LENS
Narrating and Listening to Narration   61

3 CHALLENGING HIERARCHIES THROUGH
TRAUMA STORIES AND USING CONFLICT
AND AMBIGUITY AS TURNING POINTS
What Does It Take to Be an Effective Survivor? 95

4 THE THEORY AND PRACTICE OF
ADDRESSING SYSTEMIC INJUSTICE
On Doing Systems Maintenance as Opposed to Completely
Deconstructing and Rebuilding Broken Systems 121

5 BUILDING A TOOLBOX FOR TRAUMA-
INFORMED CONFLICT PRACTICE   147

AFTERWORD Traumatic Story as Developing Practices of
Resistance *and* Resilience to Socially
Constructed Borders 169

INDEX 185

ABOUT THE AUTHOR 189

ACKNOWLEDGMENTS

"Resentment is like drinking poison and then hoping it will kill your enemies."

Nelson Mandela, Longtime Activist, and
South Africa's First Black President

When I set out to write this practitioner's guide, I doubted that I had the language to articulate the complex interplay between trauma, emotions, and conflict intervention processes. Resentful that my analytical and process-based conflict skills had made negligible impact on those suffering from social conflict, I was thwarted from realizing the critical role played by embracing emotions mindfully and noticing trauma's important role in achieving desired change. As I wrote this guide, although I had spent much time with anti-caste activists trying to understand their strategies and narratives of overcoming marginalization and suffering, I was not sure the realities I experienced in these interactions could effectively capture the complex legacy of trauma and emotions on the protracted nature of conflict many marginalized peoples experience on an everyday basis. Thanks to encouragement from many students and colleagues (as well as series editors) I began to believe this was a book I not only could write, but one that I urgently needed to write. As many people working in marginalized spaces realize, victimhood poisons the possibility of effective movement for change in diversity, equity, and inclusion (DEI). It is because of my frustration around current DEI discourse, and this nudging and encouragement from those that had read other works I had written that you hold this book in your hands now.

Even though this appears at the beginning of this manuscript, it is indeed the last section I wrote in the work before you now. The acknowledgment is also one of the more difficult pieces to write. How do you begin to acknowledge all the people that helped you in your thinking along the way? We are all products of so many others and no one is ever a self-made person, do not let the famous titans of modern neoliberal business and industry fool you into thinking they pulled themselves up by their bootstraps! Everyone is made what they are by others; we are too interconnected as a species to be "self-made." That tired and trite narrative sticks with us like the collective traumas of the past. This book could not have come to press if not for initial internal grant funding from the University of North Carolina Greensboro that took me to a week-long training at Eastern Mennonite University called Strategies for Trauma Awareness and Resilience (STAR). It was at STAR I (there are two week-long STAR trainings—I and II—I did both) that I met Dr. Jerry Lawler, a clinical psychologist. Subsequently we published an article together in *Peace and Conflict: The Journal of Peace Psychology*,[1] followed by a co-edited book entitled *Realizing Nonviolent Resistance: Neoliberalism, Societal Trauma, and Marginalized Voice*.[2] This training and these works had an immense impact on my thinking about the missing dimensions of trauma and emotions in our collective understandings of social conflict and conflict intervention. Despite studying the sources and dynamics of conflict for over twenty years, I had learned little about human emotion and the impacts of trauma. Jerry challenged me to think in new ways about traumatic sequalae, and even if we wear our political stripes in drastically different ways, we developed a friendship through an accountable writing process that spurred critical thinking and insightful analysis.

Then Covid hit. What a traumatic disruption to so many of our lives. Sitting in my home office and zooming into the 2020 ACR conference I decided to go to an information session about this very book series. There I met Michael Lang and Susan Terry for the first time. I pitched an idea about a book on a restorative youth-based sports project that a colleague and I were then trying to re-ignite after Covid impacts. Uninterested in the case I describe, it was clear that the series editors were interested in comments I made in passing about the collective traumas of these underserved high school students I was working with in the project. From that Covid-era starting place the idea of this book was born. Appreciation is also due to mentors Dr. Daniel Rothbart and

Dr. Douglas Fry for their support and encouragement of the project as I went through my own tenure process. Daniel Rhodes, Justin Harmon, Joe Cole, and Gloria Rhodes all also functioned as cheerleaders along the way. Daniel Rhodes (whose excellent photography graces the front cover) has been a long-time partner in crime—that is, if you call running community peace circles together a crime. Drs. P. D. Satya Pal and Vivek Kumar remain important translators of Dalit knowledge, social movement, and passionate collective yearning. Dr. Lalit Khandare regularly suffered through listening to me complain about the writing process and simultaneously acted as a vast source of knowledge on Dalit activism. Friends and students at Symbiosis University in Pune, India, as well as members of the TBMSG, an Ambedkar Buddhist social movement organization that I have been studying for over twenty years, were also instrumental in my thought process while writing this practitioners guide.

Finally, I come to the least appreciated but most important support—my family. To Stephanie Kriner, Kylor, and Tarin, thank you for giving me space and support to not only write but travel and explore a culture that does not see time in the same way that we do. Although your support is always there, I do not say often enough how much I appreciate your support and love you all. It is from a place of love that I authored this book, hoping that my small contribution will help conflict interveners see the importance of past traumas and, often disconcerting, emotions as key resources for lasting intervention and change. Thanks to the many unnamed readers who have helped me hone these ideas over some time. A colleague once told me a book is not required for tenure, but it often takes ten years to write a good one! Although it did not take me this long for the writing of this practitioners' guide, it did take longer than I originally thought it would. I am indebted to so many colleagues, students, activists, and practitioners who encouraged me along the way. I dedicate this work to all those working for peace around the world.

The front cover photo was taken in the Church of the Nativity in Bethlehem, Palestine. The Church of the Nativity is built around the spot believed to be the birthplace of Jesus Christ. Contemporary Bethlehem is home to 25,000 Palestinians and is primarily separated by a wall from the State of Israel. Bethlehem is considered designated as Area A by the Oslo Accords, which means it is primarily controlled by the Palestinian Authority. Palestinians' lives, however, are greatly restricted by the Israeli government and movement in and out of Bethlehem is heavily restricted. Many Western pilgrims visiting Bethlehem are unfamiliar with the apartheid state that Palestinians live under inside of Bethlehem and are often bussed or taxied directly to the Church of Nativity instead of having to undergo the same restrictive protocols that Palestinians endure daily. Although Palestinian suffering is not a focus of this book, the picture articulates well the feeling of bringing traumas and emotions into the light. I thank my friend and colleague, Dr. Daniel Rhodes, for the excellent photography.

Jeremy A. Rinker
Greensboro, NC
April 18, 2024
(My mother's 84th birthday—Happy Birthday Mom!)

NOTES

1. J. Rinker and J. Lawler, "Trauma as a Collective Disease and Root Cause of Protracted Social Conflict." *Peace and Conflict: Journal of Peace Psychology* 24, no. 2 (2018): 150–64.

2. J. Rinker and J. Lawler (eds.), *Realizing Nonviolent Resistance: Neoliberalism, Societal Trauma, and Marginalized Voice* (New York: Peter Lang Publishers, 2020).

INTRODUCTION

Trauma-Informed Response to Community Legacies of Violence: Refocusing Peace Work on Trauma and Emotions to Level Social Disparity

". . . emotion is not opposed to reason; our emotions assign value to experiences and thus are the foundation of reason."[1]

CENTERING TRAUMA, EMOTIONS, AND STORYTELLING IN CONFLICT INTERVENTION PRACTICE

There are two key claims that this book aims to make: 1) that conflict intervention work (especially framed as conflict management and/or resolution) have traditionally been averse to emotions and have framed the "work" as evidence-based and scientific rather than relational and trauma-informed, and 2) that if conflict intervention practitioners want to intervene in the systemic oppressions (conflicts over race, caste, class, gender, etc.) that are the result of rank status inconsistency, and want to alleviate the attenuate structural violence these diverse identities create, then we (conflict practitioners) must deeply explore the past traumatic experiences of collectives in "public peace"[2] processes.

This book is written for those involved in the broad work of conflict intervention practice, and both the above claims require a re-thinking of the "work" of conflict intervention "practice." In our current cultural moment, racial justice activists talk of "doing the work"[3] of antiracism. Borrowing the sentiment that such work is always ongoing and in need of crucial self-reflection, it is critical for artisans of conflict intervention to continually interrogate what we mean by our work or practice. This book is both an interrogation of conflict intervention practice and a guide for more emotionally mindful and trauma-informed conflict intervention work. Such a refocusing of peace work as attentive to trauma and emotions is critical for not only the emerging discipline of conflict resolution, but also for overcoming the ossification of polarized social identity formations.

Attempts to disempower peace work, on either instrumentalist or normative grounds, is often couched in a lack of understanding about the impacts and historic legacies of collective trauma and the emotions that violent events unleash in survivors and their communities. For too long, conflict resolution has been plagued by rationalist assumptions that the emotional resonance of trauma only gets in the way of establishing lasting peace after instances of destructive conflict and violence. An attitude of "get over it" pervades understandings of trauma in most conflict intervention practice and emotions are seen as toxic to sound judgment and rational decision-making.[4] Steeped in interest-based negotiation, traditional mediation practice, and rational choice conflict frameworks, the discipline of peace and conflict studies (PCS), alternatively, often variously termed conflict management or conflict resolution, is often portrayed as a set of skills and practices that can be mastered with a requisite level of training and practice. This book critically explores trauma and human emotions as an under-explored asset or resource in addressing local and entrenched community violence. While best-selling authors, like Van der Kolk (2014) have reminded us that emotions and body movement are critical assets in engaging trauma productively, our dominant paradigm continues to delegitimize trauma and emotions in favor of the rational mind.[5] More than therapeutic, emotional sharing of the past is critical to "reweave the social fabric of relationships torn apart by decades and generations of hatred."[6] While I have already introduced many contested terminologies in this book's first paragraphs, as the reader joins me on the proceeding journey, I promise the terms and ideas I use will become refined and more clear as we proceed. As I pay particular attention to conflict intervention practice at the collective level of conflict many of the insights from a sociological perspective cannot be divorced from my own interior experiences of conflict work. This nexus between the sociological and psychological is vital to the reflective introspection needed for our effective individual conflict practice and compliments well the previous volumes published in this Association for Conflict Resolution (ACR) Practitioner's Guide series.

When describing one's work or practice in the field of peace and conflict studies, words tend to get in the way. What does it mean to be a practitioner? Can we classify all third-party practice under a single term or phrase? Does "peace activism" or peacebuilder encapsulate the combination of mediation, facilitation, clinical therapeutic skills, and reflective/reflexive analytical abilities needed to truly make peace between long-standing enemies with divergent memories, needs, and interests? Whether describing one's work as third-party practitioner, peacebuilder, or peace activist it is easy to be disregarded, or deemed irrelevant, in our contemporary positivist and commodified reality. Assumed to be "subjective," or based on normative assumptions of pacifism or principled nonviolence, conflict resolution is often argued to be a set of replicable skills that require what Donald Schon has called "technical rationality."[7] Understood in common parlance as a set of skills that can be modeled and transferred to others through workshops and trainings, conflict management and resolution are increasingly seen as transferable commodities rather than soft skills that are honed through years of practice and engagement with emotional stress and trauma. Social emotional learning (SEL) and resilience, though increasingly both applied and studied,[8] remain little understood or embraced as implementable policy or action. Like other theory-informed practices in our contemporary neoliberal reality, peace activism too is rationalized and commodified, often in instrumentalist ways. Still, what Joseph Nye (2004) called "soft power"[9] is indeed the critically necessary power to persuade, rather than coerce, in international politics, but too often those studying and purporting the realization of peace, at all levels of society, fail to apprehend that persuasion requires what the South Asian Sanskrit tradition called *rasa*: an elicitation of emotion and feeling in story listeners.

My first graduate degree being in Religious Studies, I can still recall Dr. Lee Seigel's, University of Hawaii's imminent Indianologist, constant refrain in his lectures on the role of rasa in Hinduism's ancient literature: "You have to grasp the meaning and significance of the rasa of the story!" he would intone. More than descriptive of feelings, rasa is the unspeakable spark that elicits feeling in others. It is the social communication of feeling and emotions through the aesthetic medium of art. Rasa has no English language equivalent. "The difference between *tasting* the emotion and experiencing it in real life is summarized by the word rasa" (italics in the original).[10] In theater or literature, rasa is the emotive response that words elicit in an audience of readers or story listeners.

In invoking the concept of rasa, I am especially interested in a particular subset of aesthetics that is more concerned with the concept behind the art than the object of art itself. Often called conceptual art,[11] this form of aesthetics uses what I have defined above as rasa to elicit a response of challenging the status quo in the audience, or what I call here story listeners. By story listeners, I mean to invoke a broad category of social actors—those that are both party to a given conflict and those best described by what Habermas (1991) called the "counterpublic"[12]: those that stand in outward resistance to dominant social conceptions and ideologies. Some have conceived of this category as exceedingly broad—think Bill Ury's articulation of the third side[13] in conflict—but here my focus is on those most directly affected by social conflict. Conflict resolution practitioners at the micro, meso, and macro levels of human conflict must be particularly attentive to both the emotional needs of those that are parties to a conflict and those that are part of resistant counterpublics (often overlapping categories, but not necessarily so). Effective peacebuilders have an ability to both elicit and connect the emotional resources of rasa. For example, Balachandra, et al., (2005) has linked mediation to the improvisation of jazz.[14] Yet, in doing such work, an ability to read emotion and embody trauma are critical, yet, often, under-valued, soft skill sets for mediators and conflict intervenors. This aspect of how to engage emotions and trauma in professional conflict practice is woefully under-explored in Peace and Conflict Studies (PCS) literature and under-addressed in most conflict trainings. This book's aim is to explore and better understand how to engage socially constructed rank status inconsistencies (e.g., race, caste, and class in particular) by being attentive to collective trauma in story and storytelling. Being attentive to such storytelling devices is admittedly a sort of "paradigm shift"[15] in our thinking about such conflicts. As humans, we make meaning through story, but we rarely interrogate the emotive aspects of this meaning making. Stories are an invaluable, and an under-appreciated, means of resistance to systems of oppression. While the list of oppressive systems I mentioned above could certainly be expanded, I privilege these in this book as some of the most prescient examples of systemic oppression and ongoing neo-colonial attitudes in modern culture. These forms of oppression are also ones that I have most experienced in my own practice. Other researchers and practitioners should hone a narrative lens to address other forms of systemic oppression, and I encourage them to do so. Indeed, some have spent considerable time focused on the intersection of socially constructed status inconsistencies and peace—for example see Betty Riordan's works on gender and peace education,[16] or my own work on caste, among others.[17] Still an emphasis on narrative agency in the practice of change has been generally lacking in the conflict resolution discipline.

The objective here is to proactively re-think the role of trauma in peace and justice praxis and find ways to use it as opposed to fear or avoid it. The emotionally mindful and trauma-informed practices that follow aim to foreground stories of nonviolent resistance as central to a reprogramming (or recentering/refocusing) the young discipline of peace and conflict studies around the pro-social power of emotions and trauma. In entertaining this rather eclectic praxis-based endeavor it becomes clear that both systemic oppressions grounded in capitalist and neoliberal norms, as well as stigma towards the practices of mental health provision, impede effective human response and resilience to social conflict. Critical to my approach is the foregrounding of exemplars of localized activism as trauma-informed peacebuilding[18] practice. Using my experiences studying activist resistance to Indian caste discrimination as well as keeping peace circles[19] as a critical peace pedagogy, I develop the opening contours of a collective trauma-informed[20] framework for conflict analysis and resolution practice. In studying the resistance of those that are most proximate to oppression and the impact of oppressive systems, we can develop a theory-informed comparative practice framework for peace in which emotions and trauma are not an afterthought, but a critical foundation. By arguing for a revisioning of trauma's role in building collective resilience and empowering change, I develop a framework for resistance and peace activism in the twenty-first century.

MOVING PAST THE CONFLICT MANAGEMENT PARADIGM

Peace and Conflict Studies as an academic discipline has tended to ignore the trees for the forest. PCS has tried to compensate for its lack of attention to trauma, and psychology more generally, by focusing primarily on social institutions, collective identity, and a depersonalized sense of "human security." This generic term "human security," I argue is a sort of oxymoron. Humans in their natural state are secure;[21] intangible resources like power, greed, honor are what leads to insecurity. While these intangible resources are expressed in uniquely human ways, their absence does not ensure security. True human security requires more than a sense of social and psychological safety, it requires honest public reckoning with the past, empathy for those that have suffered, and an acknowledgement of both historical facts and the need for change so that suffering does not continue. Human security cannot be achieved if the experiences of the marginalized go unvoiced. Such reckoning, empathy, and acknowledgment can be psychologically precarious, messy, and difficult to empirically measure. Change is constant and practitioners must look on change as an ongoing process. Like structural violence, reckoning with collective pasts can be hard to quantify, but we intuitively know past trauma is there.

By exteriorizing conflict's dynamics, peace and conflict studies as a discipline has tried to legitimize itself as a more empirical and objective science and left the fields of psychology and counseling to deal with trauma's interior complexity. As a result, opportunities for integrating past historical trauma into the lexicon of peacebuilding has been overlooked and under attended. In moving past conflict management as a dominant paradigm of conflict practice, we are reclaiming psychology as a lay practice. As conflict practitioners in the twenty-first century we must socially construct a new paradigm of constructive social change. Conflict intervention practitioners do have innate abilities to address trauma and must not shy away from this important background reverberation in all social conflicts. Schon (1984) terms the tendency towards disciplinary specialization a "crisis in the professions."[22] I am attempting to situate our paradigm of specialization more clearly as a de-professionalization of what we as humans intuitively know. It is a call from the laity—a reformation of sorts. Psychological training and credentials are not required to be trauma-informed and emotionally aware in your conflict practice. Fear of re-traumatization should not impede conflict intervenors from exploring and engaging messy traumatic storylines and emotional detritus. We must overcome innate human fears and listen to harm, feel people's affect, and allow space for the uncomfortable realities of those living with the stresses and dehumanization of the marginalized. This, I believe, is true human security.

Paradigm shifts, of the kind that Kuhn (1962) famously describes happening in scientific community,[23] happen in every academic discipline and are especially important to an interdisciplinary field like PCS. Conflict intervention practitioners, thus, must debate theories and take cues for other academic disciplines. For example, sociologists studying social movements must be read closely. Social movement scholars have long argued that cultural framing is critical to effective social change.[24] Despite this, empirical approaches to peace and conflict resolution fail to take into full account the power of emotions, and culturally specific framing, to create change in both individual and collective behavior. Anti-smoking and anti-drug campaigns of the 1990s understood the power of rasa by evoking the fears of poor health and premature death (think of the famous this is your brain on drugs public service advertisement that aired regularly in the late 1980s and early 1990s). Emotional framing is crucial for effective persuasion and social change. Mass resistance to injustice, whether resistance to modern neoliberal forces, or calcified systems of oppression, requires emotional not rational argumentation. This book aims to be an opening shot in the paradigm shift towards humans' reclaimation of the emotional brain. To re-envision the critical importance of trauma and emotion in effective intervention practice at the micro, meso, and macro levels of human conflict is to support innate human security and give privilege to the power of emotional intelligence as on par with rational thought. PCS scholarship has relied too much on interests, needs, problem-solving frameworks, and/ or existing "political opportunity structures"[25] and, in turn, has failed to recognize the emotional impacts of both individual and collective trauma in mobilizing resistant counterpublics. Do not worry, I promise this book will not be too theoretical (though, as you can undoubtedly already tell, I strongly believe good practice requires sound reference to social theory, even if this sound social theory often demands positivist assumptions). What I aim to argue in the forgoing pages is that trauma and emotions are critical for effective conflict intervention practice. This is not just a theoretical exercise; I believe this fresh approach to conflict intervention practice has important implications for the future of humanity. I urge you to keep reading if you are working at any level of intervention in human conflict. I expect, being human, that all of us, in some way, are engaged in some form of conflict intervention work. I further suspect that we all have personal experience with emotions. So, this book is for anyone interested in improving their conflict practice: something we are professionally, but also morally, obligated to do. Whether you are a professional mediator, a lawyer, an academic, or a bereaved spouse, I believe my re-centering of trauma and emotions in conflict dynamic processes will open new insights in your life and work. Haga (2020) cites a veteran of the Fellowship of Reconciliation (FoR) and former marriage counselor as telling him that the one question everyone needs to ask to build strong relationships is "How do my partner's traumas come out, and can I live with that?"[26] We all have some level of trauma in our pasts. Effective conflict practitioners make the space and structure to positively engage these traumas. Existing gaps in the still emerging peace and conflict studies academic discipline threaten to miss important opportunities to both notice and effectively use trauma to constructively engage social conflict. This book aims to not only expose these gaps but also to fill them by empowering practitioners to run towards trauma and emotions, as opposed to running away from them.

WHAT'S AT STAKE IN NOT HAVING A TRAUMA-INFORMED CONFLICT PRACTICE?

As stated above, local peacebuilding after traumatic events has, from its inception, been plagued by rational policy-oriented assumptions that the emotional resonance of trauma only gets in the way of establishing lasting peace after social conflict. In short, trauma and its emotional resonance have been under-appreciated in favor of seemingly more "pragmatic" attempts to manage conflict parties' interests and needs in hopes of restoring social harmony. Most texts on mediation or conflict intervention spend a great deal of time on needs, positions, and interests and little to no time on emotions and affect.[27] The restoring of social harmony requires both emotion and the difficult embrace of past felt traumas. From religious and ethno-nationalist conflict to interpersonal mediation, collective historical trauma "has become fully psychologized"[28] and relegated primarily to the fields of psychiatric therapy or social/political psychology. In proactively re-thinking the role of trauma in peace and justice praxis we set the stage for effectively using trauma stories and emotions in conflict practice. Rather than shy away, conflict resolution practice must embrace trauma and emotions. As a proactive and prosocial response to legitimate critiques of the status quo in society, expressions of identity and collective trauma need to be centered as a source of prosocial peace and resilience. In other words, trauma and emotions must be reset as a resource, not just a problem. Collectively trauma has an amplifying effect and social identities are hardened over not only relative deprivation, but also shared experiences of trauma. Failure to address trauma and emotions circumvents the, however tenuous, possibility of reconciliation. Listening to collective historical traumas is an important form of giving voice to the voiceless and balancing power in conflict. More than mere truth telling, mechanisms in society that can allow for the free expression of shared trauma allow for a collective re-framing of history and its foregoing educative possibilities. This is not an end of history,[29] but a beginning of respecting all experiences of history. Without listening and responding to collective historical trauma it is impossible to ground the social significance of traumatic story and emotions in intervention practice. Without such grounding, attempts at sustainable social and political change are fleeting and intervention, like the violence it is trying to stem, becomes cyclical rather than finite.

Schirch (2001) has argued that cultural and ritualistic approaches to conflict resolution are left in the "theoretical trashbin"[30] by peace scholars and practitioners. Such short-sighted, interest-based, and policy-oriented focus leaves the creative potentials of peace activism unrealized. Steeped in interest-based negotiation, traditional mediations' positivist assumptions and rational choice conflict frameworks, the field of PCS is often portrayed as a set of skills and practices that can be mastered with a requisite level of training and "practice." This view of the discipline has been dominated by a rational worldview that privileges rational choice,[31] individual agency, contact theory,[32] and quotidian notions of positive peace[33] over more complex articulations of moving past conflict that involves re-storying the past and dialogically engaging collectively with experiences of systemic injustice and dominant ideology.[34] As a result, many peacebuilding programs focus on workshops and training as opposed to supporting locally-based dialogue, or discursive analysis of past wrongs as instances of emotional wreckage.[35] More than therapeutic, such emotional sharing of the past is critical to both effective conflict intervention and lasting conflict prevention practice. As a conflict resolution practitioner, it is easy to overlook trauma and emotions having been influenced by the objectivist biases endemic in our western academic culture. Rather than approach trauma and emotions head on we are taught to avoid these difficult conversations in favor of easily observed and quantified data. The following story from my own circle-keeping practice illustrates the pitfalls and missed opportunities of managing rather than proactively engaging emotional trauma.

ON RESISTING THE URGE TO COMFORT EMOTIONAL EXPRESSION

In February 2018, I was leading a group we came to call the *Circles of Pedagogy and Practice Learning Community*, as an inaugural University of North Carolina Greensboro, Institute for Community and Economic Engagement (UNCG/ICEE) faculty fellow. The role, which sounds more official than it really was, came with minimal financial support and aimed to explore the philosophy and pedagogy behind circle process as well as identify their potential uses as a unique form of community building. Of particular interest to this group was how circles could be used both in classrooms and the wider community to foster restorative change and engagement in our local community. As a seasoned practitioner of circle-based facilitated dialogue (also called Native American Council, Community Conferencing, or Family Group Conferencing, among many other names) my goal was to develop a community of practice, support, and co-learning that built on shared values and improved social emotional skills. The topic of discussion during our monthly meetings in a local library was chosen by those in attendance each particular night. The leadership and facilitation of the group was modeled on the egalitarian principles that we were all learning about in circle. Participants were chosen at the end of each meeting to lead the next meeting and facilitate a consensus about what those present wanted to discuss on that evening. No planning was required; the only requirement was that people showed up fully present to engage in authentic conversation. Whether presidential elections, gun violence, or local police response to violence and protest, the only stipulation for the group was that we develop some collective rituals and follow basic circle guidelines[36] for each new night of circle dialogue we began. Central to any such conflict practice is the idea that no two conflict contexts are the same. On this night in February 2018, I was the circle keeper, and the chosen topic of discussion was gun violence. As this was the first learning community meeting following the February 2018 shootings at Parkland High School in Florida, this was a topic in the forefront of many participants' minds.

As I opened the small circle of eight (including myself) I invited participants to share a little about themselves and what they were thinking about the recent news out of Parkland, Florida. As usual the first pass of the talking piece around the circle was full of platitudes and devoid of much emotion or relational connection. Even with a diverse group of participants we are all culturally trained to stifle any emotion in public settings, especially in places where there are people we have just met. Emotional expression is culturally, and colloquially, seen as weakness and even though most in the circle knew each other, there were a few who had just met one another. By the second pass of the talking piece, trust in the group began to grow as people began to express their shared frustration with what seemed like an endless string of mass shootings in the United States. As the emotional charge subtly grew in the room, I hoped to move participants away from broad policy analysis of gun legislation and towards more personal sharing of experience. On the third pass of the talking piece, a smooth stone I had chosen for its unremarkable look, yet captivating feel, I asked participants to share a story of how they have been personally impacted by gun violence. Wanting to understand both the emotions driving our collective frustration I did not know what to expect. On the third pass, once the talking piece came to a professional colleague who was to my immediate right and the last participant to speak, time seemed to slow. After a pregnant pause this colleague and friend launched into a story that none of us in the space that night had heard him narrate before. In fact, he later told me that he had never told that story to anyone. This story completely changed the dynamic of the circle and opened an engaging and heartfelt dialogic connection in the circle participants. The emotional sharing of his traumatic experience was a gift that quickly built relationship, trust, and understanding in the diverse participants of the circle.

As an undergraduate student in the Mid-West, this colleague had been on campus during a university-based school shooting. As I said, he had rarely shared this experience with others. One of his friends was killed in this shooting and many other acquaintances were nearby and psychologically impacted by the experiences on campus that day.

As my colleague began to share his experience, his emotions welled-up into tears and he choked-up, stumbling with his words. Sitting next to him in the circle, my immediate reaction was to comfort and console. As I stretched out my hand to put it on his shoulder and console his grief, I literally stopped my hand in midair and retracted it to my chest. I glanced around the room; had anyone noticed my gesture? Remembering my training at Eastern Mennonite University's Strategies for Trauma Awareness and Resilience (STAR)[37] workshop I had an important in-the-moment experience of self-reflection about my dual role as both circle keeper and friend. At EMU/STAR I had learned mammals have a physiological trauma response and that our cultural tendency is to try and control or manage this mammalian response. I realized that my almost programmed reaction to comfort my colleague was more about my own un-comfortability in the moment than his. Rather than comfort maybe what was most needed by him and others in the peace circle was space to vent, reflect, and listen. On seeing emotions, especially in public settings, humans often want to comfort to spare the traumatized the memory, or the relived experience of unwanted emotions. The possibility of re-traumatization, and/or the chance for social embarrassment if they "lose control" of their emotion's weighs heavy in listeners' minds. We tend to think that emotions, as unpredictable, need to be controlled and managed lest they lead to dissensus, tension, or further trauma. But does our natural communal urge to avoid pain and seek pleasure stop us from authentically listening and connecting on a human level?

By resisting the urge to comfort my friend and catching myself as circle keeper from trying to control the process, I opened the possibility that the "outlet and absorption"[38] of my colleague's trauma could find voice and possible connection. By responding to emotions and trauma we often act to stifle them and the innate potentials that these emotional expressions have available to articulate humanity, show emotional affect, and express identity. By giving space and creating the structure for such expressions (the role of a good peace circle keeper), the experience had a much more profound impact on participants. Trauma seeks psychological and social outlet, but people often stifle this traumagenic need. Being trauma-informed means learning to know when to comfort, when to acknowledge pain, and how to allow interlocutors to show affect and elicit human empathy. This is the fraught territory for professional counselors in individual practice, but it is also the challenge of effective conflict intervention practice. The impulse to lean into emotions without trying to manage them is counter-cultural. Among groups and collectives, this leaning in is even more fraught than in situations of one-on-one interaction.

Learning to apply a culturally aware trauma response, resistance to a fix-it mentality, and both analytical and practical skills to leverage traumatic expression to build group resilience are all trauma-informed skill sets that are explored throughout this book to improve conflict intervention practice. By connecting to pro-social understandings of trauma and recent research on post-traumatic growth (PTG),[39] I hope to frame a novel epistemological platform and set of trauma-informed problematics critical for achieving local and global peace and change. While foregrounding the centrality of storytelling practices as key to developing effective conflict practice, I develop both the centrality of emotions and trauma in conflict resolution, but also challenge our cultural tendency to avoid emotions as opposed to listen to and embrace them. Such an approach to conflict practice privileges process over outcomes, but also acknowledges that this mantra in the peace and conflict field can also be overthought. Does bringing tissues to the dialogue help or harm the ability for the community to build resilience? Like a Boy Scout it is good to be prepared but being too responsive can stifle the chance for the transformative shifts in conflict practice that all practitioners are looking for. Should I just trust the process? This is the improvisational aspect of both therapy and conflict practice; balancing preparation and flexibility is critical to effective practice. In addition to my personal example above, one more example of collective trauma in my research of modern Dalit[40] rights activism foregrounds the idea that awareness of trauma and emotions is just as important for large-scale group transformation as it is for individual and small group processes. But first, a few words about distinguishing collective trauma from its more commonly understood sibling, individual trauma.

DEFINING TRAUMA AS A COLLECTIVE EXPERIENCE

When the term "collective" or "historical" is appended to trauma, definitional problems only increase. This is a terrain that not just peace and conflict studies, but also other fields, like traditional social psychology, have spent too little time exploring due to its complexity and cultural variability. Yet, increasingly, in attempting to understand social conflict, the role of collective historical trauma is being thrust front and center in public discussion (especially post-George Floyd). From discussion of reparations in the United States[41] to Hindu-Muslim violence in India,[42] collective historical trauma plays a critical mediating role in most protracted social conflicts involving issues of entrenched structural violence. Like violence, trauma's existence gains definition by its use and invocation. From America's legacy of racial trauma to the millennial-long trauma of caste hierarchy, the marks of collective historical trauma inform social activism, social disparity, and counter-response to social activism. Still, this does not make the definition of a specific typology of collective trauma any easier for modern scholars studying trauma's impacts.[43] Despite the definitional complexity of collective historical trauma, its existence has been qualitatively and quantitatively studied in Native Americans,[44] post-Holocaust survivors,[45] postwar citizens of El Salvador,[46] Israeli youth,[47] Australian Aboriginals,[48] survivors of the Armenian Genocide,[49] and Palestinians,[50] among many other identities and contexts. Increasingly, the existence of collective historical trauma and its transgenerational transmission is well-established knowledge in the literature.[51] Still, any sense of uniform understanding of the phenomenon remains contested and locally contingent at best, and too amorphous as a social scientific category at worst.

For our purposes it will suffice to define collective historical trauma as trauma that does not originate from a single event, but rather arises out of a history of hierarchical power relations and systems of oppression. Powerful groups in conflict resonate uneven power asymmetries across generations and develop scapegoats[52] and "victimhood psychology"[53] to perpetuate or retain their power. In this sense, non-dominant groups in every society, in resisting these moves of the powerful, have some degree of collective historical trauma, that spans across generations as a consequence of a legacy of unequal power and marginalization. The trauma caused by those in powers' attempts at both social and discursive hegemony is both lasting and hard to quantify or study. Such traumas manifest in individuals and groups in a diversity of ways but is well captured in Eastern Mennonite University's STAR program's "snail" model (see figure I.1 below).

While individuals and collectives "act in" and "act out" their trauma in a diversity of ways (from alcoholism and other addictions to blaming and abuse), both get stuck in the cycles of violence represented in the two circles in the center of the spiral model (figure I.1). The aggressor

Breaking Cycles of Violence · Building Resilience

Figure I.1   Strategies for Trauma Awareness and Resilience (STAR) "snail" model for breaking cycles of violence caused by trauma.

and victim cycles represent the internal and external ways that victims respond to trauma and are both unique and nonlinear sequalae. In much the same way, acknowledgment and recognition represent unique and nonlinear responses to the residue of trauma and victimization in conflict. While clinical psychologists work to council individual patients through their personal experiences of trauma and the cycles of violence that trauma often perpetuates, how those individual traumatic experiences connect with others in their own community is rarely fully addressed by clinical psychologists outside of group therapy circles. A peacebuilders' work, on the other hand, is to get not just individuals, but collectives, unstuck and towards a process of healing and ultimately a sense of their own collective ability for sustainable change and resilience. Even though this sounds like what clinical psychologists do at the group therapy level, their theory of change is always stuck at the individual level. Those working in conflict intervention practice are taking a view of conflict that infers that both oppressor and oppressed are engaged in competing claims to identify themselves as the primary victims. This is what Volkan calls "the metaphor of the ethnic tent."[54] Much of his work aims to leverage individual psychological theories of change to develop collective theories of change. More than connecting affinity groups with similar experiences of trauma, peacebuilders/conflict intervention practitioners strive to bring together communities with divergent power positions in society to collectively process their experiences, needs, and opportunities born of traumatic conflict. The line leading away from cycles of violence in figure I.1 above shows some of the practices that can be undertaken to move towards the possibility of reconciliation.

Occupied with changing the relationships between conflicting power asymmetric groups, conflict intervention practitioners must add to the work of individual level processing of trauma by facilitating, within conflict parties, a sense of how their individual trauma gets them stuck in unproductive social feedback loops. Trauma and emotions are a crucial leverage point[55] in both individual and collective change processes. While, these individual and collective level interventions may be complimentary, they may look quite different in different social and cultural contexts. Although central to any level of healing is a common sense of human dignity,[56] peacebuilders are more intentionally interested in establishing collective relationships between conflict identity groups, while psychologists are more concerned with repairing interior and inter-personal or relational psychology of the individual patient. Even as I have made this distinction too simplistic, I illustrate it here to demarcate the work, or intervention practices, of these complimentary professions in such a way that underscores the primary emphasis of their theories of change.[57] Individual psychological well-being certainly lends to collective well-being, but collective psychological well-being has a broader aim of collective social stability and positive peace (admittedly a much more normative and less immediately quantifiable endeavor). The following brief discursive analysis of a story from my own past experiences with Dalit rights activists in India might provide further clarity of this rather arcane, yet important, conflict practice dynamic. Such rights activism is both a contestation over individual victims' stories and survivors' collective voice.

FRAMING INTERNATIONAL DALIT CONTENTION: ALLOWING VOICE AND CONTESTED POSITIONINGS OF THE "VICTIM"

The intersection of rising Hindu nationalism on the Indian subcontinent and contemporary Dalit rights activism poses an interesting case of the need to resist the urge to comfort and control emotional and traumatic expression on the national or even international level of entrenched identity conflict. Modern Hindu nationalist rhetoric and discursive constructs underscore the urgent need to understand past conceptions of collective trauma and create space for the voice of those most affected by elite conceptions of history to be heard. This is admittedly tricky terrain in our current politically polarized moment. Still, as Van der Kolk (2014) reminds us in stories from his own clinical practice, to successfully intervene in trauma, those victimized by it must make "me one of them."[58] This level of trust and acceptance in an identity group takes time to build and must be maintained. Early in my work with Dalit activists I visited members of the U.S. Congress in Washington, D.C., with a delegation of visiting Dalit activists. I distinctly remember one of them calling me an "honorary Dalit" as I stood out as the only white American in the delegation. Later, when I accepted a Fulbright-Nehru award to teach at Banaras Hindu University (BHU) in Northern Hindu-dominated India, I had to do considerable repair work to rebuild trust with Southern Indian Dalit friends who could not understand why I would teach at a Hindu-dominant institution like BHU! Identity is central to all trauma-informed practice. Being seen as within a trusted identity group allows a conflict practitioner to assist in repairing the flow of ruptured narrative in the lives of the traumatized.

Understanding what Montville called "victimhood psychology"[59] is critical to emotionally mindful and trauma-informed practice. Just as Hindu nationalist historical claims attempt to usurp victimhood from marginalized minorities in India one could make similar claims about the intersection of white nationalist concepts of history as resisting Black Lives Matter activists' claims of injustice in the United States. This question of positioning one's identity as the victimized has certainly taken on increased urgency in the U.S. context in recent years.[60] While admittedly a complicated example, I claim the distance of the Indian cultural context from most Western conflict practitioners can help to reframe our own narrative understandings about emotions and trauma in conflict. My focus on victimhood psychology and social positioning,[61] which are seemingly theoretical, lays the groundwork for developing emotionally mindful and trauma-informed approaches to group conflict intervention. Those with historical grievance need space to voice their sense of victimhood and structures to build conflict processes designed to critically question assumed power formations.

My first inkling of the need to reframe victimhood psychology as central to trauma-informed peacebuilding work came in a dialogue on caste that I led at the Manuski Center for human rights in Pune, Maharashtra in 2008.[62] There, a low-caste dialogue participant spoke passionately about the emotions he felt being in the room as high-caste classmates made impassioned arguments, about caste reservation policy, that were devoid of any caste-based understanding or analysis. While the context of his story is one similar to caste exclusion experiences in other walks of Indians' lives, the coda[63] of his narrative refrain was telling of the traumagenic cycles of systems of oppression. After asserting his own identity as scheduled caste to his predominantly high-caste classmates, this dialogue participant ended his narrative recounting with: ". . . my telling [of my scheduled caste identity] was bothering them and not me actually."[64] His identity claims had challenged the group's conception of themselves as the victims of India's reservation (affirmative action) policies. Indirectly challenging their social construction of power, his experience spoke to an experience of victimhood that they could hardly understand; an experience of victimhood they had no clear vocabulary for. He had instead claimed through his identity that he was the true victim of an actively present form of oppression that reservations aimed to help alleviate. This alternative narrative challenged the privileged claims that reservation policy was holding these sons of the elite back by limiting their professional choices. While reservations, also tellingly called positive discrimination in British parlance, is a stop gap measure that enforces the regulation of fixed quotas, it evens past systemic injustices in the present. Reservations (aka positive discrimination and/or affirmative action) are not intended to last forever, but rather to correct past inequities by reserving seats for those obstructed by structurally unequal systems. Yet one's identity shades one's perspective on such policy and reinforces the stories one both hears, and tells, about such policies. This dialogue respondent introduced an experience that challenged the wider groups' story about reservations. Such opportunities for inclusion of non-dominant narratives can act to reset the victim psychology of individuals in conflict.

This dialogue experience has stuck with me since that time, and through many experiences like this my curiosity is led to strive to develop a framework or model for engaging in trauma-informed peace-building in this uniquely marginalized community. It is partly the inadequacy that I felt in response to this colleague that led me to this desire to further develop applied theories of conflict transformation for caste-based social conflict. My own sense of inadequacy points to the difficulty in transforming past collective trauma through simply dialogue. Neutrality or impartiality here is not really an option. As Martin Luther King, Jr. famously said, "Injustice anywhere is a threat to justice everywhere. We are caught in an inescapable network of mutuality, tied in a single garment of destiny. Whatever affects one directly, affects all indirectly."[65] Being a neutral mediator or facilitator in such a dialogue is akin to being emotionally deaf. The injustice faced by a quota system cannot be compared to the injustice endured over generations of caste-based discrimination; they are not equivalent experiences. Still, hardened identity groups remain resistant to any moral devaluation of their lived experience as victims. Providing the space structure for such openings in victimhood psychology is a crucial aspect of trauma informed and emotionally mindful conflict practice. Such work is far from "neutral." One final brief example from global Dalit rights activism further illustrates the complex mix of dialogue and activism that is needed to overcome the endemic realities of caste-based oppression. Trauma-informed and emotionally mindful practitioners must be aware of their dual, and at times conflicting, roles of dialogue convener and partial activist for human justice. Being trauma-informed does not come without political ambiguity.

In 2001, at the World Conference Against Racism, Racial Discrimination, Xenophobia, and Related Intolerance (hereafter WCAR) in Durban, South Africa, the National Campaign on Dalit Human Rights (NCDHR) attempted to re-frame caste as a global human rights issue.[66] Despite this story being eclipsed by other news and activist concerns (e.g., disputes over Palestinian second-class citizenry) and 9–11 occurring three days after the conference ended, the story of Dalit activists being rebuffed by Indian elites has been treated by numerous scholars.[67] What has been largely missed in these discussions is the impact of avoiding emotions and past stories of trauma in both making (on the part of Dalit activists) and resisting (on the part of the Indian government) claims for redress and inclusion of caste as a human rights issue. Activists' moves in Durban, and even after the 2001 WCAR, have focused on framing their cry for caste justice as a global justice/human rights issue. With little discursive space for the expression of their collective trauma and victimhood psychology, Dalit activists strategically shifted their claims to the global human rights stage. In response, the Indian Government attempted to deflect attention from caste atrocity and traumatic personal stories and instead focused attention on defining caste as outside the ambit of racial discrimination (the focus of the WCAR conference) while simultaneously insinuating that such calls for civil rights in some way defames all Indians.[68] This theoretical and nationalistic turn of the debate buttressed the Indian government's claims that caste was nothing like race (but rather a spurious argument coming from powerful interests and a select few European sociologists). The irony is that both the moves on the part of India's powerful and Dalit activists decentered the power of narrative storytelling to elicit ambiguous emotions on the part of listeners and/or develop acknowledgment and reconnection over the collective historical trauma that generations of Dalits have experienced. In this public debate between Dalit activists and the Indian Government atrocity stories were nowhere to be seen in the discourse. Dalit activists at Durban, in sanitizing their contention of emotion and/or traumatic storylines, adopted a rational strategic approach that was ultimately unsuccessful. Devoid of a trauma-informed lens this emotionless approach failed to elicit rasa in global listeners. These listeners, especially human rights activists as well as potential supporters of the cause, missed the opportunity to be moved to action. The rational framing of caste as a form of racial discrimination left little room for ambiguity in listeners, yet also challenged any understanding of caste as a form of oppression that is distinct from racial discrimination. The government of India issued statements that further debated and re-hashed the rational arguments about sociological distinctions between race and caste, which in turn deflected listeners away from a connection to the emotional rasa of caste discrimination experience. Elite manipulation of discourse about caste torpedoed activists' attempts to bring caste discrimination to the world stage. This is the repeated story of anti-caste activism.

FORETHOUGHTS AND WAYS FORWARD

What is at stake here is not only foregrounding emotions and trauma for effective resistance by marginalized counterpublics, but also a full articulation of the many ways to resist marginalization and domination.

Emotions and trauma create unique options for facilitating lasting change by third-party actors. As conflict practitioners we need to embrace trauma and emotions head on and not recoil from anxiety due to its persistent and often uncomfortable social presence. By defining problems in positivist terms, the narrative ambiguity[69] of trauma and emotion is lost to both conflict parties and potential intervenors. The brief vignettes above frame my claims and approach in the remainder of this book. What is needed is a reprogramming of a new generation of peace and conflict studies scholar-practitioners that actively "treat" the unmet needs of "victimhood psychology"[70] and consistently re-center emotions and trauma as central to the work of conflict transformation. This book aims to guide both professional practitioners and trainers to develop a new generation of trauma-informed peacebuilding activists cum practitioners. It is not a book for those looking for quick and straight-forward answers to the world's protracted social conflicts. Rather, it is a call to restorative (victim-centered) attention to the emotional resonance and traumatic detritus underneath the surface of all protracted social conflict. Only with attention to the flotsam of emotions and past trauma in conflict can transformative ways forward be found.

NOTES

1. Bessel Van der Kolk, *The Body Keeps Score: Brain, Mind, and Body in the Healing of Trauma* (New York: Penguin Books, 2014), 64.

2. Harold Saunders, *A Public Peace Process: Sustained Dialogue to Transform Racial and Ethnic Conflicts* (New York: Palgrave, 1999). Saunders (1930–2016), was, first in President Lyndon Johnson's National Security Council, and then later a close aide to Secretary of State Henry Kissinger, eventually becoming the Assistant Secretary of State for Intelligence and Research (1975–1978) and Assistant Secretary of State for Near East Affairs (1978–1981). His ideas on sustained dialogue and public peace processes were influential in orchestrating the Camp David Accords and framing U.S. negotiations during the Iranian hostage crisis. For Saunders, the public peace process was an unofficial multi-level process of dialogue, negotiation, and continual interaction between citizens of warring body politics or groups. His ideas were widely influenced by Herbert C. Kelman, professor of social relations at Harvard University, among other well-known theorists in the now emergent field of peace and conflict studies. For more on Kissinger's influence on Saunders see: Gary J. Bass, *The Blood Telegram: Nixon, Kissinger, and a Forgotten Genocide* (New York: Vintage Books, 2013).

3. See for example: Ibram X. Kendi, *How to Be an Antiracist* (New York: One World, 2019) and Robin Diangelo, *White Fragility: Why It Is so Hard for White People to Talk about Racism* (Boston: Beacon Press, 2018).

4. An interesting example of the real-life importance of emotions in foreign policy and diplomacy decisions can be seen in Bass' (2013) Pulitzer-nominated account of the Nixon administration's botched handling of the 1971 East Pakistani war. In describing Nixon and Kissinger's taped conversations, Bass notes: "Alone in the Oval Office, these famous practitioners of dispassionate realpolitik were all too often propelled by emotion." Despite the story we tell ourselves that emotions get in the way of rational decision-making, in fact emotions play an important role in reasoning and rational choice. Gary J. Bass, *The Blood Telegram: Nixon, Kissinger, and a Forgotten Genocide* (New York: Vintage Books, 2013), xv.

5. Van der Kolk, *The Body Keeps Score*, 78.

6. John Paul Lederach, *The Moral Imagination: The Art and Soul of Building Peace* (New York: Oxford University Press, 2005), 42.

7. Donald Schon, *The Reflective Practitioner: How Professionals Think in Action* (New York: Basic Books, 1983).

8. See for example: Marilee, Sprenger. *Social-Emotional Learning and the Brain: Strategies to Help Your Students Thrive*, Association for Supervision & Curriculum Development, 2020; B. Dyson, D. Howley, and P. Wright, "A scoping review critically examining research connecting social and emotional learning with three model-based practices in physical education: Have we been doing this all along?" *European Physical Education Review* 27, no. 1 (2021): 76–95, and for-profit educational initiatives like Casel, https://casel.org/, last accessed January 17, 2022.

9. Joseph Nye, *Soft Power: The Means to Success in World Politics* (New York: Public Affairs, 2004).

10. Wallace Dace, "The Concept of 'Rasa' in Sanskrit Dramatic Theory." *Educational Theatre Journal* 15, no. 3 (1963): 249–54, https://doi.org/10.2307/3204783.

11. See the following definition of conceptual art from the Tate Museum, https://www.tate.org.uk/art/art-terms/c/conceptual-art.

12. Jurgen Habermas, *The structural transformation of the public sphere: An inquiry into a category of bourgeois society* (Cambridge, MA: MIT Press, 1991).

13. William Ury, *The Third Side: Why We Fight and How We can Stop* (New York: Penguin, 2000).

14. L. Balachandra, F. Barrett, H. Bellman, C. Fisher, and L. Susskind, "Improvisation and Mediation: Balancing Acts." *Negotiation Journal*, 21 (2005): 425–34, https://doi.org/10.1111/j.1571-9979.2005.00075.x.

15. Thomas Kuhn, *The Structure of Scientific Revolutions* (Chicago: University of Chicago Press, 1962).

16. See for example: Betty Reardon and Dale Snauwaert, *Betty A. Reardon: Key Texts in Gender and Peace* (New York: Springer, 2015).

17. Jeremy Rinker, *Identity, Rights, and Awareness: Anti-Caste Activism in India and the Awakening of Justice through Discursive Practices* (Lanham, MD: Lexington Books, 2018).

18. Note that throughout the book I will use "peacebuilding" and "conflict transformation" interchangeably. As J. P. Lederach has argued, peacebuilding aims to not just resolve conflict but transform the relationships which instigate and sustain social conflict. See: John Paul Lederach, *Building Peace: Sustainable Reconciliation in Divided Societies* (Washington, DC: United States Institute of Peace, 1997).

19. As we proceed, I will further contextualize what I mean by peace circles. For now, it will do to say that peace circles are a broad term for a particular type of group, or meso-level, conflict intervention. Peace circles provide a space and a structure to facilitate dialogue and discussion about difficult topics and/or conflict contexts. For a good overview of peace circles, also called peacemaking circles see: Kay Pranis, *The Little Book of Circle Processes: A New/Old Approach to Peacemaking* (Intercourse, PA: Good Books, 2005), and K. Pranis, B. Stuart, and M. Wedge, *Peacemaking Circles: From Crime to Community* (Minneapolis, MN: Living Justice Press, 2003), among others.

20. J. Rinker and J. Lawler, "Trauma as a collective disease and root cause of protracted social conflict." *Peace and Conflict: Journal of Peace Psychology* 24, no. 2 (2018): 150–64, http://dx.doi.org/10.1037/pac0000311.

21. See for example: Douglas P. Fry and Geneviève Souillac, Peaceful societies are not utopian fantasy. They exist. The Bulletin of the Atomic Scientists (March 22). Open Access: https://thebulletin.org/2021/03/peaceful-societies-are-not-utopian fantasy-they-exist/, 2021. Douglas P. Fry, Geneviève Souillac, L. Liebovitch, P. T. Coleman, K. Agan, E. Nicholson-Cox, D. Mason, F. Palma Gomez, and S. Strauss, Societies within Peace Systems Avoid War and Build Positive Intergroup Relationships. Humanities and Social Sciences Communications. Online, Open Access, January 18, https://doi.org/10.1057/s41599-020-00692-8.

22. Donald Schon, *The Reflective Practitioner: How Professionals Think in Action* (New York: Basic Books, 1983).

23. See Thomas S. Kuhn, *The Structure of Scientific Revolutions*, 4th Edition (Chicago, University of Chicago Press, 2012/1969).

24. See for example: Francesca Polletta, *It Was Like a Fever: Storytelling in Protest and Politics* (Chicago: University of Chicago Press, 2006); J. Goodwin and J. M. Jasper, "Caught in a Winding, Snarling Vine: The Structural Bias of Political Process Theory." *Sociological Forum* 14 (1999): 27–54 https://doi.org/10.1023/A:1021684610881; R. Benford and D. Snow, "Framing Processes and Social Movements: An Overview and Assessment." *Annual Review of Sociology* 26 (2000): 611–39. Retrieved April 5, 2021, from http://www.jstor.org/stable/223459.

25. Sydney Tarrow, *Power in Movement: Social Movements in Contentious Politics* (New York: Cambridge University Press, 1996).

26. Kazu Haga, *Healing Resistance: A Radically Different Response to Harm* (Berkley, CA: Parallax Press, 2020, 124).

27. See Lauren Abramson and David Moore, "Chapter 7: The Psychology of Community Conferencing," in *Repairing Communities Through Restorative Justice*, edited by J. G. Perry (Lanham, MD: American Correctional Association, 2002, 123–39), as one exception. Other practice-focused academics, like Bush and Folger (2004), focus mediation practice on empowerment and recognition but still fail to link this directly to trauma and emotions. See: Robert Baruch Bush and Joseph Folger, *The Promise of Mediation: The Transformative Approach to Conflict* (San Francisco: Jossey-Bass, 2004).

28. A. Taiwo, *Power, resistance, and liberation in therapy with survivors of trauma: to have our hearts broken* (New York, NY: Routledge Press, 2011).

29. Here I am invoking the controversial ideas of Fukuyama (2006) to resist the simplistic thinking that liberal democracy and free expression of trauma somehow end the need to discuss the critical importance of history. Francis Fukuyama, *The End of History and the Last Man* (New York: Free Press, 2006).

30. Lisa Schirch, "Ritual Reconciliation: Transforming Identity/Reframing Conflict," in *Reconciliation, Justice, and Coexistence: Theory and Practice*, edited by M. Abu Nimer (Lanham, MD: Lexington Books, 2001), 145.

31. Mancur Olson, *The Logic of Collective Action: Public Goods and the Theory of Groups* (Cambridge, MA: Harvard University Press, 1965).

32. G. W. Allport, *The nature of prejudice* (Addison-Wesley, 1954).

33. Johan Galtung, "Violence, Peace, and Peace Research," *Journal of Peace Research* 6, no. 3 (1969): 167–91.

34. For a welcomed exception to this dominant rational worldview in conflict resolution see: Sara Cobb, *Speaking of Violence: The Politics and Poetics of Narrative Dynamics in Conflict Resolution* (New York: Oxford University Press, 2013).

35. Severine Autesserre, *The Frontlines of Peace: An Insider's Guide to Changing the World* (New York: Oxford University Press, 2021).

36. The starting peace circle guidelines of speaking and listening from the heart, being lean of expression, maintaining a state of wonder, and the right of individuals to "pass" if they so desire, are repeated and added to as needed at the beginning of each new circle. While peace circles aim to privilege spontaneity, those in attendance agree to these basic guidelines of interaction to assist the flow and effectiveness of conversation and are they asked if anything is missing (often the first additional guideline to be added is the call to maintain the confidentiality of the circle). Additional emphasis and time are spent on guidelines when a peace circle involves the processing of a particular conflict

actively being experienced by participants. See: Pranis (2005), op. cit. for more on opening routines and guidelines.

37. See: https://emu.edu/cjp/star/about.

38. See: Erik Erikson, *Gandhi's Truth: On the Origins of Militant Nonviolence* (New York: W.W. Norton and Company, 1969), 98.

39. See: Marianne Amir, Lawrence G. Calhoun, and Richard G. Tedeschi, eds. *Handbook of Posttraumatic Growth: Research and Practice* (New York: Psychology Press, 2014); Richard G. Tedeschi, *Posttraumatic Growth: Theory, Research and Applications* (New York, NY: Routledge, 2018), among others.

40. The word "dalit" means "broken" or "downtrodden" in Sanskrit and was "used as far back as 1931 in journalistic writing." S. M. Michael, ed., *Dalits in Modern India: Vision and Values* (New Delhi: Vistaar Publications, 1999), 99. In his introduction to the dalit autobiography *Joothan: An Untouchable's Life*, Mukherjee (2002) says: "The term Dalit . . . comes from the Sanskrit root dal, which means to crack open, split, crush, grind, and so forth, and it has generally been used as a verb to describe the process of processing food grains and lentils . . . Jotirao Phule and B. R. Ambedkar, two towering figures in Dalit history, were the first to appropriate the word, as a noun and an adjective. . . ." Arun Prabha Mukherjee "Introduction" in *Joothan: An Untouchable's Life*, edited by Omprakash Valmiki (New York: Columbia University Press, 2003), xviii.

41. Ta-Nehisi Coates, "The Case for Reparations," *The Atlantic*, June 2014. See: https://www.theatlantic.com/magazine/archive/2014/06/the-case-for -reparations/361631/, accessed June 21, 2021.

42. Nishant Patel and Sanjay Nath, "Where identity and trauma converge: Hindu-Muslim perceptions of the 2002 Guajarati riots." *Journal of Muslim Mental Health*, 7, no. 2 (2013).

43. Vamik Volkan's work on "chosen traumas" (48) probably comes the closest to the category of collective trauma. I am trying to understand. Volkan describes chosen traumas as "the collective memory of a calamity that once befell a group's ancestors. It is, of course, more than a simple recollection; it is a shared mental representation of the event, which includes realistic information, fantasized expectations, and defense against unacceptable thoughts" (48). Vamik Volkan, *Bloodlines: From Ethnic Pride to Ethnic Terrorism* (Boulder, CO: Westview Press, 1997).

44. T. Evans-Campbell, "Historical trauma in American Indian/native Alaska communities: a multilevel framework for exploring impacts on individuals, families, and communities." *Journal of Interpersonal Violence* 23 (2008): 316–38, http://dx.doi.org/10.1177/0886260507312290.

45. S. Gottschalk, "Reli(e)ving the past: emotion work in the holocaust's second generation." *Symbolic Interaction* 26 (2003): 355–80, http://dx.doi.org /10.1525/si.2003.26.3.355.

46. J. Dickson-Gómez, "The sound of barking dogs: violence and terror among Salvadoran families in the postwar." *Medical Anthropology Quarterly* 16 (2002): 415–38, http://dx.doi.org/10.1525/maq.2002.16.4.415.

47. R. Pat-Horenczyk, R. Abramovitz, O. Peled, D. Brom, A. Daie, and C. M. Chemtob, "Adolescent exposure to recurrent terrorism in Israel: posttraumatic distress and functional impairment." *American Journal of Orthopsychiatry* (2007): 76–85, http://dx.doi.org/10.1037/0002-9432 .77.1.76.

48. A. Quinn, "Reflections on intergenerational trauma: healing as a critical intervention." *First Peoples Child & Family Review* 3 (2007): 72–82.

49. J. Danielian, "A century of silence." *The American Journal of Psychoanalysis* 70 (2010): 245–64, http://dx.doi.org/10.1057/ajp.2010.12.

50. I. G. Barron and G. Abdallah, "Intergenerational trauma in the occupied Palestinian territories: Effect on children and promotion of healing." *Journal of Child & Adolescent Trauma* 8 (2015): 103–10. http://dx.doi.org/10.1007/s40653 -015-0046-z.

51. See: Vamik Volkan, *Bloodlines: from ethnic pride to ethnic terrorism* (Boulder, CO: Westview Press, 1997); L. Kirmayer, J. Gone, and J. Moses, "Rethinking historical trauma," *Transcultural Psychiatry* 51, no. 3 (2014), among others.

52. See the work of the late humanities professor René Girard. René Girard and James G. Williams, *The Girard Reader* (New York: Crossroad, 1996), René Girard, *The Scapegoat,* Translated by Yvonne Freccero (Baltimore: Johns Hopkins University Press, 1986).

53. Joseph Montville, "Justice and the burdens of history," in *Reconciliation, Justice, and Coexistence,* edited by M. Abu Nimer (Lanham, MD: Lexington, 2001), 133.

54. Volkan, *Bloodlines,* 225.

55. See Donella Meadows, *Leverage Points: Places to Intervene in a System* (Hartland, VT: The Sustainability Institute, 1999). Meadows defines Leverage points as "places within a complex system (a corporation, an economy, a living body, a city, an ecosystem) where a small shift in one thing can produce big changes in everything."

56. Dona Hicks, *Dignity: Its Essential Role in Resolving Conflict* (New Haven: Yale University Press, 2013).

57. For more on theories of change in conflict resolution intervention see: https://www.beyondintractability.org/essay/theories_of_change, last accessed January 17, 2022.

58. Op. cit., Van der Kolk (2014), 18.

59. Op. cit., Montville (2001), 133.

60. See: Kathleen Belew, *Bring the War Home: The White Power Movement and Paramilitary America* (Cambridge, MA: Harvard University Press, 2019), among others.

61. Rom Harre and Luk van Langenhove, *Positioning Theory* (Malden, MA: Wiley-Blackwell, 1998).

62. For more of this workshop see: Jeremy Rinker, "Justpeace Prospects for Peace-building and Worldview Tolerance: A South Asian Movement's Social Construction of Justice" (Doctoral Dissertation, Doctor of Philosophy in Conflict Analysis and Resolution, George Mason University, 2009).

63. William Labov, *Language in the Inner City: Studies in Black English Vernacular* (Philadelphia, PA: University of Pennsylvania Press,1972).

64. Op. cit., Rinker, 2009, 414.

65. Martin Luther King, Jr. "Letter from a Birmingham Jail" (1963). https://www.africa.upenn.edu/Articles_Gen/Letter_Birmingham.html. Last accessed January 17, 2022.

66. Eva-Maria Hardtmann, *The Dalit Movement in India: Local Practices, Global Connections* (New York: Oxford University Press, 2009).

67. See: Op. cit., Hardtmann, 2009; Clifford Bob, "Dalit Rights Are Human Rights: Caste Discrimination, International Activism, and the Construction of a New Human Rights Issue" *Human Rights Quarterly* 29 (February 2007): 167–93; Dag-Erik Berg, "Race as a political frontier against caste: WCAR, Dalits and India's foreign policy," *Journal of International Relations and Development* 21, no. 4 (2018): 990–1013, among others.

68. A similar move by Hindu rights activists was made in more recent resistance to California Senate Bill 403. See: https://theprint.in/opinion/californias-trojan-horse-caste-bill-damages-reputations-of-indian-americans-on-unfounded-grounds/1744371/, accessed December 20, 2023.

69. Here I am giving a nod to the work of social movement theorist Francesca Polletta. She argues that narrative ambiguity is what gives activist stories power. See Francesca Polletta, *It Was Like a Fever: Storytelling in Protest and Politics* (Chicago: University of Chicago Press, 2006).

70. Op. cit., Montville (2001), 133.

1

PROBLEM SETTING TRAUMA AND EMOTIONS IN CONFLICT TRANSFORMATION PROCESSES

TRAUMA, IDENTITY, AND VICTIMHOOD

"Problem setting has no place in a body of professional knowledge concerned exclusively with problem solving. The task of choosing among competing paradigms of practice is not amenable to professional expertise."[1]

"Too many of us remain captive to a perilous cartography of color."[2]

IDENTITY AND VICTIMHOOD

We live in an historical moment when identity constructions and socially constructed classification systems are expanding and proliferating. It is a moment when the social construction of identity matters greatly. From color to caste to gender to religious creed we remain captive to social constructions and traumatic legacies of our species' own historical making. The ways we collectively understand ourselves are ever evolving with increased global interconnectedness and heightened justice awareness. At the same time, many of the progressive ways we have come to identify ourselves and our shared sense of community are little understood by those who are not members of our own identity in-groups. Progressive shifts towards "critical pedagogy"[3] assume a focus of education from below increasingly focused on historical oppression as liberatory for all. Sometimes called affinity groups, these socially constructed identities have proliferated in recent years, leading to counter resistance and pushback. The paradox of both expanding and limiting identities animates our modern lived realities. We must admit that the ways we currently classify and understand ourselves as unique from others would be largely unrecognizable to those living just a generation before us. This is not to say these senses of identity did not exist, but their articulation in public discourse and expressions was circumscribed and constrained by the powerful and oppressive systems and structures of dominant society. Such oppressive structures still exist but awareness of them has grown. Increased awareness of the systemic injustices wrought by structural and cultural violence[4] have opened a fraught and polarizing public discourse. Rather than the "color line"[5] or the "faith line"[6] current social conflict can best be described as an array of forces positioned as opposed across an ever-expanding identity line—an evolving and constantly moving target. Still, here I am less concerned with how we got here, than with what this increased bifurcation of our sense of self has done to our trust in what Hobbes called the social contract.[7] How has an increasing number and awareness of multiple identities (gender, race, creed, and global/cultural identities in particular) exacerbated or recalibrated grievance and provided new means to frame, resist, and repress both real and perceived injustices?

I argue in this chapter that expanded identity awareness and social expression has opened new avenues for resistance to dominant power relations (a point I will return to in later chapters), but the emotional underbelly of this increase in identity awareness, what in previous decades we may have called "identity politics,"[8] has been too little explored in the literature on social conflict. Furthermore, new avenues of resistance have also opened novel tactics of repression. How do the "unchosen choices"[9] of identity narratives work to construct our problem-solving attention, and delimit our ability to problem-set? In other words, while the increasing categories of social identity have largely been understood as either a progressive evolution of global democratic society and/or an added tool for resisting the marginalization and injustice of powerful systemic controls, limited focus has been trained on how these identities set new problems for conflict intervention practitioners. We have accepted identity as a useful means for mobilizing social change, but failed to fully set identity, and the increasing social space for difference, as a problem that has many important and complex social and cultural tails. With identity comes the complex emotions associated with a sense of belonging as well as the memory of traumatic pasts. Often such pasts are transgenerational and complex storylines become "flattened"[10] in the present. In noticing the rather philosophical point that the problem setting of identity has been overlooked by the professional rationality of conflict intervenors drive to problem-solve, I do not wish to decenter the important work of identity groups in expanding rights and opportunities for marginalized communities. Rather, I hope to underscore the ways in which these proliferating identities shrink the space for collective vulnerability while expanding the prospects for fear, misinformation, polarization, and "othering."[11] The flourishing and expanding of social identity is neither all positive nor all negative, but rather a mixed bag for those engaged in conflict transformation and peacebuilding work. A more nuanced understanding of this mixed bag can free us from the "perilous cartography of color"[12] of which Appiah warns.

Devoid of the space and structure to share vulnerability, victimhood identity is allowed space to grow and metastasize. If we, as conflict intervention practitioners, do not set the problem of identity, victimization can more easily be claimed by all sides in a conflict (as is increasingly clear in our current politically polarized moment in the United States). As Donald Schon's quote above implies space must be made in professional practice to challenge practice paradigms as well as theoretical and methodological assumptions. Looking at social identity as both resource and constraint allows conflict intervention practitioners the space and structure to co-construct shared meaning and reset seemingly intractable problems. When victims invoke their victimization in conflict, rarely do practitioners challenge received paradigms about victims and victimizers. The same is often true when conflict parties attempt to ascribe their victimization to the other; such first order social positioning in the contemporary context of "wokeism"[13] often goes unchallenged either through second order positioning or by mediators themselves.[14] Such challenges to victimization narratives requires close analytical reflection of received narrative tropes, cultural meanings, and situational context. It also requires an understanding of, and ability to challenge, received dominant narratives. Building on the arguments and guideposts outlined in the introduction, this chapter develops the important role that victim identity narratives play in conflict processes by analyzing selective trauma narratives from anti-caste, anti-racism, and restorative justice activism. But let's be clear, such victim narratives proliferate in all protracted social conflicts (one need look no further than Israel-Palestine for evidence of this). Rather than problem solving our current identity conflicts, how can the victim narratives found in the traumatic stories of those most affected by marginalization and oppression help us re-set our entire conflict practice? Resetting our understanding of victims cannot be separated from recentering trauma and emotions in conflict practice; victim identity narratives are traumatic expressions and acts of therapeutic processing. Claiming a victim narrative is a form of conflict expression that aims to both position the listener and gauge his/her empathetic understandings. Victim narratives are the fodder of conflict ingroups, and, if left unchallenged, can unnecessarily prolong social conflict.

Despite the over-emphasis of rational explanations, such as interests, basic human needs, or scarce resources, as the root cause of protracted social conflict, I have argued elsewhere that collective historical trauma forms the causal center of many seemingly intractable social conflicts.[15] Still, even in noticing the importance of trauma in analyzing conflict, conflict intervenors often fail to privilege the emotional stories of victims and/or rethink the way victims get socially positioned as victims, or, conversely, how perpetrators engage in second-order positioning of being positioned as a perpetrator.[16] Conflict resolution as a field has mostly failed to address the social-psychological variables of trauma and emotion as not just an individual experience, but also a collective social phenomenon with complex social sequalae. There are good reasons for this lack of critical attention to trauma's complex social dynamics and outcomes. Individual sequalae of trauma is complex and variable[17] and when you add in culture and other social determinants the density of variables proliferates exponentially and the potential for increased collective harm rises. In part due to the fears of subjective bias born from legitimate critiques of Freudian psychoanalysis, conflict resolution as a field has compensated for its lack of attention to trauma and psychology by orienting primarily towards the critical study of social institutions and human security (both, arguably naïvely, assumed to be more amenable to rational and interest-based negotiation processes than amorphous and variable beliefs or feelings). By exteriorizing conflict's dynamics as manageable categories like human security, the field has tried to legitimize itself as more empirical, professional, and objective than interior-facing fields like psychology or religious studies. Still, these humanistic disciplines are crucial to managing effective change. While values construct and undergird social institutions, policy and policy levers are privileged by conflict resolution practitioners as the primary means to transform conflicts involving competing conceptions of social injustice. But framing conflict in terms that resonate with vague concepts like policy reform or human security, rather than foregrounding psychological reasoning has turned conflict resolution farther away from the important social psychology of trauma and healing. Such frames have quarantined social conflict from the lived realities of those actively engaged in resisting dominate expressions of power. The intellectual turn away from activism, particularly in the social sciences, is an implicit rejection of any perception of subjectivism. Such a positivist turn belies a Western-centric bias toward the individual over the collective and the social. Western social science in general avoids individual subjectivity, but in a field so concerned with both academic inquiry and social intervention (e.g., what Kurt Lewin interchangeably called "action research" or "action science"[18]) such strident resistance to the messiness of trauma and emotions is, ironically, an arbitrary and subjective methodological decision. As we evolve the field from an emphasis on problem-solving (resolution) to a focus on long-term problem setting (transformation), a move already well underway, we must foreground conflicts as complex social-emotional traumas that are expressed in outward behaviors and grievances but couched in traumatic and emotional histories and sequalae. While conflict is certainly "nested"[19] in issues, relationships, sub-systems, and systems, each of these nests are also thatched via trauma and its emotional resonance.

Trauma, as a social-psychological expression of individual suffering (and a central part of the human condition), is foundational to transform all protracted social conflict. One cannot intervene in conflict without, at least, touching on trauma and the emotional responses it invokes in conflict parties. Therefore, sanitizing emotions and trauma

from the work of conflict transformation is ill advised for the following reasons: 1) Conflict transformation depends on relationship and
relationship is grounded in a human sense of vulnerability; 2) To
express vulnerability there must be safe space to express one's true
sense of social identity without being typecast/positioned as either a
victim or an oppressor; 3) Devoid of the space and structure to share
vulnerability, victimhood identity is allowed space to grow and metastasize like a cancer. 4) Once victimhood and fear take root, the space
and structure for expressing vulnerability shrinks or contracts. Not
as much of a positive prescription as Buddhism's four noble truths,
these four theorems articulate the recursive links between trauma and
conflict transformation. As a mutually reinforcing negative feedback
loop, this recursive loop, once set in motion, takes on a life of its own
and becomes self-reinforcing. Those practicing conflict transformation,
therefore, must be attentive to vulnerability and foster the space for
collectively sharing trauma and emotions across power imbalances. In
addition, through developing both an appreciation and understanding
of victim narratives, conflict practitioners can re-set conflict as a tool
for nonviolent prosocial change, as opposed to simply a problem to be
resolved. Conflict is change generative, if strategically and nonviolently
deployed. Opening irenic potentials for lasting humanistic transformation in the face of trauma represents a shifting priority from more than
simply managing or resolving conflict to embracing the vulnerability of
human suffering to foster change while limiting harm. Doug Fry would
frame this re-setting of the problem as an anthropological opening for
humanistic "peace systems"[20] to evolve. In addition to highlighting the
deep roots of an anthropological history of peace systems, I believe
that a re-setting of the problem of victimhood identity is critical to the
paradigm shift towards conflict transformation that John Paul Lederach
invoked in the late 1990s.[21]

In introducing atrocity stories from Indian Dalits as well as narratives
of resistance to systemic racism in the United States, I aim to explore,
throughout this book, methods for effectively engaging victim identity
in conflict intervention practice. More than simply framing victims as
survivors is needed to build both resilience and resistance to sustainable change in unjust systems. Conflict, like trauma, is a social and
collective experience despite often being framed in ways that privilege
individual agency and privatized victimology. What can we, as conflict

practitioners, do to move parties away from what Joseph Montville calls "victimhood psychology"[22] and develop restoration, healing, and collective resilience to the legacies of historical traumas that often drive protracted social conflict? By developing a theory-informed approach to practice, the complexities of developing trauma-informed approaches to peaceful coexistence in the context of blame, emotional hurt, and past trauma are exposed. Before we can talk of developing a trauma-informed lens (see chapter 2) we must set the complex terrain of the problem to be addressed. Resourcing both narrative and restorative values, theory can help us to foster a set of dynamic conflict practices that foreground trauma, express curiosity about personal and collective identity, and interrogate victimhood as central to both conflict resolution and conflict transformation practice. Trauma and emotions are critical and under-explored variables in all social conflict dynamics. By resetting the problem of victims, conflict intervention practitioners open new approaches to peace practice and potentials for human reconciliation. In developing an appreciation for reading/listening to victim narratives, and how to better use them for irenic ends, readers will increasingly appreciate how critical victim narratives are to the practice of effective conflict intervention in the twenty-first century.

WHOSE VICTIM, WHICH PERPETRATOR?[23]

One thing competing claims of victimhood make clear is that everyone is, in some sense, both a victim and a perpetrator. Just as we all have some forms of privilege and are simultaneously oppressed in distinct, but unique, ways, everyone both suffers and perpetuates suffering. Still, we often lose sight of these fundamental truths of the human condition and socially construct our plight as the result of being victimized by evil others.[24] As Resmaa Menakem reminds us: "Trauma responses are unique to each person. . . . However, trauma is never a personal failing, and it is never something a person can choose. It is always something that happens *to* someone."[25] Parties in conflict often loose this interdependent perspective and get stuck in binary thinking about distinct victims and offenders. The first four stanzas of Thich Nhat Hanh's famous poem entitled *Please Call Me by My True Names* succinctly and emotionally outlines the complexity of getting stuck in victimhood psychology. Nhat Hanh writes:

Do not say that I'll depart tomorrow
because even today I still arrive.
Look deeply: I arrive in every second
to be a bud on a spring branch,
to be a tiny bird, with wings still fragile,
learning to sing in my new nest,
to be a caterpillar in the heart of a flower,
to be a jewel hiding itself in a stone.
I still arrive, in order to laugh and to cry,
in order to fear and to hope.
The rhythm of my heart is the birth and
death of all that are alive.
I am the mayfly metamorphosing on the surface of the river,
and I am the bird which, when spring comes, arrives in time
to eat the mayfly.[26]

For Nhat Hahn, the idea of being in a perpetual state of arriving is a metaphor for the seemingly contradictory feelings of fear and hope actively alive in both victims and perpetrators. Life and death, human existence, are a balancing of contradictory emotions, traumas, behaviors, and actions. His poem speaks to the inseparability of victim and perpetrator identities by comparing those that are suffering as the Vietnam war raged. Nhat Hahn, possibly the most well-known Buddhist in the world, save the Dalai Lama, recently passed, but his example and compassionate awareness lives on. A Vietnamese Buddhist monk, Nhat Hahn was instrumental in resisting violence and helping the "boat people" who fled Vietnam during the late 1960s and early 1970s war in Indochina. The last stanza of his poem repeats in form and sentiment comparing frogs and snakes, a starving Ugandan child and an arms merchant, a refugee child and a sexual predator sea pirate, and a member of the Soviet politburo and a forced labor camp prisoner, in making the distinctions between victim and victimizer all but disappear. The poem carries many meanings, but critical to its impact and intent are the inseparable Buddhist concepts of both co-dependent arising and interdependence. Often described as the no first cause doctrine in Buddhism, co-dependent arising argues that any action is the result of innumerable other actions. In other words, the causal roots of actions and behaviors cannot be drawn back to one specific first cause, but rather are a result of a web of actions (karma), behaviors, and interactions. Such a worldview fits hand-in-glove with the Buddhist commitment to the interdependence of all sentient beings and acts as a sort of parable for those intervening in social conflicts and their attenuate traumas. The web of reactions and causes runs deep. In fact, Nhat Hahn created his own monastic order, the order of interbeing, to emphasize what he saw as these fundamental truths of human existence. Much of his understanding and monastic order was born in the war-time social work practices that Nhat Hahn championed.

Nhat Hahn's poem raises many questions for Western practitioners of peace and conflict (as well as modern transnational expressions of Buddhism). It challenges us to reflect on the fact that we are all both perpetrators and victims to various degrees, a reality made clearer by increased global connection and interaction. Nhat Hanh's poem does not condone the perpetrator or his/her behaviors, but rather draws us to empathize with those that make selfish and/or immoral decisions driven by desire, anger, and greed. They, like victims, also suffer; they carry with them a human history of trauma.[27] This is a testament to the first noble truth of Buddhism (suffering exists). But beyond this, such empathetic equation of the victim and the perpetrator calls us to acknowledge the human capacity for compassion.[28] Who gets to claim victimhood if all are truly interdependent carriers of trauma? What do claims of victimhood do to claims of interdependence? How can we see perpetrators as humans worthy of restoration in human community? Nhat Hanh's poem underscores the naiveté of assuming all conflicts have root causes (or first cause). Victimhood narratives often act to dismiss others, deny interdependence, and undermine compassion for the diversity of experiences. Though victimhood claims are important expressions of the witnessing of suffering, they are also emotionally charged statements of past trauma that can shut down critical analytical thinking and limit social agency. As conflict intervention practitioners how do we privilege victim's lived experience without undermining interdependence, compassion, and critical analytical thinking? This is a difficult balance for sure, and to think we can walk that balance with only rational and interest-based approaches to social conflict seems myopic at best, and asinine at worst. Trauma-informed and emotionally mindful conflict practitioners must be attentive to narrative structure, discursive ornaments, and meaning-making processes and how they act to shift emotion as well as imbricate observation with judgement,[29] and socially position[30] others. Such awareness of identity narratives is a first step to being critically reflective of labels like "victim" or "perpetrator."

But, of course, awareness of our interdependence is sadly not enough; conflict intervention practitioners must hone a reflective practice of narrative analysis to be ready for the trauma and emotions that consistently, and often subtly, come their way. Past traumas resist narration and inhabiting a victim narrative can be one way to avoid reliving trauma. Whose victim and which perpetrator must remain as constant questions for the conflict intervention practitioner who aspires to be trauma aware. Of course, practitioners' own positionality and identity complicate this awareness and conflict parties' own perceptions of that awareness. Still, by either losing site of these questions or relying on rational (and non-emotional) assessments of interests and needs, conflict practitioners miss opportunities for short-term resolution and long-term transformation. Identity justice[31] demands that conflict practitioners pay careful attention to all victimhood narratives as potentially threatening to interdependent future coexistence and the unique trauma response of conflict parties. This is being truly trauma-informed.

NARRATIVE ANALYSIS, MEANING, AND CHANGE

Before we go further, some discussion of narrative analysis as a theoretical framework and rigorous research methodology is essential. Despite the positivist turn in the social sciences, qualitative analysis of narratives has increasingly emerged as a methodology that "makes individuals, cultures, societies, and historical epochs comprehensible as wholes."[32] Put more forcefully: "If narrative analysis does not improve the quality of companionship between humans and stories, then it has failed."[33] Even as over the last decade a plethora of computer software programs have emerged to make the content analysis of narratives more accessible and easily comparable, the complexities of the life, or career, of a narrative remain rather amorphous. While narratives express meaning, they also construct and reinforce an historical discourse. And power relations "can neither be established nor function unless a true discourse is produced, accumulated, put into circulation, and set to work."[34] As a result, although often narrative is seen as benign in conflict episodes, it is important to realize that narrative is active and agentic; narrative itself is an actor. In the words of Vivian Jabri, narratives are more than texts, they "do not describe things, they do things."[35] Said another way, narratives possess agency—"they have gravitas; they are grave. They have weight."[36] Although we know

intuitively that narratives can persuade, often narratives are understood colloquially as synonymous with myths or rhetorical embellish-
ment.[37] More than this colloquial meaning, narratives lend themselves
to complex methodological and theory-building uses. This is especially
true in conflict resolution, stories (narratives) can be a powerful form of
both analytical understanding and intervention. "Narratives serve as a
rationale for action. Because cultural narratives encode the knowledge
that everyone in the group buys into, they can be reframed to comment
critically and persuasively on social life."[38] Raheja and Gold (1994) call
this "narrative potency."[39] As research methodology and action science
intervention, narratives are the foundation of how we make meaning as
humans and, therefore, are the seat of social power and change.

Of course, the study of narrative, like conflict itself, does not fit neatly
into any one discipline or scholarly field.[40] Narrative analysis is an interdisciplinary, even transdisciplinary, social science methodology; both
an epistemological starting point and active theoretical framework for
understanding and explaining social agency. Still, "narrative analysis
has no method in the sense of a canonical sequence of steps that, if
followed properly, produce an analysis."[41] Narrative and its analysis
is consequently always fragmentary and perpetually in the process
of meaning making. A primary way that individuals and social movements make sense of past experiences is to cast these experiences as
narratives.[42] This process is a sort of hypothesis testing and expression
of social identity rolled into one. In the context of social movements,
Francesca Polletta describes this process as "narrative ellipsis"[43]—a
process in which the stories activists tell compel other activists to re-tell
the story to better understand the ambiguous meaning of the events
described. Effective narration leaves room for ambiguity, and, therefore, provides direct access to understanding differences in power, identity, and perceptions of justice/injustice.[44] Still, as a genus, narratives
are rather broad and there is much debate in the scholarly literature
about what constitutes a narrative.[45] Since this is not a book on narrative
methodology per se, there is no need to belabor the many ways in which
narrative works in "ordering experience and constructing reality."[46]
Rather here the aim is to underscore both the utility and centrality of
narrative analysis in conflict resolution/transformation practice. As
"both a mode of reasoning and representation"[47] narrative is not only
transdisciplinary, but also an evolving agent in conflict praxis. Conflict
intervention professionals must, therefore, be attentive to narrative

structure, history, and dynamics. Knowing about the "career" of parties' narratives is critical to effective conflict intervention.

Still, while the methods of narrative analysis are often non-linear and opaque, one example of the theoretical utility of narrative itself can be found in Cobb's use of the concept of narrative violence.[48] The young discipline of Peace and Conflict Studies, regularly relies on Johan Galtung's seminal typology of violence to understand how to develop peaceful systems. In his seminal 1969 article entitled "Violence, Peace, and Peace Research"[49] Galtung developed a typology of violence that is often represented as the three sides of an equilateral triangle (see figure 1.1 below). With direct, structural, and cultural violence representing each side of this equilateral triangle, Galtung's (1969) violence triangle helped develop a base understanding of violence as a typology, as well as, to complicate our understandings of peace as both negative and positive.

Galtung's typology, by no means assuming either directional or proportional relations between these types of violence, has propelled much writing and thinking on peace research and social change over the half a century since its publication. His concept of structural violence, as it

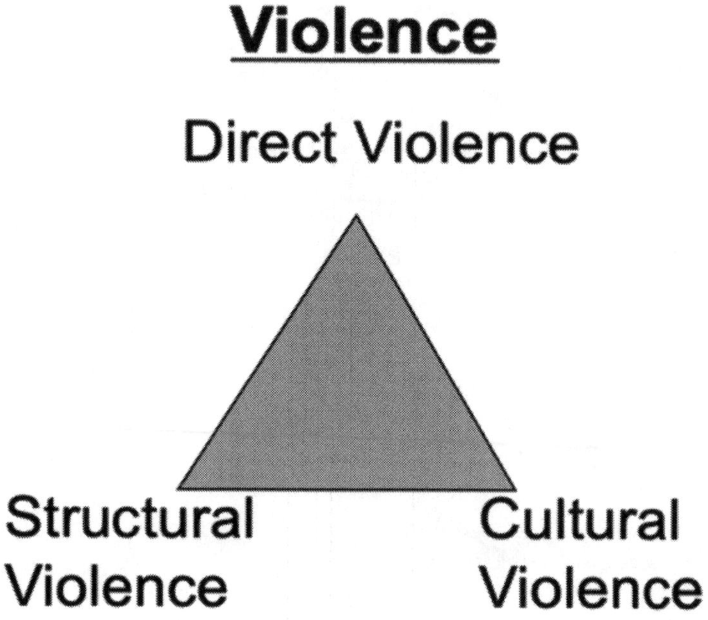

Violence

Direct Violence

Structural Violence   Cultural Violence

Figure 1.1   Galtung's Violence Triangle.

is linked closely with ideas of social justice, has particularly spawned much discussion and new ideas in not just the peace studies discipline, but also other disciplines as well [see Farmer (2004), Ho (2007), Caprioli (2005), among others as examples of this critical and interdisciplinary discussion of structural violence].[50] But Galtung's articulation of structural violence also raised important theoretical questions for peace and conflict practitioners. Most importantly, how does one challenge the agent-less and systemic beast of structural violence in conflict practice? Further, if "conflict reduces narrative complexity and increases narrative closure,"[51] then how can attention to narrative development and dynamics improve our conflict practice? Such questions cannot be answered by only looking at rational actors' interests and needs. In assuming narrative is, itself, not structured, static, and/or incapable of interest-based malleability we miss important intervention opportunities.

The complexity of narrative in conflict may become clearer if we briefly return to exploring the concept of structural violence. Structural violence refers to systematic ways in which social structures harm or otherwise disadvantage individuals in a society. As systemic and structural, unlike direct or personal violence, this form of violence does not have a clear perpetrator or social agent. It is often hidden to those attempting to expose and eradicate it and, even if victims can be clearly identified, perpetrators are more obtuse. Structural violence is also culturally and historically conditioned in such ways that its emergence is often difficult to predict or notice. One example Galtung (1969) himself uses to illustrate the concept of structural violence is the disease tuberculosis (or TB). If a person died from TB in the eighteenth century one could not conceive of this as a form of violence because it might have been completely unavoidable; with no understanding of the disease, society had no ability to cure or even control its spread. This lack of individual or collective agency marks such misfortune and suffering as distinct from anything we label as violence. Though horrible it lacks rationale or intention. But, if one died of TB today that would be an example of structural violence since we (as a global society) have the means to stop and treat TB.[52] Because we have agency (what Porter calls "the self-awareness to make self-chosen choices"[53]) any failure to act is a product of structural (whether financial, logistical, or policy oriented) rather than individual constraints. Structural violence can arise from a lack of access or systems in place to provide for the social determinants of health and wellness. For Galtung, TB death today represents an agentless form of structural violence. Note that this distinction has nothing to do with individual subjectivities of suffering—no one can doubt that death by TB in the eighteenth century would produce equal (if not more) suffering as death by TB today. What marks today's TB death as structural violence is the unrealized means with which society has at our disposal to foreclose such a possibility. Failure to use these means of foreclosure is an avoidable, though collective, failure, even if successful intervention might be structurally complex.

While direct violence is often the instrument of control to maintain injustice in the present, it is structural and cultural violence that maintain a legacy of injustice into the future. Stories of more impersonal structural and cultural violence live on. Structural and cultural violence establish the normative order for injustice while providing cover for the visible injustice and inhumanity of direct violence. Thus, one could see how important narrative is in perpetuating and maintaining violent structures and cultures. As writers in the field of Peace and Conflict Studies continue to grow Galtung's seminal typology of violence as a means of expanding our potential for achieving positive peace, they are increasingly privileging the rhetorical powers of narrative. For example, Cobb (2013) has written of what she calls "a new kind of violence"[54]—narrative violence. Rather than "new," one might better call it "newly discovered." Narrative violence is a special kind of violence that operates in the subtle spaces of storytelling, communication, and discursive listening. Cobb argues that "structural violence, by definition, is difficult to "story" in that its existence does not seem to accompany specific history."[55] As agentless and systemic, Galtung's sense of structural violence maintains an elusive connection to particular characters and/or settings and therefore makes plotlines blurry and amorphous. Unlike direct forms of violence, structural violence acts more like narrative; it leaves ambiguity and renders the relationships between social actors opaque. This leaves room for competing narratives to form and the struggle for meaning to become central to any struggle for power. An understanding of narrative violence helps conflict resolution practitioners see how direct violence and victim narratives collude to create what Cobb calls a "state of exception"[56] for those suffering within social conflict. In describing this "state of exception" as something more than the impersonal and agentless structural violence described by Galtung, Cobb describes a context and people (or identity) that many minority rights activists would readily recognize as actively describing their everyday modern lives and experiences. For Cobb this "state of exception" is "a place where law has been used to create a place without law, a place that defies narrative itself."[57] And the people that populate this "state of exception"—e.g., the victims of narrative violence—are "isolated and disenfranchised, they live in the shadows of the public sphere, their relation to state and community broken."[58] This break in social relations leads to a disruption of the narrative process; it renders victims' narrative agency useless and immobile, their meaning-making abilities thereby become unavailable. As humans use storytelling to make meaning in their lives, a lack of narrative agency leaves powerless and marginalized identities not just victims, but victims incapable of making meaning out of their victimhood. Narrative violence, thus, importantly connects direct violence in the present to its future-going structural and cultural forms of violence. Though it lives in the subtle spaces of communicative interaction, narrative violence requires the vigilant mindful attention of conflict resolution practitioners.

In privileging the present consciousness and memory of past events, narratives can help explain how an on-going "state of exception"[59] has been "incorporated into the temporal structure of relationships."[60] Narratives are socially constructed, but they are also social constructs. Applying the lens of narrative violence to conflict episodes can reveal how narrative can be both "a mode of reasoning and a mode of representation."[61] In turn, such a theoretical framework and methodology requires conflict practitioners to move beyond simply parties' interests and needs and embrace their lived trauma and emotions. This is the work of re-storying and reconnecting victims with their sense of narrative agency; it is where theory meets practice. Such a praxis approach gives life to the histories and present experiences of conflict parties who claim victimhood. Although seemingly all very theoretical, the pragmatics of this dynamic process becomes more transparent through stories themselves. Below are two stories offered as exemplars of the agentic restoring power of stories.

DALIT ATROCITY STORIES AND NARRATIVE RESISTANCE TO CASTE

As a privileged cis-gendered white American male, relaying narratives about caste-based atrocity can be quite challenging. Being unaffected by the structural and narrative violence of the caste system provides me both an important objectivity, and a problematic distance from the suffering of caste oppression. As Bryan Stevenson has written, one must be proximate to suffering to create just change.[62] Still, sometimes we are reminded how simultaneously proximate and distant we are to a particular form of suffering as we develop and reflect on ethnographic insights from chance meetings. One such meeting recently happened to me at my own University. Occasionally such short interpersonal interactions can provide important insight and perspective which corroborate the narrative accounts of those most affected by caste discrimination. These brief moments of empathetic insight, I believe, are invaluable to building the empathy and emotional intelligence needed for not only social justice resistance, but also narrative-based conflict resolution skills to unseat endemic systems of injustice and structural violence. My own positionality affords important opportunities to blur the lines between victims and perpetrators and set the problems associated with caste, rather than simply get mired in the complexity of problem-solving them. Admittedly such opportunities are fleeting and often appear only in reflection, but such reflection is critical to striving for the ideal of emotionally mindful and trauma-aware conflict practice. Such opportunities afford the possibility for the reflective awareness required to develop emotionally mindful and trauma-aware response to protracted social problems, like caste. As a sort of first step, such fleeting moments of insight underscore moments of reflective awareness that are critical to effective change. I, therefore, relay a few such stories (vignettes?) below, not to define the full scope of the caste problem (a herculean task), but rather to delineate the complex subtleties of the marginal experiences and the narrative silencing of those most affected by caste oppression. Understanding such marginal experiences as more than simply victim-hood narratives, but also as attempts to socially position collective experiences, build community, and make meaning from harm, represents a strategic starting point for emotionally mindful and trauma-informed conflict practice. Allyship is important in conflict and as practitioners we are often called to be what Lederach calls "third party partials."[63]

SEEMING INNOCUOUS INTERACTIONS AND MICROAGGRESSIONS

Recently, on the University campus at which I work, I was confronted with an unexpected social interaction on caste. Upon arriving at a social event sponsored by our Provost, I began to mingle with other guests. Soon I found myself standing next to an older Indian woman. Much of her identity was immediately clear to me as she was literally wearing it on the lapel of her Indian sari. Donning a decorative pin in the shape and national colors of the Indian state and a Bindi (the sign of a married Hindu woman) on her head, she asked me if I could take a picture of her and her colleague. I obliged and, in reaching for her cell phone, asked her where in India she was from. She, in looking me up and down, hesitantly replied "Lucknow,"[64] a city I have only traveled through on the train, but, of which, most Americans would have little geographic reference. Lucknow is best known to me as the Northernmost Indian hotspot for anti-caste activism, due in large part to the political tenure of Mayawati, head of the Bahujan Samaj Party (BSP) and former Chief Minister of Uttar Pradesh. As the chief minister, and a Dalit woman of Uttar Pradesh, India's most populace state, Mayawati courted controversy during her leadership tenure for inaugurating the Ambedkar Memorial Park in Lucknow, the state capital. Critics complained about graft and construction overruns on the multi-million-dollar state project, the optics of which were not helped by charges of favoritism and identity politics hurled towards Mayawati, the first Dalit woman to hold the chief minister position in any Indian state. Of course, my interlocutor had no means to know I would know this history of her home city and India's largest state capital. She, a mathematician on a visiting fellowship to my University from Lucknow University, and I, a faculty member in the social sciences, danced around our cultural assumptions, as is often my experience with meeting Indians for the first time.

Eventually, in finding commonalities in our mutual experiences of transatlantic travel between the United States and India, the interaction softened. Feeling comfortable and curious on my progressive campus, unsolicited I explained that I study caste and anti-caste activism in India, and this is the reason I have traveled to India so many times. This discursive move elicited an obvious non-verbal reaction in my interlocutor. Her body straightened and her response was terse and firm as she said: "Oh, well we do not have caste issues any more in India."[65] Likely noticing my shocked facial expression, she quickly followed this broad statement with some qualifiers: "Well, of course, there are random caste atrocities that occur periodically, but these are not normal occurrences like they might have been in the past."[66] Without even responding, my mind was quickly settling on a more nuanced understanding of this woman and her social and political position in India. I had "positioned"[67] her in a storyline, not of my own making, which, in turn, undoubtedly conditioned my foregoing discursive interaction with her. Like the microaggressions that Dalit friends often relay about their own interactions with higher castes, I wished afterwards that I had immediately challenged her uncritical statements and nationalist assumptions. In the flow of the moment, I did not attempt to challenge her storyline and simply let her continue speaking unabated. She persisted by narrating that India had "so much to offer the West,"[68] turning my brief articulation of my research subject into some sort of affront to India's prowess as an emerging world power (a discursive move I was not unfamiliar with in India's contemporary atmosphere of political nationalism). She continued with the over-tired trope of India as "spiritually advanced"[69] as I listened obediently not as much surprised as increasingly dismayed at the lack of critical reflection on her political and nationalistic assumptions. She continued:

> One thing I have noticed being here is that so many students in the United States are dealing with mental health issues . . . our students in India do not have these problems. I think there is so much that Americans could learn about inner peace from India.[70]

My picture of where she sat in the Indian hierarchy complete, I said one last "Well, nice to meet you" and moved to talk to a faculty colleague standing nearby. My preferred conflict style of avoidance could not shake my feeling of dislocation and disappointment for some time. The perspective of this highly educated Indian woman, reminiscent of Hindu elites' microaggressions narrated to me by Dalit friends for years, and contextually located in the right-leaning nationalism of modern India, still came as a surprise to me. In reflecting after the fact, as an ally it is clear that I should have shared the second-hand stories of my research interlocutors, not as an affront to this woman, but as witness to her uncritical assumption and counter to her obviously myopic and privileged lived experiences.

Retelling such a story provides space for analysis and reflection even if avoidance was my initial conflict style in response. While not immediately apparent that the example above is a conflict narrative if we recall the discussion above about victims and perpetrators it becomes clear that both storytellers and listeners are continually working to position themselves in competing discursive frameworks aimed at jockeying for identity recognition and narrative agency. Our interaction was like a dance where we were both listening to music with a completely different beat. In the words of Cobb (2013) "Each party tells a story in which the Other is a victimizer, thus establishing, in the process, their own position as victim."[71] Me, incredulous that this woman would discount the experiences of pain and suffering of my Dalit friends, her, adamant that India was little understood or respected in the West, our interaction was tense from the moment I raised my interest in caste. I should be clear to those not familiar with Indian politics, the subtext of our conversation is a long history of post-colonial nationalism and high caste resistance to reservations (affirmative action) in India. Colonialist frames crash up against humanistic ones and such a conversation cannot be adequately understood outside of such historical frames and "chosen traumas."[72] Failing to realize that these roles are reciprocal, and these histories are experienced from very different social perspectives, interdependent parties in conflict often get stuck in escalatory conflict dynamics; speaking past each other and almost unwittingly escalating and widening the conflict. My own reference to caste unwittingly activated some sense of national victimhood and/or collective trauma of colonization. These political histories in some sense controlled our own narrative interactions. Without disregarding the strong emotions which undergird these narrative positions, conflict practitioners must deftly negotiate these alternative storylines and help parties understand their interdependence. Often the reality that one is empowered by this interplay of victimhood psychology is illusive. Only after the interaction was I, a party to this low-stakes conflict, able to reflect on the many competing narrations we were communicating under. Failure to understand is often controlled by an inability to realize we both stand under discourses not of our own creation. The reason I retell such a story is that it articulates a central experience of what it means to be Dalit in contemporary life; a consistent devaluing of your experience by dominant high-caste society, no matter where you reside. Assumptions about my national identity conditioned my interlocutor's response just as caste status would condition many of her interactions with my Dalit colleagues. For the privileged high caste Indian, like my interlocutor, these microaggressions and devaluing of Dalit experience goes largely unnoticed. What is required here is then to share a story that flies against the socially positioned experience first shared. Telling such a story also educates those in more powerful positions in society (like my interlocutor) to be emotionally mindful of the lived experience of those with less power and social capital. With likely limited experience of interaction with Dalit communities (e.g., proximity) my interlocutor would have had little chance of understanding Dalit experience. For this reason, opportunities to share Dalit experience must be availed, even if such opportunities are seldom had for those most effected. Coupled with this hope in raising at least a faint awareness of certain past traumas of those both disempowered and outside the immediate experience of the privileged is an important belief in the power of acknowledgment. Of course, such acknowledgment that others may also feel themselves as victims does not often come to dominant groups with little proximity or shared experience with the marginalized, but this aspirational ability for human empathy is always present. This aspiration must be harnessed as an always pregnant possibility for the emotionally mindful and trauma-informed practitioner, even when one is emotionally engaging with those that see their victimhood as more primary than others' suffering.

This is a book of vignettes; how else can one really understand emotion and trauma in conflict? Emotions shift and trauma pulsates when activated in the body; stories help make meaning of emotions and trauma. Human emotions are fleeting and transitory; they come in flashes of insight, but they leave deep scars. Often those that live and work with stories of deep emotions and trauma have little space to share their own experiences of collective trauma and emotional disjuncture. This is the case with many in the Dalit diaspora in the United States. Much of the work of conflict practitioners is in creating the space for trauma to be heard. The second brief story I convey illustrates the complexity of the social isolation and traumagenic responses that past experiences of victimization engender. It comes from a focus group discussion a fellow researcher and I had with a group of nine South Asian men living in the Philadelphia/New Jersey area of the United States and who all are working in the helping professions. My colleague, a Dalit social work professor himself, has been instrumental in supporting many Dalit social workers to join the Indian diaspora in the United States. These men's willingness to join a discussion about their own vulnerability as members of the Dalit diaspora is a testament to the relationship and trust that my colleague had fostered in them over many years. My own privilege in being able to participate owes much to the trust and relationship that my colleague built with these individual focus group members, as well as his trust in me as a research collaborator. One vignette from the transcript of our hour and a half-long focus group discussion helps articulate the subtle and often hidden forms of psychological harm that those in minority social positions often face. Rather than set the problem in binary terms of victim and perpetrator, developing awareness and proximity to such social harms underscores the importance of identity, past collective trauma, and emotional resonance in working for "justpeace."[73]

SOCIAL ISOLATION AND THE LEGACY OF CASTE TRAUMA IN THE U.S. DIASPORA

My colleague and I are engaged in an on-going research project that is trying to understand what discrimination looks like in the South Asian diaspora in North America. Like other focus groups that we have run with South Asian diaspora members, our April 2022 focus group was no different in many respects. As we had previously experienced, it was difficult to steer participants away from stories of injustice back home (India or Nepal) and into how such injustices and past traumas reappear in their diasporic lives in North America. Still, eventually our nine male participants began to share about their experiences of "social isolation"[74] in their newly adopted country. Most immigrants and refugees do not make the decision to leave their home countries arbitrarily, but rather develop, over time, well-reasoned explanations that often have to do with many push and pull factors including, but not limited to, past hardships and traumas, economic opportunities, and/or the search for social or religious freedoms. Traumas, as well as positive perceptions of "greener pastures" in a new land drive the decisions of most refugee and immigrant communities.[75] The following transcript from one focus group participant is followed by some further thoughts and analysis critical for the trauma-informed and emotional aware conflict practitioner.

One focus group participant (we will call him A) follows on from a story that another participant had given in response to the following question: How do you see your social/cultural identity represented, shaped, or impacted in employment, educational, religious, housing, and/or social relations in North America?

A'S TRANSCRIPT:

(1)   . . . I have experienced [something] like [what the previous speaker] is saying.

(2)   One of my like . . . one guy, a caste fellow . . . he abused me verbally.

(3)   . . . and he threatened me, so I made a police complaint . . . that I don't feel safe, and I feel threatened . . . and I told him my background and reported that . . .

(4)   The cops then repl[ied] to me in the email, like . . . basically . . . I made the email complaint and then the cop replied that "we don't have protection against caste . . . it is not recognized here in the USA," and . . . so ultimately they did not act on it.

(5)   . . . I reported [the] incident to them, but described the incident like what happened, how he verbally abused and everything, and . . . uh . . .

(6)   . . . But then ultimately I got the response that it is not mentioned in the [law] . . . The caste is not recognized here.

(7)   . . . So ultimately nothing happened against that person . . .

(8)   . . . So, when you will be psychological . . . how it affects . . . like Okay, it is not recognized how we interact with other people you know . . .

(9)   When they know your identity . . . like, let's say if you post something on social media and immediately you know . . .

(10)   [Or say] you are like [at] an event, like [a] Dr. Ambedkar event [for example] . . . or ahhhh, any community event . . .

(11)   You do something, or talk about caste, and then you know . . . like next time your friend lists are getting less [speaker is exasperated now drawing deep breaths and eliciting nods and uneasy laughter from the other focus group participants] . . .

(12)   Because the friends who have . . . "so called friends" from uh-hhh . . . like school . . . from college . . . some are upper caste, you know . . . so immediately you'll see them . . . like they are not there anymore . . .

(13)   So, you know, like . . . uhhh . . . that way . . . like putting anything on social media [you] also have to think sometimes . . .

(14)   Because, then you think like what other people [will] react . . . means . . . we don't care . . . I don't care . . . how they are going

to react, not for them, because it is like ultimately the truth, but you . . . you're feeling that way . . . uhhh . . .

(15) The people are going to react and mostly the upper caste people are going to react they don't feel . . . AHHH . . .

(16) Connected to you, and then they feel like . . . you [do not] feel like anywhere sharing your identity, or talking about your identity in the personal sense . . . in the back of your head, you know that [is] how the other person is going to react . . . so that we have to think all the time, so it is like . . . we feel very proud of our identity . . . ahhh

(17) It is nothing, but that always there in [your] mind what [the] other person is going to react, how they are going to think . . . or how our children are going to . . . [act] when they are raised here in a free country, but then, when they go to school, how their classmates, you know the Indian classmate, is going to the interact with them . . .

(18) so, we have [such] experience.

(19) [another example is] in New Jersey and there was like one family or family from my community.

(20) They shared [their] experience that ahhh . . . a girl they were a classmate [with] . . . they were like friends, and they suddenly stopped talking . . . the other girl from the upper-caste community suddenly stop[s] talking interacting that [Dalit] girl . . .

(21) the girl from my community . . . and then when she asked her like what happened, and she said, oh no, you are like untouchable, and I cannot . . . I'm not supposed to talk to you . . . not supposed to play with you and that's what my parents told me, you know so that is the incident, and it is real, it is the recent incident . . .

(22) so, there are many incidences how kids [who were] born here are being raised and even they . . . they talk about race, race, race and when it comes to caste they. . .

(23) They just like . . . [are] still privilege[d] . . . [they] talk about their . . . how they are upper caste and how other people are lost, you know.

TRANSCRIPT ANALYSIS

Such narrations, though common in Dalit circles, rarely get told outside those networks of low caste community members. Even within Dalit communities such stories seem to do little more than elicit nods of confirmation and familiar understanding. Rarely do such stories open the space for emotional sharing and dialogue about the wider lasting social and psychological impacts of such experiences on either marginalized or privileged communities. If such space is opened it is rarely even encountered by those in privileged subject positions. Notwithstanding, one participant in the focus group discussion detailed above did express that "we understand there is a mental health [impact] and [that] traumatic mental health, and the caste discrimination has some relationship."[76] This relationship becomes apparent in direct instances of social and cultural exclusion. Still, this relationship rarely gets interrogated in any depth, even by those in our focus group, who themselves work in helping professions like social work and counseling. Many in the focus group, indeed, expressed thanks for being able to discuss these relationships stating that they regularly engage with client's trauma, but rarely have a chance to think about their own. A's transcript above is exemplar of the social psychological hesitancy of Dalit precarity, even in South Asian diasporas. Despite not knowing the specifics of the threats and abuse narrated in lines two and three above, the frustration that the authorities "did not act" (line four) and "nothing happened" (line seven) is palpable and informs future decisions and actions of those that are marginalized. The transcript also articulates the Dalit faith in the rule of law (despite its repeated inability to assist aggrieved Dalits). Dalit recourse to law conjures up connections to the modern India state and constitution, of which the modern Dalit leader Dr. B. R. Ambedkar was the lead writer. Such perspectives illustrate the pride and shame always co-present in the Dalit identity. The fact that in "the back of your head" you must "think all the time" about "your identity" (line 16 above) articulates the subtle and pervasive role that Dalit identity and residual trauma plays in the everyday decisions and behavior choices of Dalits. Unaware of this background identity distortion and sociopolitical context, conflict practitioners may miss opportunities to use trauma and build on emotional resonance to chart new paths of change forward. Being trauma-informed requires an ability to understand these socio-historical nuances and use them to frame questions and build empathy and trust. A's constant awareness of how others are "going to react" (line 17) represents a trauma response to generations of de-humanization and exclusion.

The second story that A retells externalizes victimization to a wider "community" (line 4) and is indicative of the forward-looking problem setting required to "feel safe" (line 3) and not "lost" (line 23) in a Dalit identity. At the same time, such stories of social isolation raise questions about reifying what Montville calls "victimhood psychology."[77] If Indian children born in the United States internalize casteism from their parents' experiences back home, is Dalit identity construction the best way to overcome this learned sense of domination and oppression? In other words, is doubling down on Dalit sense of identity and victimhood the solution to high caste expressions of transcultural superiority? Or are there other ways outside of identity construction to solve the problem of transgenerational Dalit trauma and oppression? While such a discussion might take us too far afield from our focus here, the focus group speakers' invocation of U.S.-born Indian Americans raises important questions about the sites of resistance to deeply embedded forms of learned structural oppression. Is celebrating cultural heritage and strengthening social identity the only, or even best, ways to push for enduring social change? Rather than simply heritage and identity strengthening of these young Indian Americans, it seems that the work of re-educating the privileged is also needed. This implies the important need for contact.[78] A trauma-informed practitioner of conflict resolution would need to dance around these internal and external community approaches to change, allowing for shared vulnerability while also maintaining trust with those with less power. This is the dance that third party practitioners in conflict must always be aware of and engaged in, even if it seems the primary work of change is only needed *within* a specific community. I have written elsewhere about the need for coordinating narrative agency and strategy in the broad and multi-faceted anti-caste movement.[79] I have come to believe that such coordination requires not only narratively coordinating advocacy for identity, rights, and awareness, but also fostering skills for emotional awareness and narratively noticing the deep impacts of collective trauma. While narratives help to set the conflict in new ways, practitioners must also be ready to create safe opportunities for contact between conflicting parties. Without emotionally mindful and trauma-informed skills, social identity and difference are privileged, victimhood psychology is strengthened, and the discursive space between victims and perpetrators is widened. While this all makes contact and dialogue that much more difficult, it also makes a well-structured process of engaged conflict intervention, critical, effective, and rewarding.

CONCLUSION: TOWARDS A TRAUMA-INFORMED LENS THROUGH BEING EMOTIONALLY MINDFUL OF BOTH VICTIMS AND PERPETRATORS

So, who is victim and who the perpetrator? Better yet, does such a question really matter in conflict-intervention practice? In one sense it does, in that "the politics of naming [sic] secures new relationships between words and bodies, between ways of being and ways of seeing and speaking within the social field."[80] Yet, still in another sense who is victim and who is perpetrator matters to the work of a conflict intervention practitioner only in the sense of establishing equidistance and impartiality between conflict parties. In other words, such labels only matter in relation to practitioners' readiness to engage in a deep social analysis of power. Narrative theory calls us to interrogate our hardened sense of subject positions and realize that we all have multiple and overlapping social identity labels, including as both victims and perpetrators. Federman (2018), in referencing Max Weber, refers to labels like victim and perpetrator as ideal types.[81] Even though such ideal types mobilize conflict responses it is the narratives that underpin these ideal types and which harden identity positions and perpetuate a psychology of victimhood.

While this chapter has attempted to highlight the important role that victim identity narratives play in conflict processes, being trauma-informed is more than just being attentive to victims. The trauma-informed practitioner must be attentive to how our ideal types solidify and reify social positions, limit reflexivity, and challenge agency. Such attentive awareness is the first step to being emotionally mindful and trauma-informed. It does not mean that victims' stories do not matter. On the contrary, they matter greatly, and they cannot be overemphasized in either setting the problem or attempting to solve it. Pride and sense of identity are crucial for mobilizing social action and they are also notorious for escalating social conflict. Trauma-informed and emotionally mindful conflict resolution practitioners must be always analytically critical and vigilant of names and labels and how they operate in tandem with power. Receiving identities and labels, as invitations to curiosity rather than social fact, are crucial starting grounds for effective conflict resolution practice. Embracing wonder and proximity are foundational starting points for emotionally mindful and trauma-informed conflict practice. The chapter that follows will continue to hone and develop this practice lens. By engaging in active listening for emotional resonance in conflict parties' narrations, conflict resolution practitioners work to set the problem and actively choose between competing paradigms of professional practice. This way conflict resolution practitioners reframe their conflict practice in trauma-informed and emotionally mindful ways that do not trap them in the "perilous cartography"[82] of hardened identity assumptions, emotions of victimhood, or legacies of collective trauma.

NOTES

1. Donald Schon, *The Reflective Practitioner: How Professionals Think in Action* (New York: Basic Books, 1983), 19.

2. Kwame Anthony Appiah, *The Lies That Bind: Rethinking Identity Creed, Color, Country, Class, Culture* (New York: Liveright Publishing Corporation, 2018), XV.

3. For more on critical pedagogy see Henry Giroux, "Rethinking Educations as a Practice of Freedom: Paulo Freire and the Promise of Critical Pedagogy," *Policy Futures in Education* 6, no. 6 (2010).

4. Johan Galtung, "Violence, Peace, and Peace Research," *Journal of Peace Research*, 6, no. 3 (1969): 167–91.

5. W. E. B DuBois, *The Souls of Black Folks* (New York: Millennium Publishing, 2014 [1903]).

6. Eboo Patel, *Acts of Faith: The Story of an American Muslim, in the Struggle for the Soul of a Generation* (Boston: Beacon Press, 2010).

7. Thomas Hobbes, *Leviathan*, ed. Richard Tuck (New York: Cambridge University Press, 1991).

8. Zillah R. Eisenstein, *Capitalist Patriarchy and the Case for Socialist Feminism* (United States: Monthly Review Press, 2019 [1979]).

9. Pierre Bourdieu, *Pascalian Meditations* (Stanford, CA: Stanford University Press, 2000), quoted in Arthur Frank, *Letting Stories Breathe: A Socionarratology* (Chicago: University of Chicago Press, 2010), 25.

10. Sara Cobb, *Speaking of Violence: The Politics and Poetics of Narrative Dynamics in Conflict Resolution* (Oxford: Oxford University Press, 2013), 81. Cobb discusses the process of what she calls "narrative compression" (266–67), a process in which dominant storylines close off other possible storylines,

thereby flattening characters (social actors) into prescribed and controlled roles. She cogently argues that the work of realizing these processes and developing the "flattened" stories of the marginalized has been under-attended, for a host of reasons, in the work of conflict transformation and reconciliation.

11. For a good discussion of how processes of "othering" and exclusion relates to protracted conflict, see Marc Gopin, *Holy War, Holy Peace: How Religion Can Bring Peace to the Middle East* (New York: Oxford University Press, 2002), 66–67.

12. Kwame Anthony Appiah, *The Lies That Bind*, op. cit.

13. See Susan Neiman, "The Fatal Tension at the Heart of Wokeism." *Time Magazine*, June 27, 2023. https://time.com/6290367/susan-neiman-tension-at-the-heart-of-wokeism/, accessed December 22, 2023.

14. See: Rom Harre and Luk van Langenhove, *Positioning Theory* (Malden, MA: Wiley-Blackwell, 1998).

15. Rinker and Lawler (2019), op. cit.

16. For detailed discussion of the position theory see Ram Harré and Luk Van Langenhove, *Positioning Theory: Moral Contexts of Intentional Action* (Oxford: Blackwell, 1999).

17. See Rinker and Lawler (2019) as well as Van der Kolk (2016) for more on these complex sequalae of trauma.

18. Kurt Lewin, "Action research and minority problems." *Journal of Social Issues* 2 (1946): 34–46.

19. Maire Dugan, "A Nested Theory of Conflict," *A Leadership Journal: Women in Leadership—Sharing the Vision* 1, no. 1 (1996): 9–20.

20. A peace system in this sense is a "cluster of neighboring societies that do not make war with each other." See: Douglas P. Fry, Geneviève Souillac, L. Liebovitch, P. T. Coleman, K. Agan, E. Nicholson-Cox, D. Mason, F. Palma Gomez, and S. Strauss, "Societies within Peace Systems Avoid War and Build Positive Intergroup Relationships." *Humanities and Social Sciences Communications.* Online, Open Access, January 18, 2021, https://doi.org/10.1057/s41599-020-00692-8.

21. Lederach, *Preparing for Peace* (1996) and *Building Peace: Sustainable Reconciliation in Divided Societies* (1998), op. cit.

22. Joseph Montville, "Justice and the burdens of history," in *Reconciliation, Justice, and Coexistence*, edited by M. Abu Nimer (Lanham, MD: Lexington, 2001).

23. This is a play on the title of an important philosophical book by MacIntyre (1988). See: Alasdair MacIntyre. *Whose Justice? Which Rationality?* (South Bend, IN: University of Notre Dame Press, 1988).

24. For more on this see: Daniel Rothbart and Karina Korostelina, eds. *Identity, Morality, and Treat: Studies in Violent Conflict* (Lanham, MD: Lexington, 2007).

25. Resmaa Menakem, *My Grandmother's Hands: Racialized Trauma and the Pathways to Mending our Hearts and Bodies* (Las Vegas: Central Recovery Press, 2017), 7–8, emphasis in the original.

26. Thich Nhat Hanh, *Please Call Me by My True Names*, found at: https://www.awakin.org/v2/read/view.php?tid=2088, accessed July 21, 2022. For more on this poem and Nhat Hanh's hermeneutics of Buddhism see: Sallie King and Christopher Queen, *Engaged Buddhism: Buddhist Liberation Movements in Asia* (New York: SUNY Press, 1998).

27. See: Resmaa Menakem, *My Grandmother's Hands: Racialized Trauma and the Pathways to Mending Our Hearts and Bodies* (Las Vegas: Central Recovery Press, 2017); Bessel Van der Kolk, *The Body Keeps Score: Brain, Mind, and Body in the Healing of Trauma* (New York: Penguin Books, 2014).

28. Only recently have those in the field of Peace and Conflict Resolution taken up the subject of compassion. As an example, see Daniel Rothbart, "Compassion for Enemy Militants? A Case Study," *Conflict Resolution Quarterly* (2021): 1–21. DOI: 10.1002/crq.21299.

29. See Marshall Rosenberg, *Nonviolent Communication: A Language of Life* (New Mexico: Puddle Dancer Press, 2003).

30. Rom Harre and Luk van Langenhove, *Positioning Theory* (Malden, MA: Wiley-Blackwell, 1998).

31. Jeremy Rinker, "Narrative Reconciliation as a Rights-Based Praxis," *Peace Research*, 46, no. 1 (2016).

32. Laurel Richardson, *Writing Strategies: Researching Diverse Audiences* (London: Sage University Paper, 1990), 20.

33. Arthur Frank, *Letting Stories Breathe: A Socio-narratology* (Chicago: University of Chicago Press, 2010), 19.

34. Michel Foucault, *Society Must Be Defended: Lectures at the College de France 1975–1976*, ed. Mauro Bertani and Alessandro Fontana. Trans. David Macey (New York: Picador, 2003).

35. Vivian Jabri, *Discourses on Violence: Conflict Analysis Reconsidered* (London: Manchester University Press, 1996), 95.

36. Sara Cobb, *Speaking of Violence: The Politics and Poetics of Narrative Dynamics in Conflict Resolution* (Oxford: Oxford University Press, 2013), 3.

37. See also Francesca Polletta, *It Was Like a Fever: Storytelling in Protest and Politics* (Chicago: University of Chicago Press, 2006).

38. Jessica Senehi, "Constructive Storytelling: A Peace Process," *Peace and Conflict Studies* 9, no. 2 (2002): Article 3. DOI: 10.46743/1082-7307/2002.1026.

39. Gloria Goodwin Raheja and Ann Grodzins Gold. *Listen to the Heron's Words: Reimagining Gender and Kinship in North India* (Berkeley: University of California Press, 1994).

40. Catherine Reissman. *Narrative Analysis* (London: Sage, 1993), 1.

41. Arthur Frank, *Letting Stories Breathe: A Socio-narratology* (Chicago: University of Chicago Press, 2010), 18.

42. Ibid., Reissman, *Narrative Analysis*, 2.

43. Francesca Polletta, *It Was Like a Fever: Storytelling in Protest and Politics* (Chicago: University of Chicago Press, 2006), 43–45.

44. See Jeremy Rinker, *Justpeace Prospects for Peace-building and Worldview Tolerance: A South Asian Movement's Social Construction of Justice* (George Mason University, Ph.D. Dissertation, 2009) and Jeremy Rinker, "Narrative Reconciliation as a Rights-Based Praxis," *Peace Research*, 46, no. 1 (2016).

45. See Catherine Reissman, *Narrative Analysis* (London: Sage, 1993), Arthur Frank, *Letting Stories Breathe: A Socio-Narratology* (Chicago: University of Chicago Press, 2010), and William Labov *Language in the Inner City: Studies in Black English Vernacular* (Philadelphia, PA: University of Pennsylvania Press, 1972) as example of some of this debate.

46. Laurel Richardson, *Writing Strategies: Researching Diverse Audiences*, 21.

47. Ibid., 21.

48. Sara Cobb, *Speaking of Violence: The Politics and Poetics of Narrative Dynamics in Conflict Resolution* (Oxford: Oxford University Press, 2013).

49. Johan Galtung, "Violence, Peace, and Peace Research," *Journal of Peace Research*, 6, no. 3 (1969): 167–91.

50. Paul Farmer. "An Anthropology of Structural Violence," *Current Anthropology*, 45, no. 3 (June 2004): 305–25; Kathleen Ho, "Structural Violence as a Human Rights Violation," *Essex Human Rights Review*, 4, no. 2 (September 2007); M. Caprioli, "Primed for Violence: The Role of Gender Inequality in Predicting Internal Conflict," *International Studies Quarterly*, 49, no. 2 (June 2005): 161–78.

51. Sara Cobb, *Speaking of Violence*, 86.

52. Johan Galtung, "Violence, Peace, and Peace Research," 168.

53. Elisabeth Porter, *Connecting Peace, Justice, and Reconciliation*, 47.

54. Sara Cobb, *Speaking of Violence*, 27.

55. Ibid.

56. Ibid.

57. Ibid.

58. Ibid.

59. Ibid.

60. Vena Das, "The Act of Witnessing: Violence, Poisonous Knowledge, and Subjectivity," 220.

61. Laurel Richardson, *Writing Strategies: Researching Diverse Audiences*, 21.

62. See: Bryan Stevenson, *Just Mercy: A Story of Justice and Redemption* (New York: Spiegel & Garu, 2014). For a nice articulation of the power proximity, see also: https://www.youtube.com/watch?v=sMKIpycFaOg, accessed June 1, 2022.

63. See John Paul Lederach, *Preparing for Peace*, 1996, op. cit.

64. Personal interaction with visiting fellow from Lucknow University, May 5, 2022.

65. Ibid.

66. Ibid.

67. For detailed discussion of the position theory see Ram Harré and Luk Van Langenhove, *Positioning Theory: Moral Contexts of Intentional Action* (Oxford: Blackwell, 1999).

68. Personal interaction with visiting fellow from Lucknow University, May 5, 2022.

69. Ibid.

70. Ibid. The irony of this quote is that India itself does, like the United States, have an epidemic of mental health issues among school-aged students. See: https://www.thehindu.com/sci-tech/health/mental-health-in-india-how-does-india-tackle-mental-health-issues-among-school-children/article67409454.ece, accessed December 20, 2023. See also: https://wp.towson.edu/iajournal/2021/05/10/indias-mental-health-epidemic-deteriorating-amidst-the-pandemic/, accessed December 20, 2023.

71. Sara Cobb, *Speaking of Violence*, 58.

72. Vamik Volkan, *Bloodlines: From Ethnic Pride to Ethnic Terrorism* (Boulder, CO: Westview Press, 1997).

73. See: Lisa Schirch, "Ritual Reconciliation: Transforming Identity/Reframing Conflict," in *Reconciliation, Justice, and Coexistence: Theory and Practice*, edited by M. Abu Nimer (Lanham, MD: Lexington Books, 2001).

74. Focus Group Discussion for UNCG internally funded, "Understanding South Asian Social Identity in North America: Justice and Solidarity Building in the Diaspora" (UNCG-IRB # 21-0115), April 23, 2022.

75. See: https://www.lirs.org/causes-of-immigration/, accessed June 20, 2022 and https://www.un.org/en/global-issues/migration#:~:text=Some%20people%20move%20in%20search,disasters%2C%20or%20other%20environmental%20factors, accessed June 20, 2022.

76. Focus Group Discussion for UNCG internally funded, "Understanding South Asian Social Identity in North America: Justice and Solidarity Building in the Diaspora" (UNCG-IRB # 21-0115), April 23, 2022.

77. Joseph Montville, "Justice and the Burdens of History," in *Reconciliation, Justice, and Coexistence*, edited by M. Abu Nimer (Lanham, MD: Lexington Books, 2001).

78. G. W. Allport, *The Nature of Prejudice: 25th Anniversary Edition* (New York, NY: Basic Books, 1979).

79. Jeremy A. Rinker, *Identity, Rights, and Awareness: Anticaste Activism in India and the Awakening of Justice Through Discursive Practices* (Lanham, MD: Lexington Books, 2018).

80. Anupama Rao, *The Caste Question: Dalits and the Politics of Modern India* (Berkeley: University of California Press, 2009), 16.

81. Sarah Federman (2018). "The Ideal Perpetrator: The French National Railways and the Social Construction of Accountability." *Security Dialogue* 49, no. 5 (2018): 327–44.

82. Kwame Anthony Appiah, *The Lies that Bind: Rethinking Identity Creed, Color, Country, Class, Culture* (New York: Liveright Publishing Corporation, 2018), XV.

2

DEVELOPING A TRAUMA-INFORMED LENS

NARRATING AND LISTENING TO NARRATION

". . . trauma can also be the body's response to a long sequence of smaller wounds. It can be a response to anything that it experiences as too much, too soon, or too fast . . . Trauma responses are unpredictable. Two bodies may respond very differently to the same experience."[1]

". . . the medical model can lead people to a sense of themselves as 'docile bodies.' Subject to knowledge and procedures in which they have no active voice. There are also subjugating stories of gender, race, class, age, sexual orientation, and religion (to name a few) that are so prevalent and entrenched in our culture that we can get caught up in them without realizing it."[2]

WHAT DO WE REALLY MEAN BY TRAUMA-INFORMED?

While many conflict intervention practitioners describe their work as "trauma-sensitive"[3] or "trauma-informed,"[4] the practices they describe vary quite widely. As was alluded to in chapter 1, simply being aware of a group's traumatic history does not guarantee a more trauma-sensitive, or trauma-informed, intervention technique. This is complicated by the fact that systematizing trauma response is a daunting task as trauma response is like a fingerprint, unique to each individual psyche. Typologies of trauma are, therefore, notoriously difficult to establish.[5] Simultaneously, dominant conceptions of emotions, and mores about their public expression, confound practitioners' responses to trauma. A trauma-informed approach requires both humble awareness of past trauma and conscious efforts to foreground treatments and intervention techniques that allow both the space and structure[6] for people to articulate the challenges and effects (as well as psychological affects[7]) of past trauma (or stress) on their unique lived experience. This requires a new-found acceptance of emotions as important drivers of reason and rational choice, not unmanageable or unpredictable variables to avoid (remember Van der Kolk's quote at the start of this book's introduction). A trauma-informed approach also privileges an awareness of the emotional intelligence to know when to step up and when to step back in conflictual situations. In a sense this is the overarching goal of all conflict resolution work; to give voice to the voiceless, especially those conflict parties that are emotionally distraught and/or traumatized. Giving voice, in turn, requires a situational and emotional awareness on the part of the conflict resolution practitioner. Consequently, central to uplifting a trauma-informed process of healing in conflict resolution practice is the development of reflexivity, deep listening, and reframing skills, which allow space for emotional expression and narration, while simultaneously limiting the possibilities of re-traumatization. I argue in this chapter that conflict resolution professionals need to move toward more strategic interventions reflexively attuned directly to a community's past trauma by using techniques of active listening, emotionally listening/noticing, and mindful reframing. Of course, the foundations of curiosity and personal proximity ground all effective conflict intervention techniques (as underscored in the introduction and chapter 1), but the intergroup skills of active listening and emotional awareness represent critical inputs for peace.

Without a base of honest inquisitiveness, trust, and relationship, trauma-informed peacebuilding cannot be achieved. Of course, with time, this base can be developed and grown through active listening and emotional intelligence/awareness. Here it may help to reframe these important foundations of trauma response slightly as an ability for reflexivity, what Jay Rothman (2014) defines as:

> an interactive process that takes into consideration the relationship between self, other, and context. This reflexive process entails engaging in

the moment as well as noticing and, as much as possible, understanding one's thoughts and feelings during an encounter with the parties in a certain time and place. Engaging in this process helps the mediator expand her or his frame of attention from a primary focus on the parties and their conflict situation to also consider how he or she encounters those parties, and what are the underlying assumptions and priorities that shape their mediated interactions.[8]

Still, all this theoretical grounding in reflexivity does not tell us how one listens and reframes in a culturally sensitive and trauma-informed way. What are the telltale signs of past trauma experiences in both speech and nonverbal communication contexts and how do our own cultural and social constructions inform both the expression of, and prosocial intervention in, traumatic pasts? This chapter aims to develop a set of meta-level guideposts for defining and developing what it means to be "trauma-informed" in social conflict practice, while simultaneously being aware of social actors' complex and dynamic expressions of power and privilege. This requires a set of abilities to engage narrative meaning reflexively and positively. Such a simultaneously backward and forward-looking set of in-the-moment conflict skills requires an ability to aggregate emotional response with concrete action, as well as an analytical ability to honor the past while being in the emotional present moment. This is not the medical model approach to trauma, but rather one that is both informed by the medical model, cultural context, and reflective process.[9] Such response is always open to ambiguity and thus difficult to definitively define outside of context.

Since there is little consensus on what is meant by trauma-informed practice, I have elsewhere written about the need for systematization of trauma-informed practices.[10] Most references to trauma in the literature of peace and conflict studies relates to the impacts of genocide and ethnic rivalry[11] instead of outlining specific practices aimed at remedying the destructive impacts of these social pathologies on communities. While many have argued along the lines that "a methodologically sensitive approach" that includes "the psychosocial assessment of trauma" is needed,[12] few have explored how such an approach would work in actual conflict intervention practice. A few notable exceptions to this practice-based lacuna include the accounts written by Resmaa Menakem (2017) quoted above and the clinical psychological approach of Duran and Duran (1995), in which the authors argue for a "postcolonial psychology" that addresses the Native American "soul wound" of past colonial genocide.[13] In both these examples, legacies of implicit racial/ethnic biases and colonial encounters with nativity are critical contexts for developing a trauma-informed practice in specific communities' identity-based conflicts. A more recent addition to this literature is Thenmoshi Soundararajan's (2022) *The Trauma of Caste: A Dalit Feminist Meditation on Survivorship, Healing, and Abolition.* While very little clinical peacebuilding literature of this nature currently exists for the world's most protracted social conflict contexts, these identity-based forays belie a need to radically reprogram the way we think about trauma and emotions in the practice of intervention in social conflicts. Trauma and emotions are key drivers of protracted international conflicts. Put another way, despite increasing use of language like "trauma-informed care"[14] and "integrated peacebuilding" and "conflict sensitivity,"[15] few scholar-practitioners of conflict resolution have engaged the concept of collective trauma in any intentional, methodical, and directly interventionist way.[16] Both the theory and practice around collective trauma is, therefore, limited in the peace and conflict field. While social scientists from other fields, in particular clinical psychology, and sociology, have provided considerable scholarly attention to, "narrative therapy,"[17] "cultural trauma"[18] and the "trauma process,"[19] few conflict practitioners are aware of either the sociological theory or its critical import for on-the-ground conflict intervention practice. Harold Saunders' ideas on sustained dialogue and public peace signal one practitioner's realization of the important role of the changing emotional context in conflict resolution processes but provides relatively little generalizable guidelines for how to effectively engage either emotions or the enduring social legacies of collective trauma in a public peace process. Having said this, Saunders' "public peace process"[20] does reveal that building peaceful relations takes time and sustained effort, not typical inputs in international diplomacy. Still, the fact is that the medical model of trauma does not map nicely to collective experiences of trauma. Figure I.1, introduced in this book's introduction (see figure I.1, the STAR Snail model, Introduction), does provide an alternative to the medical model approach to trauma, but remains primarily person-centered as opposed to expressly sociologically in vivo. What conflict practitioners mean by trauma-informed must be sociological, and not just psychological, in nature. So, as STAR's snail model can be applied to collectives, its use in collectives remains limited and under-theorized. Conflict manifests in the social expression of dissensus, and though psychological characteristics certainly impact conflict dynamics, being a trauma-informed practitioner requires having a particular ability to read the sociological situation/context, respond reflexively by reflecting on personal assumptions, and reframe conflict parties' stories in pro-social and nonviolent ways. This ability to read the situation, respond reflexively, and reframe in a trauma-informed way spans both the personal and social. Notice this is a seemingly counterintuitive turn-away from the reliance on only psychological analysis, but not a discounting of it. Trauma impacts everyone in unique ways, but when practitioners come to conflict with not only this realization, but also a deep understanding of past historical harms on all sides of the dispute, they are well positioned to develop approaches that positively impact the body politic, not just the individual body. This is being trauma-informed as a conflict intervention practitioner; it is an admittedly difficult and open-ended process of curiosity and lifelong learning.

Skills of listening and assisting in the reconstruction of narrative agency are critical practices for developing a trauma-informed lens in conflict practice. Without theoretical clarity of narrative structures, discursive processes, social theory and context, and cultural competency, a "trauma-informed" lens has little grounds to impact real intervention practice and transform protracted social conflict. Listening to stories of collective historical trauma can build a rich description of what Booth has called "memory justice"[21] and develop creative ground to establish lasting change. We must remember that trauma-informed practice requires sustained practice. Listening to such stories and developing the social and cultural competency in assessing conflict parties' speech acts is primary to any practitioner's trauma-informed lens. So, what we mean by trauma-informed is a process, not an outcome. One might say that conflict practitioners who are emotionally mindful are always already on the journey to become trauma-informed practitioners, but that they never really arrive (remember this sentiment from Thich Nhat Hanh's poem "Please Call Me by My True Names" introduced in chapter 1).[22] The following retelling of a conflict training experience I was involved in centers the importance of listening and reflexivity in trauma-informed conflict resolution practice. This example is followed by an additional analysis of a contemporary caste atrocity story. Together these narrative vignettes highlight the power of both narrative storytelling and listening, as well as practitioner reflexivity in developing what we mean by trauma-informed conflict practice.

THE TURN TOWARDS SOCIAL-EMOTIONAL LEARNING (SEL) IN EDUCATION: TEACHING SCHOOL ADMINISTRATORS TO CONSTRUCTIVELY ENGAGE CONFLICT

Since well before the COVID-19 pandemic, the field of education has been moving towards an increased awareness of what has become known as social emotional learning (SEL).[23] Progressively, SEL frameworks and approaches have been adopted by school systems increasingly aware that the existing models of discipline, success, and psychological support for their students are not working.[24] Driven by poor outcomes, SEL is increasingly seen as a model for change in school culture and discipline. SEL has been applied and studied in all aspects of the school day from overall student success[25] to physical activity.[26] Of course, like all newly introduced models and buzz words in the field of education, defining SEL is complicated and not without its critics. Hoffman (2009), as an example, argues that the hundreds of SEL programs in U.S. schools "appear to draw on a model of the emotions that sees them as internal, individual states that require active managerial control to be channeled in socially positive, healthy ways."[27] Hoffman maintains that this dominant Western bias privileges "talk" and overlooks SELs key value of community.[28] As we know, not all cultures express or share emotions in the same way, so SEL, like other trauma-informed frameworks and supports, requires great cultural reflexivity and critical reflection upon implementation. Such policy shifts, frameworks, and buzzwords, in institutionalized systems often falter due to lack of reflexivity, reflective skills, and the primary emphasis on listening for problems and speaking of outcomes as opposed to focusing attention on process. The following training experience, that I was involved in, illustrates the all-to-common absence of these primary "trauma-informed" skills.

In the Spring of 2021, a colleague and I were asked to provide a two-day training workshop on conflict resolution for teachers in rural schools who were training to become school administrators (Principals and Assistant Principals). In the training we spent an inordinate amount of time modeling and discussing reflexivity and connecting what Lederach calls an "elicitive model"[29] of intervention to mindfulness and insights from dialectical behavioral therapy (DBT) as key actionable skills/practices for administrators dealing with school-based conflict. We practiced in context-specific role play activities, engaged in meditation exercises, modeled embodied listening exercises, and trained in group dialogue about restorative school discipline. After the two days of well-received training, we were invited back to observe and act as "assessors" for an experiential role play exercise to test students' skills acquisition during their training. This "performance learning day" was administered by the Project Manager of the Principal Preparation for Excellence and Equity in Rural Schools (PPEERS) program, which is implemented through the School of Education at our University. This was the culminating experience of the conflict resolution portion of their months-long training. Each student/intern in the program was asked to play the school principal in a tightly structured and time-managed angry parent role play scenario (see figure 2.1 below for the role play scenario given to students). As my colleague and I assessed each student/intern's performance in an oral debrief and collective online assessment form, we quickly realized our primary training messages about reflexivity and close listening were lost on most of the student/interns. Of the approximately twenty students/interns only 2–3 of them exhibited the reflexivity in-the-moment to effectively de-escalate the parent and make the parents' anger recede as a central driver of the conversational and racially-tainted context.

While many of these future principals did a nice job of addressing the angry parent's immediate concerns, most jumped right to negotiation and problem-solving mindsets without deep listening or paying close reflexive awareness to the parents' felt concerns and changing emotional dynamics. While the secret instructions for the role-playing mother were to argue that her son should be allowed to play in the Friday night basketball game where college recruits would be present, the mother was also concerned about the racial implicit bias in her African American son's description about what happened with his white teacher. In many assessment observations cultural cues, made explicit in the role play's background scenario and instructions (not included herein), were overlooked or outright disregarded. Language and cultural cues in the out-of-school suspension write-up and discussion of the racial power dynamics in the classroom were breezed over in favor of issue-specific solutions. In short, most of these future school administrators rushed to solve the immediate issue-specific problem and placate the parent's anger while paying very little attention to either the racial or cultural dynamics or the emotional needs of either the parent, student, or the larger school community. Not one observed future administrator focused on the impacts to the school's emotional environment and community, but rather focused on only the individual needs of the suspended student and/or solving for these needs in a way that would not be perceived as unfair or outside of the policy of the school.

Performance Learning Day

Angry Parent Simulation (25-minute block: 12 minutes for conference; 8 minutes for verbal feedback; 5 minutes to complete the online rubric and transition for the next student/intern)

Principal (Student/Intern) Info: An actor will play the role of an angry parent who comes to the principal to discuss and ultimately appeal her son's 3-day suspension made earlier by the assistant principal. One source of information about this matter is available to you – the Suspension Form:

OUT-OF-SCHOOL SUSPENSION NOTICE
Cherry Lane Middle School

Date:___9/22/20_____ (Tuesday)
Name of Student: <u>Tyronne Johnson</u>   Grade: <u>8</u>
Teacher: <u>Miss Sissy Almsgiver</u>   Class: <u>Math 8</u>
<u>Description of Incident:</u>   Tyronne Johnson cursed at Miss Almsgiver by saying "Fuck you, Bitch" in front of the class on Tuesday. He stated that the teacher embarrassed him in front of the class by calling him "stupid" when he could not recall how he got the answer to one of his math problems.

<u>Disposition:</u>   3 days Out-of-School Suspension (Wed-Fri). May NOT play in basketball playoff game on Friday night.
<u>Handbook Reference:</u> From Section 2: Student Conduct "Students who use profane language toward any adult in the school shall receive five (5) days of Out-of-School Suspension."

John E. Stowe

Mr. John E. Stowe
Assistant Principal/Principal

CC: Parent(s)
    Student Discipline File

Angry Parent Actor: The new principal (Student/Intern) will be in possession of a copy of the suspension form (above), noting the details of an incident. The copy of this form was given to you and your son on Tuesday afternoon when the out-of-school suspension was made for the next three (3) school days (Wed., Thurs., and Fri.). The principal (Intern) has been told that this conference is at the request of the mother who wants to discuss the incident and who wants to appeal to the principal to change the out-of-school suspension because her son is a star basketball player who would otherwise be playing in Friday night's game, which is the 2ⁿᵈ round of playoffs for Cherry Lane Middle School's boys' team.

The Angry Parent Actor is encouraged to improvise within the spirit of the simulation, <u>escalating responses when poor leadership moves are made and de-escalating when more appropriate leadership moves are employed.</u>

Figure 2.1   PPEERS Training Role Play Exercise.

While the recourse to problem-solving and hard negotiation tactics is not surprising given our American cultural penchant for privileging these skill sets, future administrators/leaders' instinct to fall back on rational interest-based skills and policy over emotional intelligence and cultural reflexivity should concern us all. More than rational leadership, social conflict requires social emotional learning and skills of reflexive response and deep listening. Most future administrators, despite having two days of training that included mindfulness, listening, and conflict analysis skills, failed to take a trauma-informed stance towards the angry mother and, indeed, appeared more concerned about potential liability than student learning or healing. Instead, emotional outbursts about possible, or perceived, racial bias and lost opportunity were minimized and avoided in favor of interest-based negotiation techniques. One student/intern we assessed tried hard to impress his assessors with a clearly over-planned approach of showering the parent with kindness and offering a string of solutions without fully listening to the parents' underlying emotion-laden interests and needs. Focused on problem solving, he seemed oblivious to the trauma and emotions of the racial climate of school community or the effected classroom. This approach, devoid of emotional awareness and/or cultural/situational reflexivity proved disastrous as the angry parent felt belittled, unheard, and disregarded. Another student/intern set out an immediate logical course of action to getting the student restored to the classroom environment but seemed to miss the importance the parent put on the missed opportunity for her suspended son to play in the playoff basketball game due to the suspension falling over a weekend. Despite less than subtle hints that she was worried about her son's missing a valuable basketball recruiting opportunity, the future administrator stayed firm on policy and refused to allow discussion of alternative solutions to the parent's concerns (something these administrators are often encouraged to do so as not to make exceptions to school policy). This tension between policy and person, though not surprising, underscores a reliance on hierarchical power over relational awareness on the part of the student/aspiring administrative leaders. In each of these instances listening for tone and underlying expression of needs was missed and potential solutions, therefore, overlooked. In Fischer and Ury's popular book *Getting to Yes*, they speak of both separating the people from the problem and positions from interests in developing a principled form of negotiation, but such rational approaches of these aspiring administrators underappreciated the role of emotions and the in-the-moment emotional context and dynamics in the conflict situation. In fact, such a rational starting point tries to sanitize all emotions from conflict negotiation and misses the nuances of conflict context, narrative history, and relationship. Student/interns, familiar with this western cultural approach to negotiation, seemed unaware of the role play context's emotional dynamics and how to use them to their situational advantage in working with the angry parent. Emotional outbursts (and the stereotypes of the angry black mother) played out in predictable ways with opportunities for empathy missed by aspiring principals. Trauma-informed response required situational awareness and embodiment that these aspiring administrators seemed incapable of integrating with their problem-oriented rational focus on policy and perceived sense of fairness.

One further analytical mapping tool that can help us understand the levels of possible approaches to such interactions is Marie Dugan's nested model/paradigm of conflict (1996).[30] I find this model useful to not only analyzing and mapping a conflict, but also helping to conceptualize available conflict resolution intervention opportunities. Dugan argues that conflict issues are nested, or embedded, in relationships, subsystems, and systems of conflict (see figure 2.2 below).

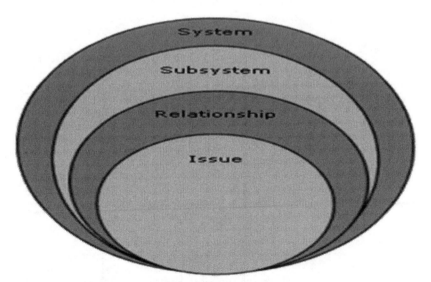

Figure 2.2 The Nested Conflict Paradigm. *Source*: John Paul Lederach, *Building Peace: Sustainable Reconciliation in Divided Societies*, 1997. cf. Dugan, "A Nested Theory of Conflict," *Women in Leadership* 1, no. 1 (summer 1996).

In each of these nested bases of conflict there are creative opportunities to intervene. Failure to be aware of the emotional and traumatic context, creates the potential to miss creative opportunities for intervention. Further, in conceptualizing conflict sources as rooted within broader social contexts, reflexive attention is focused increasingly on the impacts of structural violence as one expands outward to the outer layers of Dugan's nested model. Dugan's practice-informed paradigm provides an analytical tool to explore the complex layers of trauma and emotion which wrap around the history of a conflict context. While my training and assessment work on the PPEERs program represents a subsystem level response to school conflict and discipline, reflecting on the learning transfer from our training highlights the fact that both listening, and reflexivity, take time as well as dedicated and recurring practice. Like dialectical behavioral therapy (DBT), trauma-informed conflict resolution practice requires cognitive training to be hyper-aware of your own responses to stress and emotions.

Violent and destructive conflict we know challenges one's ability to maintain the awareness and cognitive discipline to stay trauma aware. An angry mother in an administrator's office can quickly destabilize the emotional valence of the typical school setting. So, what can conflict resolution practitioners do in the face of violence when immediate response is necessary, and reflexivity must compete with the need for both moral action and enforcement of a negative peace? Reflexivity in-the-moment is difficult and being trauma-aware does not guarantee conflict intervention professionals will always react to suffering in an emotionally mindful way. Violence speaks in an international language that transcends cultural and identity-based differences. Nonviolent resistance to violence is commonly assumed to be trauma-aware, but such a set of practices cannot always be assumed to be trauma-informed as past trauma reinscribes a practitioner's sense of meaning and subsequent reaction in violent episodes. The epistemological paradoxes of these labels of "trauma-aware" and "trauma-informed," though alluded to in earlier chapters, continues to dog attempts to neatly package and typologize these practices. The PPEERS training I delivered reinforced in me the complexity of thinking of trauma-informed as one static category. The example below aims to further complicate these labels through telling the story of a very different context of contemporary caste atrocity and the activist and conflict interventionist responses to this destructive expression of caste-based social conflict.

CHAPTER 2

THE KHAIRLANJI MASSACRE: RESISTING CASTE-BASED VIOLENCE WHILE MAINTAINING A NONVIOLENT, EMOTIONALLY MINDFUL AND TRAUMA-AWARE RIGHTEOUS INDIGNATION

The widely covered 2006 rural atrocity which has come to be known in Indian parlance as simply "the Khairlanji massacre" presents an important context to delve deeper into the lasting trauma of violent conflict and potential post-hoc intervention responses to such savagery. While the racial dynamics of American school-based discipline described above clearly have traumatic tenacles and complex legacies, violent atrocities, such as Khairlanji, speak castes' traumatic inheritance in unique ways. Think of the June 1921 Tulsa Race Massacre,[31] or the November 3, 1979, Greensboro Massacre[32] as prominent U.S. examples of racial animus that still reverberate throughout American society today. Such race-based atrocities have both left long legacies of collective trauma in the communities in which they occurred and, in the case of The Greensboro Massacre, led to the first truth and reconciliation commission in the United States. These episodes of racial violence inscribe both past and future-going events with new meaning. They also raise important questions like: how can those acting as third-party intervenors describe their practice as trauma-aware or informed in such horrific contexts? What does a trauma-aware and emotionally mindful response to such evil collective historical trauma even look like?

The, more recent, 2006 Khairlanji massacre, initially underreported in the Indian press, galvanized Dalit rights activists to protest and agitate for appropriate judicial response to the all too regular instances of violent injustices against lower caste communities on the subcontinent. This resistance nonviolently channeled low castes' emotions toward constitutional rights and judicial enforcement, as opposed to more indiscriminate violent retaliation. This channeling of emotions towards forcing the government of India to apply the 1989 Prevention of Atrocities Act (hereafter PoA Act) to this crime, while pragmatic and prosocial, also contradicted the interdependent Buddhist norms and values that are central to the identity of many Dalit rights activists. The paradoxical response and aftermath of Khairlanji reveals some important insights for conflict intervention practitioners about effectively working with trauma and emotions. In the words of academic and activist Dr. Anand Teltumbde: "Khairlanji represents the breakdown of the wicked equilibrium that has held the subcontinent historically frozen for thousands of years—and has carried India through centuries of utterly underserved self-attribution with qualities such as 'tolerant,' 'nonviolent,' and 'peace-loving.'"[33] Such a critical view from the downtrodden masses is rarely voiced in Hindu-dominated India and is regularly met with repression and further silencing violence.[34] The Khairlanji atrocity is an ongoing trigger for traumatic sequalae and feeling of indignity felt by many contemporary Dalits.

Khairlanji, September 29, 2006—Two days after my own 34th birthday, atrocity hit the Bhotmange family in a small Maharashtrian village of Khairlanji. The sequence of events now known as the Khairlanji massacre have been contested since that macabre evening. On that evening, a mob of about fifty angry caste Hindus,[35] converged on the Bhotmange's family home and attacked and killed all but one member of the family (e.g., the wife, daughter, and two sons). Portrayed as a "revenge killing" and a "Naxalite effort"[36] by local authorities, Dalit communities in Maharashtra quickly mobilized to force the state to adequately investigate the murders and bring the perpetrators to justice. In local Dalits' view there was a clear caste angle to the attack and, therefore, a need to invoke the 1989 Prevention of Atrocities (PoA) Act. The Bhotmanges were one of only two Dalit (Mahar caste) families among approximately 150 families living in the non-descript village of Khairlanji in Bhandara district of Maharashtra [the other families in this village were made up of Powars and Kalars which are classified as Other Backward Classes (OBCs) in Indian parlance].[37] While the mother, father, one daughter, and one son of the family had recently testified to the local authorities by identifying one of the attackers in a September 13 altercation in the village, Dalit activists believed that the caste dynamics of Khairlanji village had played a more important role than simply revenge in the local mobilization that eventually ended in this violent atrocity against the Bhotmange family.

Between 5:00 and 7:00 PM on the evening of the 29th, Mrs. Surekha Bhotmange (45) was cooking, and Priyanka (19) was studying with her two brothers Roshan (17) and Sudheer (18).[38] Mrs. Bhotmange had apparently heard that the crowed was amassing outside the village and informed Mr. Rajan Gajbhiye (the son of the man who the family had provided witness of on the earlier September 13 attack) by cell phone to leave the village and abort his plan to visit their home. Mr. Gajbhiye said later that he did not think the mob would harm the women in the

Bhotmange household, but nevertheless he informed the local police station by phone of the growing mob as he returned to his nearby village. When the mob learned Mr. Gajbhiye had left the village they became enraged and nevertheless continued to the Bhotmange house where they had originally expected to find Mr. Gajbhiye. According to the Manuski Center's Human Rights report, the first and seemingly most accurate report of the horrors that followed:

> They [the mob] dragged them [the Bhotmange family victims] out of their hut and removed their clothes. Roshan, bother of Priyanka, was asked to have sex with his sister Priyanka. After he refused, his private parts were thrashed by caste Hindus. Priyanka was hit with an axe on her breast, thrashed and stabbed with sticks and [an] ubhari (a stick which is one sided sharp and used to prick [a] bull while driving bullock-cart so that bullocks can run fast) [was pushed] in her private parts. Before doing this, the 19-year-old [Priyanka] was brutally gang raped by the caste Hindus, which was largely supported by Caste Hindu women. Even caste Hindu women inflamed their male counterparts to rape Mrs. Surekha and Ms. Priyanka . . . After that, caste Hindus killed all four of them and threw away their bodies in the canal.[39]

Difficult to read and beyond words, this horrific account draws a graphic picture of the traumatic violent atrocity that occurred that evening at the Bhotmange home. The gruesomeness of the account underscores the displaced trauma, anger, and rage of the perpetrators.

Soon after the attack Mr. Bhotmange, who was not home at the time of the brutal attack, began publicly arguing that the 1989 PoA Act should be invoked to investigate both the murders and the lack of local police response to the incident. Evidence compiled by the Manuski Center, a Pune-based Human Rights Center, shows that the police did not arrive on the scene until 10 PM, roughly four hours after the attack, and it took until October 1, 2006, for a First Incident Report (FIR) to even be recorded at the local police station.[40] Within days of the event Dalits in Maharashtra began to organize and support Mr. Bhotmange's, until then, futile pleas for justice. Dalit Buddhists mobilized through social media sites and social networks and took a leading role in this agitation to force the authorities to invoke the 1989 PoA Act in this case, which provides stronger penalties (including death) for crimes that are motivated by caste animus. Blogs, e-mail chains, and newsletters describing the event were circulated across the state and around the world to raise awareness of the crime and the oppressive conditions under which rural Dalits continue to live. Among Dalit friends celebrating Ambedkar's 50-year anniversary of conversion at *Dikshabhumi* (site of Ambedkar's Conversion), developing an appropriate reaction to Khairlanji was the main topic of conversation.[41] The 2006 events in the village of Khairlanji, Maharashtra became the spark for a mass Dalit-led national campaign for Dalit awareness and rights. While the 1989 PoA Act, like the Indian constitution itself, has become an important vector for Dalits' claims for social and procedural justice, the draconian punishments the act allows and condones seem to be at cross-purposes with important Dalit Buddhist nonviolent beliefs and value commitments. Dalit reliance on structurally violent judicial systems also seems to run counter to the goals of sustainable change. Such paradoxes abound in this story and complicate the traumatic dynamics and legacy of such a horrific event. In addition, many of the responses to the Khairlanji atrocity overlooked the all too ordinary reality of such horrific and all too common events in the subcontinent's history. It is not only these paradoxes which a closer look at the Khairlanji response deftly unmasks, but such paradoxes also open important questions about the interplay between local caste identities and trauma-informed and trauma-aware activism in the face of such public atrocity and communal violence. The Khairlanji massacre was an event that unleashed Dalit anger, allowing the expression of years of grievances to be publicly voiced. Khairlanji also activated an organizing network that circumvented inter-caste ideological differences in belief and identity to educate and agitate for a just response to the harm. Petitioning the Indian state (through its judicial mechanisms) mobilized a rational response to Dalit anger without fully exploring the traumatic and emotional blowback of this type of targeted, as well as retaliatory, violence. Coming just days before the 50th anniversary of Ambedkar's historical conversion to Buddhism, the event galvanized a collective and nonviolent social response from Dalits, but this interest-based response raises important questions about emotionally mindful and trauma-aware nonviolent conflict resolution in the aftermath of such emotionally triggering collective harm.

The righteous indignation of years of unheard grievances burst forth as a surprise to many, and even many Dalit rights activists were caught off guard by the outpouring of anger and protest spilling onto the streets. While the timing of these events was important, occurring immediately following the mass gathering at *Dikshabhumi* (commemorating Ambedkar's historic conversion to Buddhism) in nearby Nagpur, the sustained resistance of Dalit rights activists propelling this as a national issue was unique in India's history of caste/communal violence. Eventually winding its way with glacial speed through the Indian courts, the Khairlanji case represents a symptom of years of caste trauma. The longevity of the agitation post-Khairlanji is testament to the deep collective traumas it unearthed in the Dalit community, as well as the rising power of India's downtrodden majority. Ambedkar Buddhists' response to the July 14, 2010, Indian judicial ruling that this crime should not be punishable as a caste atrocity again sparked widespread protest in Maharashtra, the stronghold of Ambedkar Buddhism and Dalit rights activism. Ambedkar Buddhists' reaction to the court's ruling, almost four years after the atrocity, provides an important means to understanding the complex interplay between Dalit Buddhist marginalized identity and this community's collective sense of trauma. Writing about Ambedkar Buddhists' reaction to this Supreme Court decision on Khairlanji makes clear the role that emotion and trauma played, and continue to play, in this atrocity story. The story of Khairlanji and the agitation that followed also illustrates well Ambedkar Buddhists' critically inattentive exploration of the connections between their core Buddhist value commitments and their Dalit identity-based mobilization for social justice. Describing Dalit Buddhists as either trauma-informed/trauma-aware or emotionally mindful obscures our understanding of the Dalit response to these events and masks the ways in which assumptions about organizing and mobilizing response trumped more emotionally aware intervention opportunities. So, how can those acting as third-party intervenors describe their practice as trauma-aware or informed in such a horrific context? What would be a more trauma-aware and emotionally mindful response to such evil? One, obviously, cannot be "neutral" or "impartial" in the face of such violent atrocity. But how should one aiming to be emotionally mindful of the impacts of collective trauma most effectively respond? Ambedkar Buddhists' lack of attention to both means and ends of their emotion-laden activism further reified a marginalized position vis-à-vis the nation-state. Does such reactive organizing thereby put them closer to, or farther from, realizing their ultimate emancipation? Such questions, though possibly perceived as unduly critical of victims, are essential to reflective trauma-awareness of both those marginalized and those intervening. More broadly, how can conflict intervention practitioners foreground this collective trauma (be trauma aware) without allowing this trauma to inform, or rather control, their emotional affect? Detailed analysis of the events of Khairlanji, and the activist agitation that followed, raises more questions than they provide clear answers. Still, conflict practitioners cannot forgo these challenging questions and traumatic histories in their quest to be trauma aware. As insider partial intervention practitioners, we must "revive the morning process"[42] to foment sustainable change in such systems of oppression; this is a tightrope walk for sure. This is where agitating and organizing can sometimes work at cross purposes to effective conflict intervention.

While a conflict intervention professional faced with such a context must work to be proximate to the emotional suffering of those agitating for change, they also must resist the urge for quick solutions, or emotional reaction, to complex generational and structural conflict dynamics. The Khairlanji massacre is a symptom of larger system-level problems, and, thus, requires emotional attention and mindfulness. Responses to the harm can only go so far in transforming the structural violence inherent in traumatic sequalae. Attempting to address the issues and relationships in this conflict (see figure 2.2: Dugan's Nested Conflict Paradigm above) may provide short-term solutions but will not ensure lasting change in the system of caste-based oppression. Real change will require what John Paul Lederach has called a "generational"[43] view of peacebuilding and the reflexive ability to deeply listen to the transgenerational and vicarious trauma of those most effected by past harm without allowing this pain and suffering to drive reactive intervention practices. Of course, those who believe they are unaffected by the trauma of discrimination often do not realize its full impacts on their lives and trajectories. To be trauma-aware, conflict practitioners must be attuned to the many nuances of their own, as well as others, positionality. The conflict intervenor, while remaining vigilantly curious, must also have skills in deep listening, active listening, and reframing. This means deploying conflict skills without assuming or telegraphing desired outcomes; this is the work of peacebuilding that is most difficult to both teach and/or fund. No donors and humanitarians will support peace interventions with no clear professed outcomes, but lack of long-term vision, to some extent, is required to balance emotional distance with emotional mindfulness. How do we train conflict intervention specialists in such creative visioning? Such long-term irenic outcomes are often opaque and amorphous in the context of protracted social conflicts. Practitioners must trust the creative process and simultaneously resist calls for outcomes-focused measures and predetermined metrics of evaluation. Again, Lederach is useful here—he refers to this as the "moral imagination."[44] Holding these paradoxical realities is trauma-informed peacebuilding work; there is no singular definition for this set of complex practices. Focused on the present moment, conflict resolution practitioners must maintain a sense of desired outcomes while also not getting too focused on an outcomes-based approach to change. Trauma-informed conflict intervention involves what Dan Druckman calls "situating the situation,"[45] but this is a continual and ambiguous process not some one-time, or discrete, analytical practice. This on-going situational awareness is key to effective trauma-informed and emotionally mindful conflict practice even if it raises important philosophical questions for practitioners about the implications of remaining both equidistant and allied to those fighting to end historical injustices. This is what makes the work of racial reconciliation, or caste annihilation, so indefinite and daunting. The vigilance required for such trauma-informed and emotionally mindful work is unmeasurable and the necessary capability of sitting with ambiguity is immense.

IS TRAUMA-INFORMED RACIAL RECONCILIATION EVEN POSSIBLE?

By now readers may be feeling overwhelmed with the number of contextual, reflexive, and situational realities to which conflict intervention practitioners must be constantly aware and attentive to. Historical methods, situational awareness, and an emotional intelligence to read trauma are all critical to a reflexive response. Humans can only be attentive to a finite flow of information even if every second we are faced with millions of possible social stimuli calling for our undivided attention. Transforming socially constructed systems of oppression, like either race or caste, requires not only conflict resolution skills, but also emotional intelligence, situational awareness, and alertness to the historical dynamics of social trauma. As everyone has different experiences of, and with, these socially constructed identities, not all will have the same awareness and measure of emotional intelligence of these complex conflict dynamics. In the context of centuries (or millennium) long culturally constructed systems of oppression, social stigma, and discrimination, healthy skepticism about whether racial or caste-based reconciliation is truly possible is certainly both appropriate and legitimate. In our current age of oversaturated information, this skepticism about the goal of racial (or caste) reconciliation becomes even more pronounced. No simple solutions or silver bullets are provided here; only reflexive perspective and theoretical distance to honestly interrogate our own conflict practices can mark a gradual shift away from both racial and caste-based discrimination and hierarchical domination. While direct experience and the open expression of feelings and emotions are often shorthand for creating theoretical distance in our society, they do not have to be. Effective conflict resolution practice deconstructs any distance between the theoretical and practical. Here "theoretical distance" signals less a disavowal of social conflict theories, than a stance of what Schon (1983) calls "reflecting-in-action."[46] When working to transform past trauma, theory is useful only as it can help map a means of practice. This integration of theory and practice requires creativity and moral imagination. As Varma (2018) has argued: "While trauma is used as a shorthand for collective suffering, it is also used to make calculations about 'good' and 'bad' victims of violence and how these individuals might be transformed through the gentle hand of medical humanitarianism."[47] Less than transforming victims, trauma-informed and emotionally mindful conflict practice is about engaging unjust structures of society. For Schon, "reflecting-in-action" is using theory-driven knowledge while simultaneously not forgetting social context and personal experience.

Social media outrage rarely distinguishes the nuances of social identity, the diversity of personal experience, and/or the complexities of context, but rather claims victimhood from all sides or viewpoints (as was discussed in chapter 1). Victimhood claims garner "likes" in the world of social media but do little to effectively level the playing field for those that feel marginalized and disempowered. Political, cultural, and moral calculations often shift under the conflict practitioner's feet, making any medical model of trauma intervention next to impossible across cultural, situational, and linguistic contexts. Like a jazz musician who has played with colleagues for years, trauma-aware racial justice activists "manifest a 'feel for' their material and they make on-the-spot adjustments to the sounds [read racial/caste dynamics] they hear."[48] Social media reactions often miss that "feel for" context and the diversity of personal experiences of a situation. Conflict resolution, or transformation, of entrenched social hierarchies, like race and caste, require vigilant attention to the micro-shifts in the socio-cultural dynamics of the situation. This constant "reflecting-in-action" requires vigilant attention to story narration, subtle acts of reframing, and communicative dynamics of deep listening.

To further illustrate this shifting terrain of trauma, identity, and victimhood (as was highlighted in chapter 1) just think of how different the racial justice conversation in the United States is today than it was just roughly fifteen years ago when the election of the first Black U.S. President established new public discourse, and beliefs in many, of a "post-racial"[49] America. Presuming outcomes and refining our sociological and anthropological explanations of oppression will only get us so far. It seems that to engage in conflict resolution on racial and/or caste oppression we need more than historical, or systemic, understanding of these complex social systems of oppression; the goal of conflict resolution, much less the distal goal of reconciliation, requires an ability to internalize one's own reflexive social positionality in these systems and externalize effective problem solving without foregoing this internalization. Racial reconciliation will require of social justice practitioners an ability for reflection-in-action in what Schon (1983) calls "the 'action-present,' the zone of time in which action can still make a difference to the situation."[50] While this action presence is a shifting landscape, trauma-informed conflict intervenors can make progress towards reconciliation through both their physical and discursive actions. Theory, like critical race theory, matters, but it is such theories' integration with action, and change in habituated behaviors, that will eventually transform.

In recent years the use of the term "racial caste," and its nuanced understanding, has become more prevalent in American public discourse. From activists to political pundits to academics, the term racial caste is now set in our collective psyche as a reconfigured shorthand for a hardened system of oppression that locks people of color into inferior hierarchical positions in American society based on the color of their skin. In this popular telling, racial caste is a unique system of structural violence that the legacy of slavery and systemic racism after the reconstruction era has constructed and encoded in society. While there have been important scholarly connections drawn between race and caste since at least the late nineteenth or early twentieth century,[51] if not before, consensus on what is meant by a "racial caste" remains broad and contested. Does the addition of caste to socially constructed descriptions of race provide a new lexicon or understanding that makes people more trauma-aware? It seems that although comparison can be theoretically instructive, this hybrid lexicon does not necessarily assist in developing either emotional awareness or social emotional learning about what it must be like to be marginalized in a subordinate social or economic hierarchy. To get people educated and aware of the experiences of those not in their social identity groups, more than shared language and/or contact with those others is needed.

In their early work on race and caste Davis, Gardner, and Gardner (1941) state that:

> "Caste" is, then, no mere conceptual device for analyzing Negro-white relations in the Old City. It is a vigorous reality, as the sanctions for the subordination of the Negro and the maintenance of endogamy have revealed. The caste system is at work in every aspect of life in the Old City.[52]

For these early anthropological chroniclers of America's post-reconstruction and Jim Crow deep south, caste provided a clarification of social practices that race, and racism, did not fully provide. The popular and complex connotations of structural racism continue to drive a searching for new language. For evidence of this search one only need note the recent publication, and acclaim, of Pulitzer Prize winning author, Isabelle Wilkerson's *Caste: The Origins of Our Discontent* (2020).[53] While I will have more to say on Wilkerson's contribution to the term "racial caste" below, Fuller (2011), in summarizing the anthropological debates about caste and race comparisons that gained credence well into the 1960s in the United States, aptly concludes:

> In sum, irrespective of behavioral similarities between black-white relations in America and caste relations in India, the two systems differ fundamentally because, first, their ideologies or value systems are divergent and, secondly, the relationship between ideology and social structure is differently articulated in the two cases.[54]

Put another way, the racial boundaries between whites and blacks in the United States, though socially and behaviorally similar, are religiously, culturally, and structurally quite different than the barriers of castes in India. Discriminatory practices in the context of being black or low caste, may look and feel very similar in the "action-present,"[55] but the structures and ideologies that re-enforces them are culturally distinct. Whereas the racial hierarchy of the United States creates two castes with slight gradients within these "castes" that relate to color tones (colorism), the hierarchy of South Asia is based on thousands of caste subgroups in a complex-graded hierarchy in which religious texts have provided traditional sanction for the hierarchy, and endogamy has sustained the boundaries. While Christianity is used to both resist and justify racism, the racial system has clearer, and more recent, historical connection to economic interests and hierarchies of colonial domination. While this is not to say colonial era economic interests and hierarchies did not help build and perpetuate modern caste in South Asia, the origin of that system of discrimination are less clearly tied to simply elite colonial economic interests. While historical and structural antecedents of these systems of oppression differ, modern parallels can still be discursively effective.

For fear of losing the forest for the trees, lets return to the "action-present" and the use of the hybrid term "racial caste." Probably the most influential recent re-emergence of the term comes from the work of Michelle Alexander (2010). In her own words Alexander (2010) used the hybrid term "the way it is used in common parlance to denote a stigmatized racial group locked into an inferior position by law and custom."[56] For Alexander, mass incarceration in the Unites States, since the 1960s civil rights movement, has acted as a new Jim Crow system; another innovation aimed at subjugating people of color after an era of chattel slavery. As she says: "We have not ended racial caste in America; we have merely redesigned it."[57] Alexander's connection of mass incarceration of black bodies to racial caste stratification stigmatization is instructive and rhetorically powerful. Capturing the above critique about American racial caste as a distinct structural reality from India, Alexander's description of racial caste as grounded in the rule of law that "justifies a legal, social, and economic boundary between 'us' and 'them'"[58] grounds an understanding caste in a distinct American form. Whereas Jim Crow was grounded on custom, the new Jim Crow of mass incarceration is based on law and early on Alexander reminds us that "It is possible—quite easy, in fact—never to see the embedded reality."[59] Here one can begin to both feel and understand theoretically what a system of racial caste can do, as well as what becomes necessary to dismantle it. Here is where the terminology of racial caste gains meaning in the "action-present." This is a naming and reframing of the on-going traumatic realities of a history of racial segregation. Unlike Wilkerson's (2020) discussion of "our discontents" Alexander's idea of racial caste outwardly calls for a "new social consensus" and asks for "dialogue, a conversation that fosters a critical consciousness" as a "key prerequisite to effective social action."[60] This, I believe makes an important distinction. While it is an intrinsic good that Isabel Wilkerson's *Caste: The Origins of Our Discontents*, released at the height of protests over the killing of George Floyd, introduces many American readers to the concept of caste, her understanding of caste leaves too much to the imagination. Having studied caste and anti-caste social movement in India for more than a decade, reading a Pulitzer Prize winning author articulate the importance of B. R. Ambedkar to American readers feels exciting and long overdue. Still, Alexander's linking the idea of caste directly to the structure of the carceral state is much more useful in practice. Long ignored by major publishers, having caste in the title of a Random House *New York Times* bestselling book feels like a coup. However, as a work of social and historical scholarship much remains missing in Wilkerson's thick reportage, but thin argumentation. Such a critical statement should not be read as reason enough to forego reading this important book; it does us all a great service by re-opening early connections between the social and emotional impacts of both race and caste. But to focus on the "action present" goal of transformation, calling out specific structures of oppression can have a greater impact on agency for change.

To her credit, early in the book Wilkerson (2020) explains that "Caste and race are neither synonymous nor mutually exclusive."[61] Still, a few pages earlier, in describing the "three caste systems" she plans to compare, Wilkerson describes the "race-based caste pyramid in the United States" as "shape-shifting" as compared with the "caste system of India" as "lingering, millennia-long."[62] The orientalism so deeply embedded in this characterization should not be easily discounted.[63] Ironically, such unreflective and enduring assumptions form the foundation of the hierarchical systems Wilkerson is actively striving to unmask. I draw on this theoretical critique as it has practical implications for how we intervene in caste conflict and aim to work towards the ideal of a trauma-informed racial reconciliation. Although the critique may seem theoretical, rhetorical, and esoteric, it has real impacts on both conflict practice and the psychology of victimization and harm. Without clear referent to actual structural inequities, the emotional and rhetorical

emphasis of the term "racial caste" is lost. This may seem like splitting hairs but taking notice of such distinctions underscores the need
to listen carefully and be intentional in reframing conflict narrations
for conflicting parties. Laden with emotional context, conflict narrations articulate nuanced and complex identities and belie complex
expressions of "structuration."[64] Listening and reframing these narrations requires trauma-informed awareness, emotional intelligence, and
radical empathy. Racial and caste reconciliation will be illusive without
such awareness, intelligence, and empathy.

CONCLUSIONS: TURNING TOWARDS STRUCTURAL CHANGE
IN OPPRESSIVE HIERARCHIES

The narrative illustrations I have provided in this chapter, though complicated and nuanced, articulate the need for close listening, trauma-
informed questioning, and reframing/resetting of the context of social
conflict. One final vignette from recent political identity battles on U.S.
college campuses will help to frame the complex terrain of the trauma-
informed lens and recall the discussion about the need for emotional
awareness and victimhood psychology that was introduced and discussed in chapter 1. As articulated above, Peace and Conflict Studies
and Conflict Resolution professionals often miss the way in which
emotions and trauma are foundational to what Marie Dugan termed
"nested"[65] conflict (see figure 2.2 above). If conflict issues are truly
nested in relationship, systems, and subsystems then these were created
(or, I like to say, "thatched") via human emotion—not simply interests
and assumed "truths." Emotions and trauma are the metaphorical tree
that holds the nest. Building on this metaphor, we do not want to miss
the forest for the trees. This foundation of the nested conflict, if noticed,
draws us to ask targeted trauma-informed and emotionally mindful
questions about difficult conflict episodes.

This awareness of trauma and emotional harms becomes particularly
evident when one explores ongoing identity conflicts on U.S. college
campuses. On September 24, 2021, an identity conflict went viral on
the Arizona State University (ASU) campus in Tempe, Arizona. A
seven minute and forty second video, posted on Instagram and eventually seen by over 6 million people, showed "four students: two white
men seated at a study table, and facing them, two students of color."[66]
The two students of color film their confrontation with the two white

men over both a sticker ("Police Lives Matter") on one of the student's laptop, and a tee-shirt ("Did Not Vote for Biden") that the second white male student was wearing. The conflict escalates quickly and as Viren (2022) explains: "The space is also an important character in this drama."[67] Not just any space, this was the newly labeled multicultural space on ASU's campus.

For over a year and a half, the students of color on campus (including the two filming the video) had been asking the University administration to provide space for a multicultural center and activities on campus. After the killing of George Floyd in Minneapolis, and nationwide protest that followed, these students argued that there was a need for a safe space for students of color to feel safe on campus. In the video, one can hear the sense of past harm: "this white man thinks he can take up our space and this is why we need a multicultural space" says one of the students of color.[68] One of the white students seems shocked by this assumptive outburst and the other gets defensive, refusing to leave. Explaining to the white students they are not being kicked out, but rather being asked to leave, one of the students of color explains that the whole rest of the campus was set up for them and says: ". . . this is the only space that you are not centered."[69] The whole interaction, though quick, is impactful; the emotions of all involved are palpable. All the students involved would ruminate on the interaction even years later because of the firestorm the viral video created when it went public on social media. Both telling of past harm and harm-inducing for the way in which it was received by others, the episode is a cautionary tale of reading such conflict episodes devoid of an understanding of either the collective historical trauma or the local context of the conflict situation. It also speaks to the reality that just knowing this history and being trauma-aware and/or trauma-sensitive is not enough. In the moment of the interaction, social actors are setting the problem and making in-the-moment judgments; this is human. Still, more than awareness of past historical trauma, or being sensitive to it, conflict resolution practitioners must listen actively and read conflict parties' emotional affects. Failure to do so can make practitioners complicit in conflict escalation. Failure to choose your words and affects carefully as an intervenor could have the opposite of the desired effect. This is the case with a few students nearby that became emergent interveners, trying to calm tensions of the four arguing students. In the ASU video that went viral, there is an Asian-American student that tries to come play a sort of emergent mediator role. Unfortunately, he fails to internalize the lessons I am articulating here and allows his own anger of being interrupted from studying (his own interests) to dictate his own emotional response to the conflict. Instead of reframing and validating both sides' concerns, this emergent mediator debates the students of color that were expressing long-held traumatic frustration. Both social emotional learning and resistance to violence as a solution to any conflict must provide moral grounding (or what Lederach 2005 calls the moral imagination) for any emotionally mindful and trauma-informed conflict practice. No silver bullet can be given to handle such deeply personal, emotional, and traumatic episodes of conflict, but humble awareness and radical empathy that all have experienced harm is an important starting point for conflict resolution practitioners to reflect on prior to any response. Again, the map is not the territory and conflict practitioners must navigate the situations, attitudes, and behaviors of conflict actors to inculcate a way of being that invites nonviolent perspective. Givens calls this "radical empathy" and argues that it involves both emotion and cognition. "Understanding how a person feels also provides insight into how the person understands the world."[70]

When victims invoke their victimization in conflict, rarely do practitioners challenge received paradigms about victims and victimizers. Collective sympathy for "true" victims is thereby conferred.[71] Conflict transformation, or effective conflict resolution practice, depends on relationship and relationship is grounded in a human sense of vulnerability. To express vulnerability there must be safe space and "process-structure"[72] to express one's true sense of social identity without being typecast/positioned as either a victim or an oppressor. Devoid of such safe space and structure to share vulnerability, victimhood identity is allowed the space to grow and metastasize like a cancer. Following tragic events like the killing of George Floyd, victimhood was given space to metastasize. Further, once this victimhood and fear take root, the space and structure for social expression of vulnerability shrinks (and conflict escalates and becomes protracted). Practitioners of conflict resolution must draw attention to victim identity in conflict narratives, but this requires more than just being attentive to victims. Victims' stories do matter, but we cannot over-privilege, or over-emphasize them. The fact is pride and sense of identity are crucial for mobilizing social action; they are also notorious for escalating social conflict. Embracing wonder, being proximate to suffering and listening attentively to narration are foundational starting points for emotionally mindful and trauma-informed conflict practice, especially in contexts where victimhood psychology has been firmly anchored on all sides. By engaging in active listening for the emotional resonance in conflict parties' narrations, conflict resolution practitioners work to set the problem and actively choose between competing paradigms of professional conflict practice. This is what it means to be trauma-informed as a conflict resolution practitioner. Trauma and emotion can be powerful allies in conflict resolution practice if we can humbly listen and redevelop "radical empathy"[73] for those that are both perceived as victims and those that are marked as victimizers. Failure to do this work of partial equidistancing misses opportunities for de-escalation and transformation.

NOTES

1. Resmaa Menakem, *My Grandmother's Hands: Racialized Trauma and the Pathways to Mending Our Hearts and Bodies* (Las Vegas: Central Recovery Press, 2017), 14.

2. Jill Freedman and Gene Combs, *Narrative Therapy: The Social Construction of Preferred Realities* (New York: W.W. Norton & Company, 1996), 57.

3. Craig Zelizer, "Trauma sensitive peace-building lessons for theory and practice." *African Peace and Conflict Journal* 1, no. 1 (2008): 81–94.

4. See as examples: M. Harwood and J. Almond, "On trauma-informed peacebuilding & development assistance." MBB Consulting (2017). Accessed January 12, 2020 at: https://medium.com/@MBBconsulting_22368/on-trauma-informed-peacebuilding-development-assistance-e8a4162df82c; B. Hart and E. Colo, "Psychosocial peacebuilding in Bosnia and Herzegovina: approaches to relational and social change." *Intervention* 12, no. 1 (2014): 76–87, among others.

5. As one example, see: Bessel Van der Kolk, *The Body Keeps Score: Brain, Mind, and Body in the Healing of Trauma* (New York: Penguin Books, 2014). In his bestselling book, Dr. Van der Kolk speaks of trauma as more than a past event, but rather is the "imprint" left on the "mind, body, and brain" (21). Like a birthmark, trauma is unique to each survivor.

6. See Abramson and Moore (2002), where they discuss the role that space and structure as critical for the third-party practice of community conferencing. L. Abramson and D. Moore, "Chapter 7: The Psychology of Community Conferencing," in *Repairing Communities through Restorative Justice*, edited by John Perry (Lanham, MD: American Correctional Association, 2002), 123–39.

7. Silvan Tompkins posited that affects were the biological portion of emotions and included nine (two positive, one neutral, and six negative) affects

that can be seen in babies' faces as responses to various stimuli. These affects include: Enjoyment/joy, excitement/interest, surprise/startle, anger/rage, disgust, dissmell, distress, fear/terror, humiliation/shame. For more on Tompkins' affect theory see: Silvan Tompkins, *Affect Imagery Consciousness: Volume I. The Positive Affects* (New York: Springer, 1962). In total between 1962 and 1992 Tompkins wrote four volumes on these nine affects.

8. Jay Rothman, "The Reflexive Mediator," *Negotiations Journal* 30, no. 4 (2014): 441–53, 443.

9. Rothman (2014), for example, acknowledges the important influence of Donald Schon's (1983) *The Reflective Practitioner* in his thinking and argues that reflection is the first step in being reflexive. "Reflexivity goes deeper as people reflect upon their own reflection, and how this in turn influences their ongoing experience as it unfolds through co-constructive and dynamic feedback loops." Jay Rothman, "The Reflexive Mediator," *Negotiations Journal* 30, no. 4 (2014): 441–53, footnote 1.

10. Jeremy Rinker and Jerry Lawler, "Toward Best Practices in Trauma-Informed Peacebuilding: Systematizing Interventions in Protracted Social Conflicts," *Realizing Nonviolent Resilience: Neoliberalism, Societal Trauma, and Marginalized Voice*, edited by J. Rinker and J. Lawler (New York: Peter Lang, 2020), 47–77.

11. See for example: Vamik Volkan, *Bloodlines: From Ethnic Pride to Ethnic Terrorism* (Boulder, CO: Westview Press, 1997); Joseph Montville, "Justice and the burdens of history," in *Reconciliation, Justice, and Coexistence*, edited by M. Abu Nimer (Lanham, MD: Lexington, 2001).

12. B. Ba and B. LeFrancois, "Ethnic Genocide, Trauma Healing, and Recovery: The Case of Identity Ruptures and Restoration among Bosnian Refugees," in *Critical Issues in Peace and Conflict Studies*, edited by Thomas Matyók, Jessica Senehi, and Sean Byrne (Lanham, MD: Lexington Books, 2011), 81–96.

13. See: Resmaa Menakem, *My Grandmother's Hands: Racialized Trauma and the Pathways to Mending Our Hearts and Bodies* (Las Vegas: Central Recovery Press, 2017); E. Duran and B. Duran, *Native American Post-Colonial Psychology* (Albany, NY: State University of New York Press, 1995).

14. Lucy Berliner and David J. Kolko. "Trauma Informed Care: A Commentary and Critique." *Child Maltreatment* 21, no. 2 (May 2016): 168–72.

15. Craig Zelizer, ed., *Integrated peacebuilding: innovative approaches to conflict transformation* (Boulder, CO: Westview Press, 2013).

16. One exception might be Leonard Doob's Tavinstock Model. See: Ronald Fisher, *Interactive Conflict Resolution* (Syracuse, NY: Syracuse University Press, 1997) and Leonard Doob, ed., *Resolving Conflict in Africa* (New Haven: Yale University Press, 1970).

17. In describing narrative theory Freedman and Combs (1996) write: "Instead of seeing ourselves as mechanics who are working to fix a broken

machine or ecologists who are trying to understand and influence complex ecosystems, we experience ourselves as interested people—perhaps with an anthropological or biographical or journalistic bent—who are skilled at asking questions to bring forth the knowledge and experience that is carried in the stories of the people we work with." Jill Freedman and Gene Combs, *Narrative Therapy: The Social Construction of Preferred Realities* (New York: W.W. Norton & Company, 1996), 18. For more on narrative theory as a tool for overcoming and reconciling marginalization see: Jeremy Rinker, "Narrative reconciliation as rights-based peace praxis: Custodial torture, testimonial therapy and overcoming marginalization." *Peace Research: The Canadian Journal of Peace and Conflict Studies* 46, no. 1 (2016): 121–43.

18. Ron Eyerman, *Cultural Trauma: Slavery and the Foundation of African American Identity* (Cambridge, Cambridge University Press, 2001).

19. Jefferey Alexander, *Trauma: A Social Theory* (Malden, MA: Polity, 2012).

20. Harold Saunders, *A Public Peace Process: Sustained Dialogue to Transform Racial and Ethnic Conflicts* (New York: Palgrave, 1999). Saunders (1930–2016), was first in President Johnson's National Security Council, and then later a close aide to Secretary of State Henry Kissinger, eventually becoming the Assistant Secretary of State for Intelligence and Research (1975–1978) and Assistant Secretary of State for Near East Affairs (1978–1981). His ideas on sustained dialogue and public peace processes were influential in orchestrating the Camp David Accords and framing U.S. negotiations during the Iranian hostage crisis. For Saunders, the public peace process was an unofficial multi-level process of sustained dialogue, negotiation, and continual interaction between citizens of warring body politics or groups. His ideas were widely influenced by Herbert C. Kelman, professor of social relations at Harvard University, among other well-known theorists in the then-emerging field of peace and conflict studies. Foregrounding intervention as a sustained process, Saunders' intervention approach assumed more than simply contact; it assumed emotional relations, or what he called a "human dimension of conflict" (xvii).

21. James Booth, "The Unforgotten: Memories of Justice," *The American Political Science Review*, 95, no. 4 (2001): 788.

22. Nhat Hanh's poem indeed begins with the prescient line: "Do not say that I'll depart tomorrow because even today I still arrive," Thich Nhat Hanh, *Please Call Me by My True Names*, found at: https://www.awakin.org/v2/read/view.php?tid=2088, accessed July 21, 2022. This insightful sentiment expresses well the struggle to reach the ideal of being trauma-informed. For more on this poem and Nhat Hanh's hermeneutics of Buddhism see: Sallie King and Christopher Queen, *Engaged Buddhism: Buddhist Liberation Movements in Asia* (New York: SUNY Press, 1998).

23. One of the leading collaborative organizations focused on spreading the value of social emotional learning defines social emotional learning in the

following way: "SEL is the process through which all young people and adults acquire and apply the knowledge, skills, and attitudes to develop healthy identities, manage emotions and achieve personal and collective goals, feel and show empathy for others, establish and maintain supportive relationships, and make responsible and caring decisions." The Collaborative for Academic, Social, and Emotional Learning (CASEL), see: https://casel.org/fundamentals -of-sel/, accessed August 1, 2022.

24. Guilford and Winston-Salem/Forsyth counties in North Carolina, as my own local examples, have since the onset of the Covid-19 pandemic instituted SEL specialists or coaches in their school systems. Guilford County North Carolina supports two "Social Emotional Learning Specialists" in a Department of Social Emotional Learning and Character Education (see: https://www.gcsnc.com/Page/58420, accessed August 1, 2022) and Winston-Salem/Forsyth County Schools now supports three "Social Emotional Learning Coaches" under a director of the Department of Social and Emotional Learning (see: https://www.wsfcs.k12.nc.us/Page/122271, accessed August 1, 2022).

25. See: Susanne A. Denham and Chavaughn Brown, "'Plays Nice with Others': Social–Emotional Learning and Academic Success," *Early Education and Development* 21, no. 5 (2010): 652–80, DOI: 10.1080/10409289.2010.497450.

26. See: Don Hellison, *Teaching Personal and Social Responsibility through Physical Education*, 3rd ed. (Champaign, IL: Human Kinetics, 2011).

27. Diane Hoffman, "Reflecting on Social Emotional Learning: A Critical Perspective on Trends in the United States." *Review of Educational Research* 79, no. 2 (June 2009): 533–56, 540.

28. Hoffman, ibid., 540–41.

29. John Paul Lederach, *Preparing for Peace: Conflict Transformation Across Cultures* (Syracuse, NY: Syracuse University Press, 1995), 55.

30. Marie Dugan, "A Nested Theory of Conflict," *Women in Leadership* 1, no. 1 (Summer 1996).

31. For details of the Tulsa Race Massacre, see: https://www.tulsahistory .org/exhibit/1921-tulsa-race-massacre/, accessed August, 12 2022, and a recent *New York Times* feature section from May 24, 2021 about the history of the Tulsa race massacre, https://www.nytimes.com/interactive/2021/05/24/us/ tulsa-race-massacre.html, accessed August 12, 2022.

32. For more on the Greensboro Massacre see the final report of the Greensboro Truth and Reconciliation Commission (GTRC) found at https:// greensborotrc.org/, accessed August 22, 2022, and Spoma Jovanovic, *Democracy, Dialogue, and Community Action: Truth and Reconciliation in Greensboro* (Fayetteville: University of Arkansas Press, 2012).

33. Anand Teltumbde, *The Persistence of Caste: The Khairlanji Murders and India's Hidden Apartheid* (New York: Zed Books, 2010), 43.

34. Anand Teltumbde himself has paid a personal price for such blistering criticism of the Indian State response to caste violence. In 2017, this came to a head in the state repression following the Hindutva inspired violence at the annual celebration of Bhima-Koregaon. In celebrating the victory of Dalit (ex-untouchables) soldiers who fought alongside the British against the Peshwas (High caste/Brahmins) in the battle of Bhima Koregaon in 1818, every year on January 1st Ambedkarite Dalits gather at the Victory Pillar in Koregaon, Pune. However, on December 31, 2017, such a gathering of Dalits called "Elgar Parishad" (congress for speaking out loud) was faced with violence from right-wing groups. The arrests of more than a dozen human rights activists and advocates of Dalit and tribal emancipation followed the violence. The Bhima-Koregaon violence and subsequent arrests of activists and intellectuals represent a clear case of how dissent is stifled in a majoritarian Hindu nationalist country under the increasingly draconian leadership of Narendra Modi. In the First Incident Reports (FIRs) following the violence, it was alleged that activists at the Elgar Parishad events used highly divisive language with the intent to incite hatred in society. Further, it was alleged, and widely reported, that these activists had "Maoist links" and were planning to assassinate Modi and destabilize India. Evidence of these allegations remains illusory, and the Government of India has produced no concrete proof of these plots to date. Still, the FIR language has familiar undertones of enemy images and nationalist othering now widespread in the contemporary Indian polity. These activists still languish in jail awaiting trial, despite India's recent Covid-19 upsurges. Among those arrested is Dr. Anand Teltumbde, a Marxist social theorist of caste and prolific writer and public intellectual (cited in the previous note). For more on this context see: Apoorva Mandhani, "2 years, 3 charge sheets & 16 arrests—Why Bhima Koregaon accused are still in jail," *The Print*, October 31, 2020, https://theprint .in/india/2-years-3-charge-sheets-16-arrests-why-bhima-koregaon-accused-are -still-in-jail/533945/, accessed June 23, 2021; Mridula Chari, "Bhima Koregaon charge sheet: Focus on plot to kill Modi, silence on caste violence," *Scroll.in*, November 16, 2018, https://scroll.in/article/902374/bhima-koregaon -chargesheet-focus-on-plot-to-kill-modi-silence-on-caste-violence; https://en .wikipedia.org/wiki/Anand_Teltumbde, accessed June 23, 2021, https://www .amnesty.ie/bhima-koregaon-9/, accessed June 3, 2021.

35. The term "caste Hindu" is used here to denote those Hindus (of both high and low caste) that benefit in social, economic, and/or political ways from the current caste-based status quo in Indian society and therefore consider themselves within the Hindu fold. Again, in quoting Teltumbde, "through four decades of caste carnage, there has in fact been no direct involvement of the brahminical castes at all. Rather, it can be said that the manifestation of caste violence as atrocity is a post-1960s phenomenon, connected with the rise of the Backward classes" (Teltumbde, *The Persistence of Caste*, 2010, op. cit., 46).

36. The Hindu Opinion Online, "Khairlanji: The crime and punishment" (August 23, 2010), https://www.thehindu.com/opinion/Readers-Editor/Khairlanji-the-crime-and-punishment/article16149798.ece, accessed August 8, 2022.

37. http://www.europe-solidaire.org/spip.php?article410, accessed February 11, 2011.

38. https://atrocitynews.files.wordpress.com/2006/10/khairlanji.pdf, accessed August 17, 2022. This Manuski Centre for Human Rights Report was the first and most complete account of the murders as the local media and police took much time to respond to the crime.

39. https://atrocitynews.files.wordpress.com/2006/10/khairlanji.pdf, accessed August 17, 2022.

40. https://atrocitynews.files.wordpress.com/2006/10/khairlanji.pdf, accessed August 17, 2022. A First Incident Report (FIR) is required in the Indian legal system for any police investigations to begin.

41. Personal correspondence with Dalit rights activists during research trip to Nagpur, India, September/October 2006.

42. Joseph Montville, "Justice and the Burdens of History," in *Reconciliation, Justice, and Coexistence*, edited by M. Abu Nimer (Lanham, MD: Lexington Books, 2001), 133.

43. See: John Paul Lederach, *Building Peace: Sustainable Reconciliation in Divided Societies* (Washington, DC: United States Institute of Peace Press, 1997).

44. John Paul Lederach, *The Moral Imagination: The Art and Soul of Building Peace* (Oxford, MA: Oxford University Press, 2005).

45. Daniel Druckman "Chapter 6: Situations," in *Conflict: From Analysis to Intervention*, edited by S. Cheldelin, D. Druckman, and L. Fast (New York: Continuum, 2003), 96.

46. Donald Schon, *The Reflective Practitioner* (New York: Basic Books, 1983), 54.

47. Saiba Varma, "From 'terrorist' to 'terrorized': How Trauma Became the language of Suffering in Kashmir," in *Resisting Occupation in Kashmir*, edited by Haley Duschinski, Mona Bhan, Ather Zia, and Cynthia Mahmood (Philadelphia: University of Pennsylvania Press, 2018), 147.

48. Donald Schon, *The Reflective Practitioner* (New York: Basic Books, 1983), 55.

49. See: Bettina Love and Brandelyn Tosolt, "Reality or Rhetoric? Barack Obama and Post-Racial America." *Race, Gender & Class* 17, no. 3/4 (2010): 19–37, among many others.

50. Schon, *The Reflective Practitioner*, ibid., 62.

51. For example, see: B. R. Ambedkar (1916), "Castes in India: Their Mechanism, Genesis and Development," in *Dr. Babasaheb Ambedkar: Writings and Speeches*, edited by V. Moon (2nd ed., Vol. 1). New Delhi: Reprinted by Dr. Ambedkar Foundation. (First publication by Education Department,

Government of Maharashtra in 1979); Allison Davis, Burleigh Gardner, and Mary Gardner. *Deep South: A Social Anthropological Study of Caste and Class* (Chicago: University of Chicago Press, 1941); John Dollard, *Caste and Class in a Southern Town* (New York: Yale University Press, 1937); O. C. Cox, "The modern caste school of race relations." *Social Forces* 21 (1942): 218–26. Each of these represent some of the earliest examples of comparisons between caste in India and race in the United States of America. The earliest reference to the concept of caste by African Americans seems to be W. E. B. Du Bois, "Evolution of the race problem" (Paper presented at the National Negro Conference, New York, 1909).

52. Allison Davis, Burleigh Gardner, and Mary Gardner. *Deep South: A Social Anthropological Study of Caste and Class* (Chicago: University of Chicago Press, 1941), 44.

53. Isabel Wilkerson. *Caste: The Origins of our Discontents* (New York: Random House, 2020).

54. C. J. Fuller, "Caste, race, and hierarchy in the American South." *The Journal of the Royal Anthropological Institute* 17, no. 3 (September 2011): 617.

55. Donald Schon, *The Reflective Practitioner* (New York: Basic Books, 1983), 62.

56. Michelle, Alexander, *The New Jim Crow: Mass Incarceration in the Age of Colorblindness* (New York: The New Press, 2010), 12.

57. Alexander, *The New Jim Crow*, ibid., 2.

58. Ibid., 12.

59. Ibid.

60. Ibid., 15.

61. Isabel Wilkerson, *Caste: The Origins of Our Discontents* (New York: Random House, 2020), 19.

62. Ibid., 17.

63. Edward Said, *Orientalism* (New York: Vintage Books, 1978).

64. For more on the complex sociological relationship between structure and agency see Anthony Giddens, *The Constitution of Society: Outline of the Theory of Structuration* (Berkeley, CA: University of California Press, 1986). In his theory of structuration Giddens argues that structure's rules and resources along with actions of social agents (agency) are dependent on the other for their existence in social life. In other words, structures both re-constitute themselves and actions can change structures. It is the combinations of these sociological effects that constitutes modern society as an evolving interplay of both structure and agency.

65. Maire Dugan, "A Nested Theory of Conflict," *A Leadership Journal: Women in Leadership—Sharing the Vision* 1, no. 1 (1996): 9–20.

66. Sarah Viren, "When a Campus Clash Is Caught on Video," *New York Times Magazine*, September 11, 2022, 28. Full article found here: https://www

.nytimes.com/2022/09/07/magazine/arizona-state-university-multicultural -center.html, accessed September 19, 2022. The full seven minute and forty-second video can be seen here: https://www.youtube.com/watch?v=1BzraMl-g9Ek, accessed September 19, 2022.

67. Viren, "When a Campus Clash Is Caught on Video," ibid., 31.

68. See: https://www.youtube.com/watch?v=1BzraMlg9Ek, accessed September 19, 2022.

69. Ibid.

70. Terri Givens, *Radical Empathy: Finding a Path to Bridging Racial Divides* (New York: Polity Press, 2022), 28.

71. Daniel Bar-Tal, Lily Chernyak-Hai, Noa Schori, and Ayelet Gundar. "A Sense of Self-Perceived Collective Victimhood in Intractable Conflicts." *International Review of the Red Cross* 91, no. 874 (2009): 229–58.

72. John Paul Lederach, *Little Book of Conflict Transformation: Clear Articulation of the Guiding Principles by a Pioneer in the Field* (New York: Good Books, Ltd., 2003).

73. Terri Givens, *Radical Empathy,* op. cit., 2022.

3

CHALLENGING HIERARCHIES THROUGH TRAUMA STORIES AND USING CONFLICT AND AMBIGUITY AS TURNING POINTS

WHAT DOES IT TAKE TO BE AN EFFECTIVE SURVIVOR?

"Canonical story lines and institutionalized ways of knowing may limit storytelling's influence, but activists have sometimes succeeded in extending those limits. . . . So, with the right narrative tools, disadvantaged groups today may be able to style victims as guides to the social bases of inequality."[1]

"Narrative interventions promote positive peace not only by addressing protracted conflicts, but also by upending latent conflicts and dynamics left unaddressed in more traditional mediation and dialogue processes, dynamics that wreak havoc on many well-intentioned traditional conflict approaches. In fact, unless marginalized groups can recreate their identity and relocate themselves in relation to their community, conflict tends to resurface."[2]

This chapter returns to narrative theory to take a deeper dive into the trauma story as a tool for both conflict mapping and conflict resolution. Resourcing Francesca Polletta's (2006) work on social movement framing, quoted above, as well as Sara Cobb's writings on narrative in conflict (2006, 2013) among other narrative conflict theorists, this chapter develops a set of narratively effective practices for survivors to frame resistance and use ambiguity and irony to change conflict systems and relational dynamics.[3] Trauma stories act as turning points, or are sometimes called critical moments, in conflict by both challenging hierarchies and opening space to acknowledge past collective harms and express emotions. Conflict practitioners must realize the centrality of trauma as an emotional narrative fulcrum of conflict resolution practice and sustainable peaceful change. Failure to listen to and witness past "chosen traumas"[4] has clear impacts on present and future conflict escalation. Specifically, this chapter asks how conflict practitioners build the cultural competency, embodied awareness, and narrative skills to empathize with the historical trauma of conflict parties and empower disempowered parties as survivors rather than victims. This chapter aims to develop a sort of road map to reflective and "radical empathy"[5] in conflict practice by building on the theoretical foundations developed in the early chapters of this book. Narrative interventions, although representative of a broad range of social activities, can be strategically deployed in ways that decenter hardened identity constructs that have been built up in social conflict and thereby challenge received hierarchies and uncritical social constructions. Such work is complicated by the media mobilization potential of particular types and emotionally resonate stories as well as the modern proliferation of false narratives targeted for economic or political gain. Why do some stories lead to mass mobilization, anger, and outrage, while others do not? As Polletta has argued, "To put it another way, some stories are more potent than others not because of their content or the skill with which they are told but because of assumptions made about their tellers."[6] Ambiguous or ironic variables can have either escalatory or de-escalatory effect on a social conflict. Being emotionally mindful and trauma-aware involves living into this ambiguity and using irony, and other narrative devices, as means to developing irenic conflict intervention practices.

Decentering hardened identities and challenging received hierarchies are neither easy to achieve or quick to overcome. Many of Polletta's (2006) examples are from political campaigns, but this does not signal that narratives are only important because of their collective meaning and/or abilities of rhetorical persuasion. Narratives elicit emotional response as primary to rational reflection. Often these emotional responses are subtle expressions of irony or ambiguity and express not listeners' sense of meaning, but rather their confusion or cognitive dissonance. Whether in politics or social protest, in Polletta's words the social conventions of stories "encourage us to pay attention not just to meaning but also to the social organization of the capacity to mean effectively."[7] For conflict resolution practitioners to "mean effectively" entails part persuasion and part an ability to articulate a shared nonviolent vision of coexistence post-harm. Admittedly, those that are marginalized rarely feel as if they are post-harm—harm is constantly active and present in their minds and experience. Trauma impacts our cognition and memory, and unaddressed trauma lives in the body[8] and reemerges in nonuniform ways. When I first began studying Ambedkar Buddhists in India, I remember asking one of their spiritual leaders and movement organizers, at what point organizing around Buddhist identity would no longer be necessary. His immediate response was that "we are not there yet!"[9] By this he meant that organizing and mobilizing around Buddhist identity was still critical to low-caste activists' success as many in the community still had low self-esteem and social fear of losing relationships and social capital if their low caste identity were publicly exposed. In this context of fear and traumatic memories, Buddhist identity helps to provide collective identity and meaning, an ability to "mean effectively."[10] Buddhist identity limits the felt ambiguity among poorly educated low-caste followers of B. R. Ambedkar and provides a stable platform from which to make meaning. Noticing trauma stories as critical moments for communities' ability to make meaning is crucial for effective conflict transformation practice.

More than a mobilizing and organizing tool, the reliance on Ambedkar Buddhist identity is critical for healing and re-developing a sense of collective meaning in that community. Although difficult to fully understand as a white-bodied American researcher, this fear of the public outing of caste identity is real for even the most socially aware of Dalit professionals. One Dalit intellectual friend of mine, even though a ten-ure track professor in the United States, explained that his psychological fear of losing social standing and/or relationship was still strong in him and, indeed, determinative of many of his own social behaviors. Thus, a positive identity (as opposed to a negative one like Dalit) was crucial to his own survival.[11] Humans are social animals; we demand relationships and a sense of validation. Such anecdotes point one back to story as a vehicle to helping those that are traumatized and oppressed to "mean effectively" in Polletta's sense. Art is also an important vehicle in this regard; indeed, it is in story where art meets science. The emotional engagement that stories elicit have unique powers to challenge social identities, arrest cognitive dissonance, and re-construct unequal hier-archies. Of course, how social actors and conflict intervention practi-tioners use their "moral agency"[12] involves a plethora of complex social variables involving social position, class, structural context, systems of hierarchy, and historical dynamics of privilege. But what this illustrates is that when listening to emotionally charged stories and atrocity tales, conflict practitioners must suspend judgment and evaluation and live into simply observation as witnesses. Conflict intervenors' job is not to judge the story, but to hold the emotional space for all parties to hear better the needs and emotional experiences of each other. This is not an observation devoid of emotion or morals, but rather mindful of practi-tioners' power to condition empathic response and expose tightly held assumptions. As conflict practitioners our job is to think strategically and intentionally about the social positions, contexts, assumptions, and historical dynamics inherent in these stories and help parties to do the same. We cannot do this without being attentive to ourselves and our own socially situated positionalities.

Reflecting on her own anthropological writing, the anthropologist Ruth Behar articulates an important tension between academic writing and emotions (a tension that readers have likely already seen clearly visible in this practitioner's guide):

Should I feel good that my writing makes a reader break out crying? Does an emotional response lessen or enhance intellectual understanding? Emotion has only recently gotten a foot inside the academy and we still don't know whether we want to give it a seminar room, a lecture hall, or just a closet we can air out now and then. Even I, a practitioner of vulner-able writing, am sometimes at a loss to say how much emotion is bearable within academic settings.[13]

Behar's sense of being "at a loss" is telling, and clearly the objective academy still struggles to figure out what to do with traumatic expressions and emotional debris. Conflict intervention practitioners should not get caught up with such struggles. Primary to any conflict intervention (action), practitioners must, to the best of their objective scientific abilities, immerse themselves in the conflict positions, contexts, and histories in order to integrate (reflect) this knowledge with their lived experience and values. This "reflective action"[14] is not done by maintaining a "strict boundary"[15] between emotion and reason as two distinct ways of knowing. Critically reflecting on irony, ambiguity, and narrative turning points from both rational (ethnographic) and emotional (autoethnographic) perspectives is critical for effective conflict intervention practitioners. This is when the work of literary criticism provides an illustrative example. Literary criticism is valued as more than mere criticism because it is critical reason from a human empath aimed at raising questions about a text. Holding space for both criticism and objective empathy is an important skill for effective conflict practitioners. Authentically balancing emotional and rational sentiments in conflict can help victims to recraft themselves as survivors and use emotions, morality, and radical empathy to challenge traumatic social hierarchies and "chosen traumas."[16] This requires emotionally mindful observation and awareness first and foremost. Only after this can social actor's narrative agency be exploited to help victims of traumatic experiences "actively re-author their lives."[17] As with anything in conflict practice, this is a process, not a destination or outcome. Trusting a process of intellectual curiosity, understanding, and empathy is primary to pushing for specific conflict intervention outcomes; ambiguity and irony draws one to critically question, and revisit, processes rather than outcomes thereby unmasking assumptions and building the potential for change over time. The story of Rohit Vermula, which went viral globally in 2016, provides an illustrative example of how sticking with a story as it evolves is crucial to effective conflict intervention processes.

THE STORY OF ROHIT VERMULA: INTENT AND IMPACT

One illustration of social movement activists' use of irony, ambiguity, and narrative turning points can be seen in the tragic story of the suicide of Rohit Vermula, and the movement his story helped invigorate among Indian Dalit rights activists worldwide. On January 17, 2016, doctoral student Rohit Vermula committed suicide, but this is neither the end nor the beginning of his story. "The fatal accident of my birth,"[18] as Rohit himself described in his suicide note, was more than that he was simply born untouchable. Vermula, a doctoral candidate in Social Sciences, in his final piece of writing pointed not only to the injustice of being born "unappreciated,"[19] but also the cumulative traumas or being socially and economically marginalized throughout his life. Writing his final letter, as opposed to his aspiration of being "a writer of science, like Carl Sagan" Rohit Vermula emotes: "I am not hurt at this moment. I am not sad. I am just empty."[20] This is a telling insight into the traumatic sequalae of a person that has grown tired of fighting the socially normalized indignities of living as a Dalit in modern Indian society. The daily microaggressions and constant need to justify one's identity and worth took both an individual and collective toll on Vermula. In the words of Peter Levine, "Trauma is not what happens to us, but what we hold inside in the absence of empathetic witness."[21] For Rohit Vermula, this lack of feeling empathetic witness coupled with the wounds of being in a constant "state of exception"[22] left little room for Vermula to develop his own narrative agency or express his emotional dissonance with the status quo. The sense of self and diminished self-esteem this marginalized context empowers can eventually be deadly, if not by suicide, then in the unequal social determinates of health for those in marginal positions in any society. In Rohit Vermula's case this lack of agency and voice led to an individual choice, but evidence abounds that such social marginalization eventually kills in a collective sense too.[23] Feeling alone, unseen, and devoid of the moral agency[24] to express his trauma resulted in the ultimate tragic decision of suicide for Rohit Vermula. In one sense Vermula's story makes clear that emotional awareness is directly related to one's awareness of social agency. Emotions are not just personal, but collective in this sense. In another sense, the irony and ambiguity in Vermula's story were a catalyst for change and an awakening for many on the periphery of anti-caste movements for change. As a critical moment activists capitalized on his choice as a turning point in Dalit rights activism. Rohit's story was a catalyst for developing new emotionally intelligent understanding of the lived experience of caste and its real impacts on the lives of those striving for betterment. One Dalit journalist put it this way: "[Rohit Vermula] made me 'come out' to the people I grew up hiding from, wanting to fit in with. He made me recognize that my history is one of oppression and not shame."[25]

But, even with his suicide letter in hand, we will never fully understand the full intent of Rohit Vermula's final act. Was he hoping to spark outrage? Was he seeing his ultimate decision as a collective tactic or a personal response to the indignities of his caste oppression and the systemic push-back his institutional resistance within his university had unleashed? Though we will never have completely clear answers to such questions of intent we can certainly see the social impacts of his ultimate decision. The sense of injustice and the perception of his act as an ultimate sacrifice mobilized a nation to ask important questions and morally reflect on the ambiguous meaning of his decision. Rohit's decision gave him back some level of moral agency; it allowed him to write the coda to his own story; a privilege he did not feel he had in life. Though not a nonviolent, or even scalable, solution to his suffering, his decision opened a public discussion about the collective suffering of Dalits. Although this opening might not have been as wide as the one opened by the unjust police killing of George Floyd in the United States, it was an opening, nonetheless. The ambiguity and uncertainty that Vermula's act unleashed opened social space for uncomfortable questions. The impact of his choice was an immediate and spontaneous expression of empathic solidarity. There was an emotional outpouring of the realization that this could easily have been any member of the Dalit community.[26] Near the end of his final letter, Rohit signs off with the words: "From shadows to the stars."[27] This entreaty self-referentially frames Rohit Vermula's life as metaphorically that of a shooting star burning bright across the dark sky of caste suffering and oppression. Simultaneously inspirational and tragic such metaphorical symbolism in India is extremely powerful. Given Rohit's love of Carl Sagan the salutation is packed with meaning and a striving to mean effectively. One may argue that in this last phrase and act Vermula was finally able to mean effectively. In a country where dharmic icons and idols stir deep emotion and devotion (bhakti), this image of the spent potential of a young scholar had the power to mobilize the anger and frustration of marginalized generations as well as grow allies. The image of a shooting star both conjured pride and shame. The irony of life through death, change through giving into the pain, moksha (liberation) through dharma (duty), resistance through the ultimate relent, galvanized Dalit rights activists to focus on not being victims, but rather celebrating the improbability of their communities' survival amidst being stamped by the historical trauma of caste. Trauma provides such perspective. More than "pathetic victims or corrupt, immoral opportunists"[28] Dalits saw in Vermula a brave hero that exhibited complete bhakti (devotion) to the cause of Dalit rights. Such hagiographic narrative framing recasts victims as heroic survivors and reimagines the possibility of egalitarian as opposed to hierarchical society.[29]

Rohit Vermula's name became a household one as both activist-oriented and average Indians alike tried to understand why it had to happen this way? Rohit's story has what Polletta calls an "elliptical quality,"[30] which is a critical ingredient for mobilization for collective change. "The impossibility of logically explaining events compels us to tell stories, which in turn preserve the ambiguity that compels us to tell more stories."[31] This is an emotional and collective response, not a rational or logical one. The emotional uncertainty of fully understanding Rohit Vermula's ultimate decision mobilizes a reframing and retelling in a hope that it will bring fuller clarity to what happened. Becoming aware of the power of emotions to drive our behaviors of retelling is critical to conflict intervention professionals "because once you move a heart, you've moved the mountain."[32] This is not an objective, logical, or analytical rationalization of conflict causes and intervention strategies, but rather a grappling with the emotional resonance of an act within its social context.[33] The elliptical ambiguity and rhetorical irony in his story, and suicide letter, best articulate the impact that Rohit Vermula's suicide had on the wider Dalit social movement. The story, and Rohit's letter, were powerful indictments of the status quo of caste marginalization.

Noticing and witnessing these emotional responses is critical to effective conflict intervention practice (as well as trauma healing). Attempting to repair the harm caused by Rohit Vermula's suicide would be impossible without acknowledging the emotional realities of both his ultimate act and the legacy of traumas which led to it. In this sense conflict intervention practice is no different than trauma healing. Echoing the words of Thenmozhi Soundararajan: "we can no longer avoid the wound [of caste oppression], but we can let it be our teacher."[34] Rohit's final act helped remind and teach Dalits, and their allies, that this "soul wound"[35] of caste lives in us all. It also reminds us that caste can be invoked at any time in the service of power. "Once the core from which soul emerges is wounded, then all of the emerging mythology and dreams of a people reflect the wound."[36] Rohit's dreams became an emotional reflection of the trauma of the collective, while his marginalization, all too ordinary, seems normal to the dominant communities in power. So, noticing and acknowledging is certainly step one, but then the work of meaning-making with his marginalization begins. How do individuals and collectives embrace and embody the long suffering of the soul wound? This is no simple question to answer. Ambiguity and irony are often seen in negative light, but here they must be embraced and celebrated as tools of resistance and change. Cobb, in her study of irony and turning points in negotiation processes, argues that "the 'unexpected' exists independently of our ability to predict, control, or even describe it."[37] As conflict intervention practitioners our role is not principally to explain or understand as a social scientist would, but rather to transform and intervene in systems, direct, structural, and cultural, that perpetuate violent conflict (of course these two roles are intricately intertwined). The conflict intervention professional is engaged in a higher order of psycho-sociobiological complexity than the social scientist looking for explanation and understanding. One might argue that some level of understanding, and explanation is primary to this conflict transformation and peacemaking, but often we get caught up in the intellectual or curious questions and miss the unique opportunities to use uncertainty, ambiguity, and irony as positive tools for conflict transformation. Here Ruth Behar's writing is again instructive. She speaks of reaching "a point where these forms of knowing [e.g., emotional and objective] were no longer so easily separated."[38] Certainly, we must seek to theorize and create knowledge to be good conflict intervention practitioners, and also knowledge and meaning making are not all we must do to effect lasting change. We, as conflict intervention practitioners, must sit in the emotional ambiguity and irony of a story like Rohit Vermula's. To intellectualize and rationalize this tragedy is to miss the ways that collective suffering is embodied and reified in a collective. This is not to say intellectualization and rationalization are not necessary steps to either grieve or empower transformation, but they are not the end goal of lasting systemic change.

There is one final aspect of Rohit Vermula's story that cannot be left unsaid. As a Dalit intellectual, Rohit Vermula suffered a particular form of injustice, one that Thenmozhi Soundararajan terms "epistemic injustice," the "exclusion and silencing; invisibility and inaudibility" of Dalit voices. Rohit's voice was particularly silenced in a way "where someone is wronged in the capacity as a knower."[39] Soundararajan takes this definition from the work of Miranda Fricker, who argues "any epistemic injustice wrongs someone in their capacity as a subject of knowledge, and thus in a capacity essential to human value. . . ."[40] This level of injustice may have been the final straw that broke the proverbial camel's back in Rohit Vermula's case. Beyond the ambiguity of Rohit's shocking choice of death is an irony that much of this decision was informed by his experiences of epistemic injustice (or more specifically what Fricker terms "testimonial injustice"[41]) and its curtailing of his desire to live and create. If one cannot feel audible as a doctoral student and aspiring intellectual, then how can one hold onto a sense of agency and self? If one feels invisible in the academic discourse, where might one feel visibility can come from? In this sense killing himself was seen by Rohit Vermula as his last chance at making audible and visible his voice and agency in the context of the epistemic and institutionally bound injustices that he faced. While even Fricker (2007) admits that "Eradicating these injustices would ultimately take not just more virtuous hearers, but collective social political change,"[42] one can sympathize with, and indeed, be mobilized by, Rohit's final act if adequately armed with a better understanding of the processes of epistemic silencing. The complex harm of being socially positioned as incapable of creating knowledge, coupled with the real barriers imposed by the structural violence of institutional academic "gate-keeping"[43] has far-reaching impacts on collective self-esteem, sense of agency, and individual traumatic sequalae. "It is one thing to keep a people down; it is another to have the audacity to position yourself as the authority on those people's lives, experiences, and histories."[44] More than the "accident of his birth,"[45] Rohit's final choice came from a confluence of factors that have a long historical and collective social trajectory. Like other major decisions and accomplishments in life, nobody achieves them alone; both difficult decisions and accomplishments are social and collective by nature. Humans are social animals and all behavior, in some sense, is deeply connected to the collective. Rohit's final decision was not his alone and the irony of this realization calls one to push for social change in much the same way that the ambiguity of the decision compels one to retell his story. The epistemic injustice he faced, was a silencing of his lived experience. The injustice was that his testimony seemed invisible to the vast majority of even the marginalized. Being a witness or made newly aware of this complicity drives one to either deny its reality or call for change. How conflict intervenors react at such critical moments or turning points in social conflict is determined largely by a subset of social power that Fricker terms "identity power."[46]

IRONY AND TURNING POINTS[47] IN CONFLICT PRACTICE: AWARENESS, DRAWING ATTENTION, AND RESILIENCE

Of course, our hope as conflict intervention and prevention practitioners is to ensure voice and equalize agency, for all parties in conflict, prior to any acts of social violence occurring. This preventative a priori gaze of conflict intervention professionals is a critical resource for conflict resolvers, despite most often being called in only once conflict and/ or violence has occurred. Irony and ambiguity provide important turning points (also called critical moments in the literature on mediation and negotiation[48]) if we are aware and open to them. If we are simply emotionless, objectively focused, rational actors then these turning points are regularly missed and, along with this oversight, opportunities to draw attention to them are lost, and often forgotten. Within marginalized communities this awareness is honed on long histories of "microaggressions"[49] and systemic marginalization, which in turn develop into important coping and resilience techniques and measures within these communities. As practitioners we must be aware of these dynamics, even if we come from dominant communities. "The cumulative 'day-to-day stress' caused by microaggressions has been reliably associated with negative physical and emotional health outcomes for decades."[50] In the context of these microaggressions and code switching many other social/collective coping skills have evolved in these communities to ameliorate the negative impacts of the microaggressions, and systemic biases experienced by those within marginalized groups. As conflict practitioners we can learn from these coping skills and hone our own sense of trauma awareness and emotional mindfulness by leaning into irony and turning points (e.g., critical moments) in our conflict practice. "It is through our bodies, as well as our minds, that we discover the key to [trauma] healing."[51] This awareness of the mind-body connection is central to effective conflict intervention practice and irony and ambiguity provide windows to access this awareness. In Peter Levin's *Walking the Tiger: Healing Trauma*, the reader is introduced to role play and reenactment as means through which mammals cope with trauma. For example, becoming aware of repeated "accidents" can be a sign of an individual's trauma response. "The clue to identifying them as symptoms of trauma lies in how often they are repeated and the frequency with which they occur."[52] So what appears as ironic can often be a chain of complex sequalae of trauma experiences that live in the body of the marginalized. Conflict practitioners' attention to detail and awareness of behavior patterns as possible reenactments of past trauma can be critical tools for social healing and resilient change. What appears as ironic and/or ambiguous may be expressions of trauma re-enactment and signal an important tool for change as opposed to an uncertainty to be avoided by the conflict practitioner. As Judith Herman has argued: "The conflict between the will to deny horrible events and the will to proclaim them aloud is the central dialectic of psychological trauma."[53] This dialectic often makes the traumatized express their suffering in ambiguous, or socially awkward, ways. Rather than run from trauma, here is a prime example of the importance of noticing and being critically aware that social behaviors and conflict situations can be the culmination of legacies of individual and collective trauma. These critical moments in a person's memory and perceptions of past events can be useful if they are able to be understood in new perspectives by conflicting parties. Noticing and reflecting on critical moments (conflict turning points) is, therefore, obligatory for good conflict practice.

> Critical moments help practitioners and stakeholders move from a stream of experience to a rudimentary story. Critical moments' capacity to move between the distinct worlds of a researcher and a practitioner or a stakeholder facilitates interaction across the boundaries between these worlds. The give-and-take that they anchor can, in turn, facilitate the elaboration of stories and the thickening that makes these stories useful.[54]

Critical moments are plastic[55] in the sense that they can help a conflict practitioner develop story and sequence historical (and often traumatic) events in ways that help conflicting parties realize assumptions and differing perspectives. This plasticity creates the space for what the renowned anthropologist, Clifford Gertz, would call "think description."[56]

Social-historical awareness and keen observation skills are critical to the trauma-informed and emotionally mindful conflict resolution practitioner; indeed, they cannot be divorced from analysis. Irony, metaphor, and ambiguous storylines all open avenues for awareness to the critical moments laden with trauma and emotions. Rather than see these expressions as negative, uncertain, or expressions of limited use or understanding, instead these ironic, metaphorical, and ambiguous representations or utterances may be constructive openings for the trauma-aware and emotionally mindful practitioners to build resilience, self-esteem, and overcome fears that often drive escalatory behaviors. Embracing the awareness and close interrogation of these expressions also challenges dominant hierarchies. All trauma stories involve power and therefore they open opportunities to challenge dominant social power relations and push parties towards conflict resolution. In name or deed, such awareness is critical to all interpersonal and systemic change. While being critically observant of these dynamics and dialectics may seem like only a tertiary soft skill, or character trait, for an effective conflict intervention practitioner, it is indeed an invaluable and scalable primary skill set of effective conflict resolution. Any effective long-term peacebuilding efforts hinge on a collective ability to notice these critical moments and use the irony, assumption, and ambiguity inherent in all testimonies of past events to re-story, re-organize, and, in some sense, re-program collective social response. I want to be clear; I am here arguing that there is a moral and political stance to effective conflict intervention work because without challenging the unjust structures of asymmetric power, conflict will only be managed and not transformed. Irony, ambiguity, and turning points in conflict provide the openings for lasting change. Admittedly, this is a political and social stance towards asymmetric power and oppressive systems; it cannot be objective and non-normative. Just as nonviolence is a state of mind, oppression and marginalization by powerful parties must be noted at every opportunity. Irony, ambiguity, and turning points provide these opportunities for naming and framing. Naming and framing then requires practitioners to square action with ethical values. Conflict intervention practitioners nervous by such a stance should remind themselves that practitioners' normativity is not directed at any one person or community, but structurally violent systems of oppression and asymmetrical hierarchies.

CRAFTING EFFECTIVE SURVIVORS FROM CONFLICT PRACTICE

Of course, many, if not all, social conflicts are driven and fed by competing narratives about critical moments in history. Once these narratives about shared events are socially constructed or developed, and socially solidified, changing them can be extremely difficult, if not impossible. When I began teaching at Guilford College in Greensboro, North Carolina, early in the 2010s, I taught a conflict resolution freshman seminar on narrative in conflict. At the same time, I began learning about the Greensboro Massacre, a critical moment in the history of this small southern city of Greensboro, North Carolina, which happened on November 3, 1979 and was largely lost to other historical events at the time.[57] For my class I asked the Reverend Nelson Johnson, the organizer of the 1979 March that ended in bloodshed that day, to come to deliver a guest lecture on his experiences of the event and his work in helping to organize a first of its kind truth and reconciliation commission in Greensboro many years later. Not more than five foot three, Reverend Johnson's short stature belies his energy and electric persona. With his cadence as a Southern preacher and the energy of a legendary football coach, he immediately grabbed the attention of most (if not all) of my social media distracted freshmen students. But the most powerful and memorable story he relayed that day was about his years of arguing with writers and journalists at the *Greensboro News and Record*, the local daily newspaper, about what to call the events of November 3, 1979. Describing how for years he had been reading in the *News and Record* stories about the 1979 "Greensboro shootout," he explained how he kept arguing to them: "you just cannot call it that . . . that is not accurate!"[58] Then one day Reverend Johnson woke to a story in the *News and Record* about the "Greensboro Massacre." He was elated and remarked that he thought: "I have finally gotten through to them!"[59] His elation lasted for only about a week, as while enjoying his morning breakfast one morning a week or so later, he encountered the *News and Record*'s next mention of the events of 1979, referring to them by returning to the all-too-familiar "Greensboro shootout." In his retelling of this story, Reverend Johnson lamented how he thought he had finally changed the narrative about what happened only to see the inaccurate description of a "shootout" re-emerge! He explained to my students that once a historical narrative sticks in the collective consciousness of a community, changing that narrative is extremely difficult, if not impossible. He encouraged them to be skeptical of the ways past events are described and retold. He argued for the need for victim's voices to be heard. In short, he argued for victims to be seen as survivors with important truths and lived experiences to tell. Being critical of the dominant narrative is an important stance for effective peacebuilders. This is also being trauma-informed and emotionally aware; not oblivious to these collective histories and past traumas and looking for openings to privilege the voice of those most effected by critical moments of trauma and violence.

So how do we cast victims as survivors and use irony and ambiguity as turning points toward a process of lasting pro-social change? A word of clarification is in order here. By "victims" I am not thinking specifically of Rohit Vermula (whose story was discussed above) or the Bhotmanges of Khairlanji (who stories were discussed in detail in chapter 2). Although these victims cannot be excavated from their eternal suffering and death, their stories can still act as resistance and as a mobilizing strategy for rethinking and reframing future activism. By victim here I am thinking more of the everyday victims of caste oppression and/or racial micro-aggressions. Victims that through their resilience have survived but are nevertheless changed by their multiple experiences of trauma (including the above mentioned atrocities perpetuated against their identity group). A roadmap for conflict intervention practitioners to engage in radical empathy requires awareness of "identity power" and "epistemic injustice"[60] as inherent in the complex processes of "social positioning"[61] of those with limited power in society. But more than simply awareness to "mean effectively" in Polletta's sense, conflict intervention practitioners also need to develop narrative skills and cultural/communicative competence in dealing with trauma and emotions in "conflict-in-process."[62] Empowering narrative agency and voice requires an embrace of ambiguity, what Donald Schon calls "reflection-in-action,"[63] and the use of turning points to orchestrate (or facilitate) irenic ends.

We know that pride and sense of positive identity are crucial for mobilizing social action. They are also notorious for escalating/protracting social conflict (e.g., solidifying social identity groups and a hardened sense of in-group identity). So, what is needed is a roadmap for conflict intervention practitioners to engage in the work of building radical empathy, requiring the awareness of "identity power" and "epistemic injustice"[64] inherent in the complex processes of social positioning.[65] Such a roadmap does more than build awareness across communities, it also helps conflict practitioners in developing the skills of "radical empathy"[66] towards those with whom they disagree or with those that come from divergent social positions and experiences. This cross-community interaction is often lacking in protracted social conflicts, and this is especially so in movements of marginalized identity politics. Devoid of contact, social actors get dehumanized and socially positioned, while "solutions" get mired in structure and policy as opposed to the lived experience of those most affected by social trauma. Jeffrey Alexander, in his work on social or cultural trauma has argued that traumatic social conflict and violence often leave ineradicable marks on communities.[67] But more than being aware of this fact, these marks must be used to explore "victimhood psychology"[68] in on-going conflicts. Rather than be repulsed by these blemishes we must embrace them. Trauma and emotion can be powerful allies in social conflict, acting as opportunities for change (turning points), not just emotionally filled contexts to be avoided. Denial is not a recipe for healing or conflict transformation. If conflict resolution practitioners can humbly listen and create the space and structure in society to redevelop radical empathy then, and only then, can social change be sustainable, and transformation be lasting. In other words, framing victims as survivors, along with developing cultural/communicative competence to develop radical empathy in the "Other," during critical moments in conflict, is both key to systemic social change and lasting conflict resolution. Turning points (or critical moments of past trauma or atrocity) represent important vectors for transformative change (as opposed to just negative peace or meeting of immediate interests and needs) by empowering narrative agency in marginalized speakers. The Rohit Vermula tragedy is an opportunity to recast everyday victims of caste injustices as survivors of an oppressive system that does not have to result in the ultimate silencing of suicide. Opening the space for radical empathy and shared understanding, activists can rethink the annihilation of caste in this modern moment. This moving beyond the modern realities of precarity challenges hierarchies and power asymmetries. This allows social change activists to recast their resistance thereby developing opportunities for more inclusive forms of peace and peacebuilding. The works of peace are interconnected with the works of justice in complex and imbricated, or inseparable, ways.

CONCLUSION

In a 2017 *Forward Press* piece on the Indian intellectual giant, Dr. B. R. Ambedkar, I wrote:

> Unless activists work to complicate the story of his [Ambedkar's] life and work, his legacy and full impact are done a grave injustice. Ensuring his

revolutionary legacy requires more than memorialization through the thousands of statues erected in low caste bastis across India. How activists make Babasaheb new and innovative for this time hinges on how they strategically tell his story; how much they complicate and interrogate it.[69]

In quoting this now, I would only add that this requires a humble sense of ambiguity, critical thinking, and a fraternal desire to be ever open and curious in critical conversational turning points. Telling the story of past movement leaders requires this humble sense of ambiguity, critical thinking to adapt past leaders' ideas to our new age, and a fraternal desire to be ever open and curious. For Dr. Babasaheb Ambedkar fraternity, not nationalism, ideology, or ideological orthodoxy of any sort was the primary call to social action. Fraternity does require positive self-esteem in marginalized communities, but building such self-esteem and confidence walks a fine identity line. Strengthening personal sense of identity hardens collective identity, and positions social identities as opposed to an "Other." Hardened collective identity is important for organizing and agitating for change, but often gets in the way of education and developing a sense of fraternity. In Ambedkar's case he was looking for ways to achieve both organizing and agitation alongside educating and developing fraternity in Indian society. Developing fraternity was the primary means of challenging the graded hierarchy of the caste system for Dr. Ambedkar. By encouraging white allies into the movement in the summer of 1964 (freedom summer) to register black voters in the south, the Student Nonviolent Coordinating Committee (SNCC) and Dr. Martin Luther King Jr. similarly realized the centrality of developing fraternity in the American struggle for civil rights. Civic engagement with those from the identity group with which one disagrees is critical for any lasting social change. We know from Tajfel and Turner's famous 1979 study of social identity theory that the mere presence of the outgroup can create a discriminatory response in the in-group.[70] The only way to engage this discriminatory response is to create contact[71] and open spaces for empathic sharing and spaces for dialogue and joint action. Ambiguity, irony, and critical moments provide leverage to open these important spaces.

Such collective wisdom moves beyond individual leaders and hero-worship; it assumes that we all have important lived experience to share and grow from. Rather than shy away from painful pasts, we need to engage them in creative and proactive ways. Trauma-informed and emotionally aware conflict resolution practitioners realize this and work creatively to build trustful spaces and structures to collectively engage across identity lines. The Indian academic and political prisoner (see chapter 2, note 34) Anand Teltumbde has lamented that "the entire Dalit emotional charge is concentrated in the Ambedkar icon."[72] Beyond Rohit's story there are many other victim narratives in the anti-caste movement, not least of which are the many stories of Dr. B. R. Ambedkar's own hardships.[73] But the emotional charge of movement stories is not unique to Dalit anti-caste social movement. The civil rights movement in the United States also abounds with such stories. Emmett Till, Michael Brown, and George Floyd are names that conjure traumatic imaginaries and deep back stories; they are both a movement resource and a movement constraint. Such atrocity stories run the risk of taking us down a slippery slope of in-group identity formation and a victim psychology exclusively focused on failed justice. For B. R. Ambedkar, like Martin Luther King Jr., fraternity, born of the idea that I am you and you are me, is the root of all positive social change and, thus, the root of collaborative democracy, consensus making, constructive social change. Such fraternity cannot be birthed if victimhood psychology is allowed to proliferate without critical questioning. This perspective was in complete congruence with Ambedkar's adopted religion of Buddhism as well as King's own Christian faith, but one does not have to be either a Buddhist or a Christian to appreciate the importance of social fraternity for the creation of lasting social transformation in society. Social contact, and indeed fraternity in the sense of being bound to others, is critical for democracy and indeed social transformation of any kind. Religious leaders often understand this need for fraternity before others, as religion, in its literal meaning, is the ties that bind, and each of the worlds' faith traditions realize the importance of community to maintaining healthy society. As such religious traditions are storehouses of collective wisdom about challenging hierarchies and creating ties that bind diverse identities to others. Like emotions and trauma, we should not be afraid of religious worldview as conflict resolution practitioners. These traditions are full of ambiguity and irony. They too are a resource for lasting change; yet this does not mean you have to believe in a religion to see, or embrace, its healing powers.

As peacebuilders, or conflict transformers, the religious leaders discussed above challenged social hierarchies through framing their followers as in a historical narrative that accessed critical moments, or turning points, in a shared and interconnected human trajectory. Ambedkar and King were not only ahead of their times, but they were also re-crafting traumatic stories as tales of survivorship, perseverance, and resilience. Their creative narrative interventions were key to the movements these leaders began. They are an ongoing legacy and lived example of radical empathy, fraternity, and humility. In this way these leaders' work is not done, but rather is a model of how to progressively develop the beloved community. Our binded-ness to each other and emotional awareness of our fundamental interdependence is a primary resource in critical moments of social conflict. Conflict resolution practitioners must avoid thinking of these resources as divine outliers and use their own stories as access points for irony, ambiguity, and discussion about critical conflict moments. Leaders like King and Ambedkar were not divine saints with special powers, but rather creative leaders with narrative skills and trauma-aware emotional mindfulness.

Still, while this may be theoretically easy to see, how we put these access points of irony, ambiguity, and critical moments into practice is much more complicated in real time. What are words and emotional expressions to look out for in conflict practice that will moor us to our emotional awareness and trauma-informed selves? How do we empower our emotional awareness/intelligence and not get too caught up in our rational casual desire to understand and explain social conflict or solve problems? The following three phases can assist the conflict practitioner in accessing emotions in critical moments of traumatic retelling:

Phase 1—Self-reflecting on what you are feeling as a traumatized event is retold: This requires listening and simultaneously scanning your body for signs of emotional response. We embody our own and others' trauma, this is not unique to anyone, but is a normal mammalian response. But *how* we embody trauma is unique to us individually. It requires listening to and noticing the micro shifts in mood, perspiration, muscle pains and tightening, and involuntary responses to the pain and anger, as feeling is expressed by others. It also requires self-reflection about past traumas we have ourselves experienced and how they are informing our reactions to what is being shared in-the-moment.

Phase 2—Arresting the desire for sympathy and attempts to control of others' emotions: This is easier said than done. Remember my own circle story shared in the introduction to this volume? This practice requires one to slow down emotional response and trust that you can listen and self-reflect (phase 1) at the same time. Listening with the whole body is intuitive and will provide the grace that one often fears will not be there. As a conflict practitioner, faced with a perceived need for response on the part of parties sharing their deeply held emotions and trauma, this can be challenging. Sometimes less really is more; silence is a salve. Of course, authenticity and how you nonverbally convey your connection is critically important. This phase can be a space of great discomfort but helps us realize that that discomfort is me-focused and, not, other-focused. Re-directing towards others and not self, though not easy, is critical for trauma-informed response to conflict.

Phase 3—Creating ways to actualize your core values within local context as needed: This phase often comes in an epiphany. It involves trusting yourself in the first two phases and having faith that creative solutions and reactions to trauma and emotions are innate in each of us. These creative responses cannot be rationalized and theorized, they just are, waiting to be discovered if we can reflect (phase 1) and arrest (phase 2) effectively and authentically. This last phase, often, though not always, can involve engaging with the openings created by ambiguity, irony, and reflection on critical moments in conflict. Such engagement with ambiguity, irony, and reflection is an invitation to creativity (which, like emotions, are innate within us).

These three phases, which will be discussed further in the next chapters expose the need for both rational and emotional response to conflict. As we explore how to change the system without destroying what works in our current system in the next chapter we will return to these simple, yet complex, processes and try and put some language to them. Balancing Systems maintenance with radical change requires both thought and action, both theory and practice. While nonverbal and intuitive, there is language and "training" that can help us learn to be more present in the moment and open to ambiguity; in an elemental sense it just takes practice. The praxis of trauma-informed and emotionally aware conflict practice requires walking on Occam's razor. It is not easy, and we are always learning—so I profess no special expertise here. Still, irony, ambiguity, and critical moments can be turning points for building effective survivorship while simultaneously not getting mired in a tribal identity as victim.

NOTES

1. Francesca Polletta, *It Was Like a Fever: Storytelling in Protest and Politics* (Chicago: University of Chicago Press, 2006), 140.

2. Sarah Federman, "Narrative Approaches to Understanding and Responding to Conflict" *The International Journal of Conflict Engagement and Resolution* 4, no. 2 (2016).

3. See: Sara Cobb, "A Developmental Approach to Turning Points: 'Irony' as an Ethics for Negotiation Pragmatics." *Harvard Negotiation Law Review* 11 (2006): 147–97; and Sara Cobb, *Speaking of Violence: The Politics and Poetics of Narrative Dynamics in Conflict Resolution* (Oxford: Oxford University Press, 2013).

4. Vamik Volkan, *Bloodlines: From Ethnic Pride to Ethnic Terrorism* (Boulder, CO: Westview Press, 1997).

5. Givens defines radical empathy as "encouraging each of us not only to understand the feelings of others, but also to be motivated to create the change that will allow all of us to benefit from economic prosperity and develop the social relationships that are beneficial to our emotional wellbeing." See: Terri Givens, *Radical Empathy: Finding a Path to Bridging Racial Divides* (New York, Polity Press, 2021), 1.

6. Francesca Polletta, *It Was Like a Fever*, op. cit., xi–xii.

7. Ibid., xii.

8. Bessel van der Kolk, *The Body Keeps Score*, op. cit.

9. Personal correspondence with TBMSG founder and Chief Executive, Lokamitra, October 2006.

10. Francesca Polletta, *It Was Like a Fever*, op. cit., xii.

11. Personal correspondence with Dalit academic colleague, Summer 2021.

12. Sara Cobb, *Speaking of Violence*, op. cit., 29.

13. Ruth Behar, *The Vulnerable Observer: Anthropology That Breaks Your Heart* (Boston: Beacon Press, 1996), 16–17.

14. Donald Schon, *The Reflective Practitioner*, 1983, op. cit.

15. Ibid., 19.

16. Vamik Volkan, 1997, op. cit.

17. Jill Freedman and Gene Combs, *Narrative Therapy: The Social Construction of Preferred Realities* (New York: W.W. Norton and Company, 1996), 11.

18. The Wire, January 17, 2019. Accessed November 18, 2022. See: https://thewire.in/caste/rohith-vemula-letter-a-powerful-indictment-of-social -prejudices.

19. Ibid.

20. Ibid.

21. Peter Levine, *In an Unspoken Voice* (Berkeley, CA: North Atlantic Books, 2012) xii, quoted in Thenmozhi Soundararajan, *The Trauma of Caste* (Berkeley, CA: North Atlantic Books, 2022), 19.

22. Sara Cobb, *Speaking of Violence*, op. cit., 27.

23. Over the years a vast body of literature in what has become known as the "social determinates of health" has arisen. While broad and all-inclusive in many respects this concept is an important and increasingly respected variable in understanding public health outcomes. The World Health Organization defines social determinants of health as "conditions or circumstances in which people are born, grow, live, work, and age. These conditions are shaped by political, social, and economic forces" (CSDH *Closing the Gap in a Generation: Health Equity Through Action on the Social Determinants of Health*. Final Report of the Commission on Social Determinants of Health. Geneva: World Health Organization, 2008). For a nice overview of the complexities of the concept of the social determinates of health see: MM Islam, "Social Determinants of Health and Related Inequalities: Confusion and Implications." *Front Public Health* 7 (February 8, 2019): 11.

24. By using moral agency here I am not questioning the morality of Vermula's many attempts to challenge the structural violence he experienced prior to taking his life. "Rather 'moral agency' refers to the way that Others elaborate the capacity of actors to be moral agents and the consequences for those subjected to structural violence to narrate that violence. Narrative violence reduces moral agency both for those who create the state of exception and for those who are victims of it." Sara Cobb, *Speaking of Violence*, op. cit., 29.

25. Yashica Dutt, *Coming Out as Dalit: A Memoir* (New Delhi: Aldelp Book Co., 2019), xix.

26. Dutt (2019) articulates this well when she writes: "under a slightly different set of circumstances, his short life could have been mine." Yashica Dutt, *Coming Out as Dalit,* op. cit., xvi.

27. The Wire, January 17, 2019. Accessed, November 18, 2022. See: https://thewire.in/caste/rohith-vemula-letter-a-powerful-indictment-of-social -prejudices.

28. Yashica Dutt, *Coming Out as Dalit,* op. cit., xvi.

29. This points to the structuralist approach of Louis Dumont's *Homo Heirarchicus: The Caste System and Its Implications* (Chicago: University of Chicago Press, 1970). In this important work of sociology Dumont strives to distinguish Indian society as a hierarchy between pure and impure as opposed to western (French?) society as egalitarian. For further discussion of this see also: TN Madan, *Pathways: Approaches to the Study of Society in India* (Delhi: Oxford University Press, 1994).

30. Francesca Polletta, *It Was Like a Fever*, op. cit., 39.

31. Ibid., 43.

32. Thenmozhi Soundararajan, *The Trauma of Caste* (Berkeley, CA: North Atlantic Books, 2022), 123.

33. For readers that are familiar with social theories of human violence this is reminiscent of the writing and work of Rene Girard. Girard spent his career

writing about the human urge to imitate each other as the cause of rivalries and violent conflicts. For him, this mimetic desire could be partially resolved by scapegoating others. Rohit Vermula's intent was not to have others imitate his final act, but rather his choice does expose the collective and social impacts of the trauma of caste oppression by challenging the idea that we can be separated as members of the human race. For more of Girard's ideas see: Rene Girard, *Violence and the Sacred* (Baltimore: John Hopkins University Press, 1979).

34. Thenmozhi Soundararajan, *The Trauma of Caste*, op. cit., 39.

35. Eduardo Duran and Bonnie Duran, *Native American Postcolonial Psychology* (Albany: SUNY Press, 1995), 24.

36. Ibid., 45.

37. Sara Cobb, "A Developmental Approach to Turning Points: 'Irony' as an Ethics for Negotiation Pragmatics," *Harvard Law Review* 11, no. 147 (2006): 148.

38. Ruth Behar, *The Vulnerable Observer*, op. cit., 19.

39. Thenmozhi Soundararajan, *The Trauma of Caste*, op. cit., 43.

40. Miranda Fricker, *Epistemic Injustice: Power and the Ethics of Knowing* (New York: Oxford University Press, 2007), 5.

41. Ibid., 1.

42. Ibid., 8.

43. Thenmozhi Soundararajan, *The Trauma of Caste*, op. cit., 43.

44. Ibid., 43.

45. Ibid., The Wire, January 17, 2019. Accessed, November 18, 2022. See: https://thewire.in/caste/rohith-vemula-letter-a-powerful-indictment-of-social -prejudices.

46. Miranda Fricker, *Epistemic Injustice,* op. cit., 14. Fricker argues "Whenever there is an operation of power that depends in some significant degree upon such shared imaginative conceptions of social identity, then identity power is at work" (14).

47. This language is indebted to: Sara Cobb, "A Developmental Approach to Turning Points: 'Irony' as an Ethics for Negotiation Pragmatics." *Harvard Negotiation Law Review* 11 (2006): 147–97.

48. See: David Laws, "What Use Is a Critical Moment?" *Negotiation Journal* 36 (2020): 107–26. https://doi.org/10.1111/nejo.12323.

49. "Microaggressions are defined as the everyday, subtle, intentional— and oftentimes unintentional—interactions or behaviors that communicate some sort of bias toward historically marginalized groups." NPR Interview with Kevin Nadal found here: https://www.npr.org/2020/06/08/872371063/ microaggressions-are-a-big-deal-how-to-talk-them-out-and-when-to-walk-away, accessed December 12, 2022.

50. M. T. Williams, M. D. Skinta, J. W. Kanter, et al., "A qualitative study of microaggressions against African Americans on predominantly White campuses." *BMC Psychol* 8, 111 (2020). https://doi.org/10.1186/s40359-020-00472-8.

51. Peter Levine, *Walking the Tiger: Healing Trauma* (Berkeley, CA: Northern Atlantic Books, 1997), 34.

52. Ibid., 183.

53. Judith Herman, *Trauma and Recovery: The Aftermath of Violence: From Domestic Abuse to Political Terror* (New York: Basic Books, 1997).

54. David Laws, "What Use Is a Critical Moment?" *Negotiation Journal* 36 (2020): 107–26. https://doi.org/10.1111/nejo.12323.

55. Ibid.

56. Clifford Gertz, "Thick Description: Toward an Interpretive Theory of Culture," in *The Interpretation of Cultures: Selected Essays* (New York: Basic Books, 1973), 3–30.

57. To learn more about the Greensboro Massacre, see: https://greensborotrc .org/exec_summary.pdf as well as: Spoma Jovanovic, *Democracy, Dialogue, and Community Action: Truth and Reconciliation in Greensboro* (Fayetteville: University of Arkansas Press, 2012). The day after this event (e.g., November 4, 1979), which made national news on November 3rd, the hostages were taken at the U.S. Embassy in Iran and the Greensboro story went cold.

58. Reverend Nelson Johnson, class presentation in FYE 101: Narrative Conflict: The Myth of Serenity, freshman seminar, Fall 2012, Guilford College, Greensboro North Carolina.

59. Ibid.

60. Miranda Fricker, *Epistemic Injustice,* op. cit.

61. For detailed discussion of the position theory see Rom Harré and Luk Van Langenhove, *Positioning Theory: Moral Contexts of Intentional Action* (Oxford: Blackwell, 1999). See also: Fathali Moghaddam, Rom Harré, and Naoim Lee, "Positioning and Conflict: An Introduction," in *Global Conflict Resolution Through Positioning Analysis*, edited by Fathali Moghaddam, Rom Harre, and Naoim Lee (New York: Springer, 2008), 3–20.

62. Dennis J. D. Sandole, "A Comprehensive Mapping of Conflict and Conflict Resolution: A Three Pillar Approach," *Peace and Conflict Studies* 5, no. 2 (1998), Article 4. DOI: 10.46743/1082-7307/1998.1389.

63. Donald Schon, *The Reflective Practitioner*, 1983, op. cit., 54.

64. Miranda Fricker, *Epistemic Injustice,* op. cit., 5.

65. Rom Harré and Luk Van Langenhove, *Positioning Theory: Moral Contexts of Intentional Action* (Oxford: Blackwell, 1999). Ibid., 5.

66. Terri Givens, *Radical Empathy: Finding a Path to Bridging Racial Divides* (New York: Polity Press, 2021).

67. See: Jeffrey Alexander, "Toward a Theory of Cultural Trauma," *Cultural Trauma and Collective Identity* (Oakland, CA: University of California Press, 2004) and Jeffrey Alexander, *Trauma: A Social Theory* (Malden, MA: Polity Press, 2012).

68. Joseph Montville, "Justice and the burdens of history," in *Reconciliation, Justice, and Coexistence*, edited by M. Abu Nimer (Lanham, MD: Lexington, 2001).

69. https://www.forwardpress.in/2017/04/reading-dr-ambedkar-as-a-narrative-for-social-change/.

70. H. Tajfel and J. C. Turner, "An Integrative Theory of Intergroup Conflict," in *The Social Psychology of Intergroup Relations*, edited by W. G. Austin and S. Worchel (Monterey, CA: Brooks/Cole, 1979), 33–47.

71. G. W. Allport, *The Nature of Prejudice: 25th Anniversary Edition* (New York, NY: Basic Books, 1979).

72. Anand Teltumbde, "Bathani Tola and the Cartoon Controversy," *Economic and Political Weekly* 47, no. 22 (2012): 10. Quoted in Hugo Gorringe, "Ambedkar Icons: Whys and Wherefores," in *The Radical Ambedkar: Critical Reflections*, edited by Suraj Yegende and Anand Teltumbde (New York: Penguin, 2018), 330.

73. See: Dr. Babasaheb Ambedkar, *Writings and Speeches*, Vol. 12, Vasant Moon, ed. (Bombay: Education Department, Government of Maharashtra, 1993), Part I, 661–91.

4

THE THEORY
AND PRACTICE
OF ADDRESSING
SYSTEMIC INJUSTICE

ON DOING SYSTEMS
MAINTENANCE AS OPPOSED TO
COMPLETELY DECONSTRUCTING
AND REBUILDING BROKEN
SYSTEMS

I began my higher education teaching career at small liberal arts
colleges in the United States. That atmosphere presents a unique
cloistered opportunity for study and reflective introspection. Hired as
a visiting assistant professor of peace and conflict studies provided a
unique opportunity from which to explore, along with students, the
processes of prosocial systems change and societal transformation. In
such an academic environment people theorize and analyze the collective problems of the world and identify the many fissures in complex systems which intersect with policy, activism, hierarchical power,
decision making, and contentious politics. The cloistered life of the

mind, a privilege at increasingly elite liberal arts institutions of higher education, allows time for dialogue, debate, and critical thinking. As a scholar-practitioner of social movement activism and conflict transformation, the liberal arts environment afforded me unique opportunities to explore social justice and systems change from the positionality of both radical resistance and privilege. Working for radical change while simultaneously maintaining the positive aspects of a flawed and unfair system is a challenging balancing act. Theorizing about such processes is more than academic; such theorizing has real world utility. Space and opportunity for reflective introspection is critical for conflict intervenors keen on having lasting real-world impacts. The patient work of reflection is not, as is often assumed, the sole purview of the privileged, rather it is a necessity for just change in the modern world.[1] Liberal arts institutions, even though increasingly attacked by the political right are ripe with local politics and on-going institutional battles over funding, policy, and leadership. Despite increasing attacks, the liberal arts context fosters a leisure of thinking that can grow analytical awareness necessary to birth creativity. Such a context can act as a testing ground for young students interested in the local and global "problems" of the world. Often realizing the global connections to local problems for the first time, young students in liberal arts environments often begin to develop a sense of the depth and reach of their own identity and social agency. This often leads these students to adopt disruptive strategies of local activism to effect what they see as slow-moving solutions to major global problems.[2] This disruption is contrary to the patient liberal arts deliberation and often acts to further radicalize young activists impatient for change. Still, a reflective young activist can begin to see that their actions have impacts that are both intended and unintended. While only sometimes the realization of the negative impacts of disruption comes too late, the specter of disruption should always give pause. The common response to a growing critical awareness of potential impacts, cracks, and systems openings is often to call for the destruction and rebuilding of entire systems labeled as having failed a particular identity group, or the society as a whole. But, in addressing problems of systemic injustice, this may not always be the most efficient or effective means of sustainable social transformation. Rarely is destructive disruption an effective long-term conflict resolution or peacebuilding strategy, despite its value as a source of moral shock and/or social issue mobilization. Young activists often don't have the long view that a trauma-aware and emotionally experienced approach requires.

As a Peace and Conflict Studies professor at Guilford College, a small progressive Quaker liberal arts college in Greensboro, North Carolina, I used to have to repeatedly remind socially aware and politically angry students that burning down the house does not fix its many structural problems. The emotions of anger and frustration often drive issue mobilization, social organizing, political opportunities,[3] and resistance/response to "wicked problems."[4] This is especially true when one's goal is to establish social justice for marginalized low-power communities in the late capitalist era. The roadblocks, and ingrained and habituated systems of oppression, lead to frustration and aggression, especially in young activists not yet defeated by pessimism borne of failed attempts at social justice activism. Such emotions, often dismissed as "the passion of youth," are not necessarily a bad thing,[5] but unchanneled and undisciplined they can be destructive as opposed to constructive to long-term transformation. The key is not to deny these emotions but to use them in prosocial as opposed to antisocial ways. If social change is the goal, then channeling anger and frustration towards constructive transformation of existent systems is critical to success. This is an important reminder to young student-activists who see the problems of the world and impatiently desire change yesterday.

While effective social change has historically been led by younger generations channeling this frustration productively (and most often nonviolently[6]) such change has also strategically worked within (not outside of) systems. Still the line between acknowledging trauma, social harm, and destructive emotions without destroying systems as you aim to disrupt them, at times, can feel like walking on Occam's razor. This chapter aims to develop effective equilibrium between trauma-informed and emotionally aware response to past harms and the complex realities and tensions of maintaining systems in conflict.

Conflict resolution must not only help parties reach consensus on just ends, but serve as the means to get there as well. As distasteful as it may be for some social justice theorists, transformative conflict resolution (in the social justice sense) requires being attentive to the proletarian goings-on of systems maintenance, for it is here where outcomes of a resolution-ary agreement will be determined.[7]

Like Schoeny and Warfield (2000), quoted above, I argue that sys-tems maintenance and social justice are interdependent and intercon-nected goals, not separate ones. Systems have functions, but if a system is not functioning well it does not mean the entire system is broken. Inputs, outputs, and flows in systems must be understood to suggest and implement effective and lasting change in systems. In the words of system theorist Donnella Meadows: "If you understand the dynamics (behavior over time) of stocks and flows, you understand a good deal about the behavior of complex systems."[8] While often the emotional resonance of calls for social justice and desires for systems maintenance can appear to be at cross purposes it is my contention that effective con-flict resolution practice embraces systems maintenance as inseparable from a trauma-informed and emotionally aware intervention practice. Effective change requires a sense of grounding and feeling grounded. Emotions of anger, frustration, and helplessness can be used to effect change in systems but are often framed in ways that assume, and, in turn, bring out, the worst in both people and systems.[9] An emotionally mindful and trauma-informed conflict resolution practice mediates between disrupting and repairing broken systems, not disavowing them entirely.

In their study of urban planning, Rittel and Webber (1973) coined the idea of "wicked problems" and speak of these as "malignant (in contrast to 'benign') . . . or 'aggressive' (like a lion, in contrast to the docility of a lamb)."[10] For Rittel and Webber, there is no definitive for-mulation of a wicked problem, but "the formulation of a wicked prob-lem *is* the problem."[11] Wicked problems are thereby invoked simply by naming them: climate change, social inequalities, racial or decent-based caste discrimination, protracted social conflict (think ongoing conflicts in Israel-Palestine, Syria, or Ukraine as examples). These are all prob-lems "whose causes and consequences are so inextricably intertwined that one can't understand them, let alone cope with them separately."[12] Wicked problems are, by definition, a type of ethical dilemma where one intervention impacts other potential interventions; a sort of cascad-ing and interconnected set of problems. To address wicked problems, one must go beyond theoretical or practical frameworks, epistemologi-cal squabbles, or raw emotions and think collectively and creatively of not just solutions, but the way problems are set in the first place.[13] Here both language and social stability matter greatly. To resolve such wicked problems, we must widen the descriptive/linguistic tent and explore collaboratively those parts of systems and their complexity that have been too long neglected (like emotions and trauma), but we must also not throw out the proverbial baby with the bathwater. In other words, to "solve" wicked problems, systems must continue to operate/ function (however poorly they do) while simultaneously being challenged to change and adapt. This can be sort of like fixing an airplane while flying it. We must manage emotions, and emotionally laden calls for destruction, while simultaneously transforming the ways we think and talk about effecting change in the system. Such an approach requires complex comparative analytical skills, patience, and emotional intelligence for success. Some have described this as an approach that is responding to "syndemic conditions."[14] In describing the creation of peace, justice, and healing in the wake of an epidemic of police shootings of African Americans in the city of Chicago, Hooker and Bedi (2021) argue that such conditions require not simply analysis skills but creative comparative theory creation. "Syndemic theory recognizes that when multiple pandemic or epidemic conditions co-exist, the context is shifted beyond any additive analysis, a new set of conditions emerge that are not fully predicted by the current theories regarding either condition."[15] This suggests that while conflict intervenors must be creative theory builders they must also realize applying new theory requires careful and incremental trials of creative solutions. Think of the early civil rights era strategic testing of nonviolent actions of disruption and civil disobedience to effect change. Often renaming or relabeling wicked problems can be an important first step in the preliminary work of theory creation for peaceful systems change. In their book *The Trauma of Caste*, Thenmozhi Soundararajan creatively reframes victims of caste oppression as survivors and argues for the sufferers of caste to develop "embodied" responses as "empathetic witnesses to each other's pain"[16]; this is an example of the reframing and relabeling of wicked problems that modern anti-caste activists are actively engaged in. Such activist work realizes the shortcomings of current theory and practice, but also acknowledges that the outright destruction of the unjust system will not serve the more distal goals of peace, justice, or collective healing of survivors from legacies of harm. When harms have happened we cannot deny their impacts, but rather must reframe them in ways that foreground the means by which these harms can be instrumentalized for constructive systems change. This reframing reclaims and reinscribes agency of those that are most effected by injustice. Rather than rhetoric of destroying problematic systems outright, creative theory-building and applied practices are needed to simultaneously build awareness and overcome such wicked problems.

Another important example of this critical reframing of language can be found in Isabelle Wilkerson's recent (2020) book *Caste: The Origins of our Discontents*. Wilkerson makes an important claim for reframing in her attempt to redress American ideas of race and racism in the more ancient language of caste hierarchy. She writes: "In America, race is the primary tool and the visible decoy, the front man, for caste."[17] She argues that race and racism conjure tropes and assumptions that hinder effective responses to the wicked problem of racial injustice. The term race in fact elicits emotions and collective historical traumas that can get us stuck in a loop of retaliatory victimization (remember the discussion in chapter 1 of this book for more on these, often retaliatory, cycles of violence). To achieve real structural change in racial conflict we need to rethink what Wilkerson calls the "grammar" of what we know through experience. "If we have been trained to see humans in the language of race, then caste is the underlying grammar that we encode as children, as when learning our mother tongue."[18] Rethinking this grammar provides creative opportunities for agency for the oppressed. Addressing injustice, as a wicked problem, is complex and requires deep social and cultural rethinking. Wilkerson's work provides an important expression of this complexity, but this alone does not "solve" the problem. Relabeling and reframing are just initial steps towards transforming unjust systems. Caste and race, as wicked problems that are socially constructed and ever adapting to new social conditions, are systems that need to be dismantled, but doing so is a process that requires careful attention rather than an assumption of one-time change or simple massive overhaul solutions. Cobb (2013), indeed, draws important attention to the role of "path dependency" in unmasking the complexity of what she terms narrative violence. She writes: "Given the complexity of institutionalized exclusion, vigilance, as a mental attitude, is a weak prophylactic against the enactment of narrative violence; it is much more likely that the existing patterns of interaction, anchored in the language of agency, institutionalized through the state of exception, persist. They have a path dependency (Boas, 2007)."[19] Still, a series of

subtle shifts, starting with narrative reframing, can represent a powerful step towards lasting change, although such steps also require collective vigilance and can take time. Such a gradual approach that embraces
emotions and trauma will prove to be a more effective means to lasting
systems change than emotionally-driven and reactive disruption. This
is a call for pragmatic and strategically planned activism, not reactive
attempts to dismantle interconnected systems.

Practitioners of conflict resolution must not only be aware of the
critical importance of language and framing/setting of social problems,
but also they must be adaptive-reactive to complex and subtle shifts
in wicked problems as interventions are attempted. This is the work
of paying close attention to conflict-in-process. John Paul Lederach
calls this "the moral imagination" and argues that this requires "the
ability to sustain a paradoxical curiosity that embraces complexity
without reliance on dualistic polarity."[20] Too often humans get stuck in
such polarities. The social awareness of violence and injustice must be
coupled with a critical awareness that the language, and the language
rules and norms that we reproduce, are more than productive of us
versus them identity positions but part of dynamic processes of shifting
meaning. Good/bad, evil/morally upright, victim/perpetrator, etc., are
not absolutely real polar opposites (again remember the poem by Thich
Nhat Hanh referenced in chapter 1). This idea that practitioners rely on
curiosity without getting stuck on dichotomies like victim-offender or
oppressed-privileged is a critical insight for conflict resolution practitioners working for sustained systems change in unjust systems. Practitioners of the art of conflict resolution are in a sort of existential space that
is present focused, but future oriented at the same time. Holding this
space involves skills in systems change that centers the lived experience
of injustice and disempowerment, but also models inclusive futures
that embrace creative understanding of the dynamic interrelationships
between opposites. This leaves little room for practitioners to get stuck
in particular identities, or retaliatory loops. Amid the pain and emotions of "victims" of past trauma or "perpetrators" of suffering, this
can be a difficult "middling" space to hold. Anger, shame, guilt, and
sorrow can stifle curiosity, empathy, and lead to assumptions of quick
fixes to complex wicked problems. Often, such quick fixes are based on
assumed psychological theories that hold little validity in practice. For
example, solutions to environmental degradation that assume a behav-
iorist bias and neglect the social construction processes of shared values

like acceptance of neoliberal consumption norms. Still, system maintenance does not mean that emotional anger and traumatic response should be stifled or forgotten; this is not what I mean by managing emotions. Rather systems maintenance must be foregrounded in such a way that is inclusive, forward-looking, and critical of assumed knowledge. This is the uneasy balance, or polarity,[21] that needs to be experimented with, tested, and consistently pin-pointed in specific conflict contexts. This is the artistic and multi-disciplinary side of peacebuilding and conflict intervention that makes success so difficult to quantify and practitioner guides so difficult to write! Theories, like for example psychoanalysis, are helpful here, but practitioners must not let the theory alone drive the practice. That emotionally mindful and trauma-aware systems change without tearing down the system, is possible, but it is also a constantly moving target that requires creative acts of "moral imagination."[22] "The creative act brings into existence processes that have not existed before. To sustain them over time, processes of change need constant innovation."[23] This focus on process, not outcome, is critical to trauma-informed and emotionally mindful conflict practice, as we have discussed in previous chapters. Too often as practitioners we move to outcomes at the expense of process. Reflection on process, as opposed to getting fixated on desired outcomes, requires practitioners to be constantly innovative and change adaptive. Such theoretical curiosity and critical vigilance without developing theoretical blinders, or outcome biases, is challenging. This creative vigilance requires a tense equilibrium of pushing for systems change and being attentive to the "proletarian goings on of systems maintenance."[24] While these goals often work at cross-purposes, they require faith in a process of creative reflection that embraces emotions and trauma, as opposed to running away from them. The goal of peace with justice requires ongoing management of peace processes rather than one-off solutions.[25]

CHANGE AND MOVING FROM RESOLUTION TO TRANSFORMATION

In exploring how collective trauma and opening space for either emotional sharing and/or cultural collaboration is critical to balancing social movement strategies, both system's maintenance and social justice should be understood not as "polar opposites," but rather complimentary polarities. Polarities are interconnected and dance with each other; they move in tandem or are affected, and not entirely separate from, the other. More than opposites attract, opposites are, to a certain extent, defined by each other. Johnson's (1996) ideas about managing polarities mirrors a "both-and approach" to both "prefigurative" and "harm-reduction politics," which Bohrer (2022) also argues for in effective social movement work for change.[26] There is room for both revolutionary and more incremental tendencies in both social movement work and conflict resolution practice, and neither is exclusive of the other. Dang (2022) also articulates this idea well when she writes: "Incremental change is required to improve immediate and short-term living conditions, but revolution of the system is required for long-term, intergenerational change."[27] Still, the human tendency toward collective identity formation often makes these complimentary approaches seem radically divergent from, or even at cross-purposes to, each other. Humans are attracted to others like, or similar, to them, but getting too focused on the similarities we miss opportunities for the cosmic dance of polarities. Both incremental and revolutionary strategies and tactics often too easily become linked with ideological identities, but such strategies are human. In social justice movements especially, identity concerns tend to supersede all strategy and planning. But the fact is conflict transformation aims to do more than simply maintain or resolve protracted and festering problems in society. Transformation is forward looking and present focused, a polarity that is often a challenge for identity-based movements for social justice. Conflict transformation requires aligning reactive and proactive approaches to change; balancing desires for resolution with strategies for longer-term revolutionary transformation. This calls on both social movement actors as well as conflict resolution practitioners to bracket identity concerns— not forget them, but make them a lesser concern than peace, equality, humanity, and justice. This, of course, is no small task, in the face of either emotional suffering and trauma or in a context of collective anger over public and historical injustices.

Putting identity concerns on a back burner is often easier said than done. As we have already seen, putting complex social-psychological theory into practice and engaging in the art of the moral imagination is, indeed, tricky work. Comity is as important a foundational value of conflict intervention practice as nonviolence, but rarely practiced in social movement circles. The foundational narratives of conflict practice underscore these seminal values of nonviolence and comity. But to understand these values, we must interrogate the stories we tell about our own practice.

Bush and Folger (2005) start their important practice-oriented book, *The Promise of Mediation,* with four stories to help illustrate their argument for what they call transformative mediation. In framing what they call the "four stories of the mediation process," Bush and Folger argue that "the existence of divergent stories suggests that although everyone sees mediation as a means for achieving important private and public goals, people differ over what goals are most important."[28] In other words, implicit values of a practitioner's practice do not always align with perceived intervention goals or values; practitioners' espoused theories are not in alignment with their theories in use.[29] The focus on these stories here is not to suggest all conflict transformation work is synonymous with mediation practice, but rather to illustrate how stories help frame the inherent values-based tensions in conflict intervention work more broadly. Bush and Folger (2005) outline the four stories of mediation as focused on satisfaction, social justice, transformation, and oppression.[30] While the first three stories see mediation as a positive prescription for responding to social conflict, the fourth, the oppression story, sees mediation as a "serious threat to disadvantaged groups."[31] It is this oppression story that deserves more critical attention from conflict resolution practitioners. While the satisfaction story argues that mediation is "a powerful tool for satisfying human needs"[32] and the social justice story argues mediation builds "stronger community ties and structures,"[33] the oppression story is largely avoided as inconvenient by mediators. Branding the story, they want to tell as "the unique promise of mediation"[34] the transformation story, according to the authors, gives conflict parties the agency to define problems and set their own dispute resolution goals through both the recognition of the humanity of the "Other" and personal empowerment. The authors of *The Promise of Mediation* make the bold claim that empowerment and recognition lead to the constructive transformation of social conflict, but they never fully deliver a full-throated critique of the oppression story. The oppression story argues that mediation only "reinforce(s) the status quo"[35] and "consolidate(s) the power of the strong"[36] over the weak. While they admit these stories are not monolithic and overlap with each other, they never fully address the all-to-present realities that conflict interventions often maintain unjust systems. Another way to say this is that mediation, at times, can have destructive impacts, as well as unintended consequences on developing socially just systems.

Though Bush and Folger (2005) commendably acknowledge this reality of mediation, they do not fully explore its implications. If the goal of conflict resolution is increased equality in society, is mediation the best, or only, means to achieve it? Of course, mediation is not the only means to work for equality in society, but it is one effective way to balance the power of conflicting parties and use the generative power of conflict. Balancing the power of conflict parties, a key building block for equity, can also act to give legitimacy to unjust historical relationships. Mediation can, given the correct context and conflict ripeness,[37] be effectively used to develop and uphold equality between people. But is it a good method of developing or upholding equality in instances of collective historical trauma and public expression of the emotional sequalae of traumatic histories? Another way to ask this question is to ask if a process can sideline identity concerns enough that emotions and trauma can be harnessed for constructive (as opposed to destructive) social change? Centering injustice and disempowerment are like opening Pandora's box; such centering requires a change in mindset from mere resolution to conflict transformation for sure, as Bush and Folger (2005), indeed, argue. It also requires a set of system analytical skills that notices the micro-impacts of interventions and how acknowledging and engaging trauma and emotions impacts a long-term intervention process.

Working for systems maintenance while simultaneously working for social justice is complicated and at times appears to be at cross purposes in practice. Embracing collective historical trauma and opening space for emotional sharing is critical to balancing the goals of equality and the maintenance of a systems' functioning. Conflict resolution, cum transformation, practitioners must navigate a complex terrain, sometimes unknowingly, that is littered with trauma and emotions that are often hidden in a labyrinth of individual sequalae of conflict parties.[38] How we navigate this terrain depends on values of equity, equality, and comity as well as a creative reflexivity that is process, as opposed to outcomes, oriented. The goal for conflict practitioners must always be to develop effective resolution mechanisms/processes aimed at acknowledging harm and disrupting systems so change can occur over time. Of course, this is far from neutral work and emotions often complicate the argument for gradual change.[39] Conflict intervention practice is political and normative advocacy that must take hierarchy and other power imbalances constantly into account. As stated above, disrupting systems without destroying them can be like walking on Occam's razor, but it need not be work that is unknowable or a practice that is untrainable. Emotionally mindful and trauma-aware conflict intervention is a learnable set of practices. To acquire these skills and practice processes one must practice them regularly and be open to a sense of ambiguity.

HOW TO EMBRACE TRAUMA AND EMOTIONS IN YOUR TRANSFORMATIVE CONFLICT PRACTICE AND PROCESS

So, thus far, the discussion of practices has primarily been theoretical. However, how do conflict intervention practitioners apply creative reflexivity, comity, and simultaneously reframe the language of trauma and emotions to improve their intervention processes? To answer this pragmatic question, I must return to my own personal experiences as a scholar-practitioner working alongside anti-caste activists. Since I can never fully know the emotional state of others, speaking of my own emotions in conflict intervention practice processes can provide some guidance for how to apply this theory to transforming systemic oppression and injustice.

Jenkins (2008) argues that social identity is not a "thing," or something that we have, but rather something we do, a process.[40] In this sense we identity, rather than we have an identity. This is as true for conflict intervention practitioners as it is for conflict parties themselves. In 2023, as a Fulbright-Nehru scholar in India, I organized a series of focus group discussions and dialogues on the trauma and experience of caste with students and human rights activists in Pune, Maharashtra. The first of these four group dialogues took place at an Ambedkar Buddhist human rights center called the Manuski (literally translated as "humanity" from Marthi language) Center in Pune city. The small group discussion, comprised of four men and one woman and facilitated by me, was framed as a chance to engage in discussion of the traumas of caste oppression and explore their impacts on society as a whole. Staring with having participants self-define their own samaj, or community, I asked them if they felt justice was distributed equally in their self-disclosed community. Although all participants were from low-caste communities, they were not all from the same caste, sub-caste, or geographic region. Immediately one of the men launched into a long and heart-wrenching story about the social exclusion and social boycott his family faced as landowners in his home village in eastern

Maharashtra. While his emotional pain and family trauma over the events he described were palpable through his visible psychological affect, as a facilitator I became increasingly aware of my own sense of frustration with the focus groups' dynamic of monologue as opposed to circle dialogue. This frustration, upon reflection, emanated from two different process dynamics. Firstly, I was clearly frustrated by the fact that this single voice took over the discussion. Secondly, as I actively attempted to find a way to include other voices in the group, I became aware of my frustration with this respondents' rational, as opposed to emotional, interpretation of my questions. In other words, this second level of frustration emanated from my own dismay with how the emotional aspects of my question had been sidelined by the rationalizations of this speaker. This, coupled with the speakers' seeming disregard for others' stories hampered my ability to react in the moment, even as I reflected in the moment. Although not atypical, parties' reliance on rational rather than emotional reflection is deeply embedded in our cultural perceptions about the expression of emotions publicly. As I became increasingly aware of my rising level of frustration over this single voice taking over the discussion, my own interests and perceptions began to try and manage the situation. My own limited time and ongoing frustrations with Indian patriarchy (females rarely takeover talk) certainly conditioned my actions. Feeling that I had to jump in to facilitate a change in dynamic, the discursive direction weighed heavily on me, and time seemed to slow down. The communicative values I was trying to model for the group, in my mind, seemed to be highjacked by this one participant. As seconds ticked by, my own sense of anxiety rose—how would I redirect to others to encourage dialogue as opposed to monologue? This sense of my own victimhood as a researcher grew by the moment, to the point that I was even having trouble following what the participant was articulating (thank God for recorded transcripts!). My rising frustration that other voices in the group were being silenced hampered my own ability to empathize or actively listen and my attempts to redirect the speaker were repeatedly rebuffed, or not embraced by others in the group. Upon reviewing the recording, three fourths of this first focus group "dialogue" was this one participant talking. Upon post-facilitation reflection my own perceptions and emotions as a facilitator and researcher were clearly disrupting my goal, and desire, for what I consider an inclusive dialogue process. Was my framing and setting of ground rules at fault, or was the need to be heard as victims so prevalent in these participants that my questions, and attempts to inclusively redirect, were just unrealistic? As I re-listened to the recordings of my own re-directive questions I can see how my own emotional frustration was not a passive player in this communicative dynamic; knowing this think how disruptive participants' emotions must have been. The insistence on telling their own personal stories of injustice, despite my continual re-directive requests for participants to focus on wider collective community impacts of their experiences, while not new to me in work with both Indian and Indian diaspora survivors of caste oppression and social ostracism, pushed me to try and manage the process, as opposed to just trusting the process to transform (and eventually "include") others. Limited resources, especially time, often mitigate against the patience and creativity required to change systems while working within them. It was as if participants' need for emotional outpouring, by focusing them inward and towards their own injustice narratives, clouded my own ability to trust the process of unmasking the collective impacts of such traumatic events.

As a conflict intervention practitioner how do I use such frustration to my advantage, as opposed to letting it derail a facilitated intervention process, as it did in this case? Firstly, and most obviously, the critical reflection of my own emotions must be done in-the-moment. It is one thing to learn from the process through reflection after the fact and another to act on that reflection in-the-moment. It is easy to sit back now, with hindsight, and critically reflect on my own emotional responses to the dynamics of participants' storytelling. Conversely, reflecting in-the-moment allows a practitioner to not only learn but act effectively on their emotional frustration by gracefully expressing it (as opposed to bottling it up). The critical reflection in-the-moment takes practice and an ability to give oneself grace when your set-up and intervention process dynamics do not go as you planned or envisioned. It also requires a fearless leadership to redirect the conversation empathetically but forcefully. In addition to this critical reflection in-the-moment, there must also be what Schon (1983) calls "reflection-in-action"[41] for professional practice of conflict intervention to be lasting and effective. In other words, one cannot simply critically reflect in the moment, which, in fact, my own field notes attest I did in this case, but also act appropriately on that in-the-moment reflection. This requires a trust in self and others that allows the conflict intervenor to voice their own emotional reactions to participants' rationalizations of trauma without imposing their emotional understandings on other participants; this is indeed a dance of identities and polarities. This also goes against how we humans are socialized—we shy away from trauma and try and manage it rather than respond emotionally to it. Even theoretically understanding this we must also practice it. Done well, this is not necessarily conflict generative, though it can be, but rather connecting, constructive, and supportive of the positives of the system as it is. One might call this asset-based as opposed to deficit-based intervention. While it may seem philosophical and esoteric in writing about this process, in practice it is this emotional connection and trust that works to manage conflictual polarities and create pathways toward collective social change. We are, by human nature drawn to our personal experiences, but trauma and emotions bring us back to our interconnected and collective sense of our experience as humans. Application of our values to our experience is part of the human condition; making these values explicit through action is achieved through real emotional sharing and connection—a critical dynamic that is often underappreciated in social reality. Attempting to practice the sharing of emotion-laden values is at the core of effective conflict intervention practice and we must give ourselves grace as practitioners when we miss opportunities to engage this core. As a social constructionist, I believe that continual practice can lead to dynamic change in habituated path dependency. The emotionally laden sharing of values can disrupt our habituated tendency to rationalize and manage social conflict, but this does not mean such disruption needs to disable or destabilize the system. It also does not mean this shift to emotion-laden sharing is easy.

So as not to misinterpret emotional cues in conflict process, we need to be constantly aware of them in the room. Although exhausting, this vigilance to our innate emotional intelligence is crucial and requires direct questions about feelings, emotions, and how conflict participants are defining these feelings. I know this is beginning to sound like a therapy session rather than conflict intervention, but conflict intervention practitioners must do more than simply manage emotions, which assumes they know the intended meaning and impacts of emotional outbursts. They must negotiate them with participants, much like a trained therapist would do to help patients mean effectively. We, as conflict resolution practitioners, need to get past the perception that emotions are not "professional" and/or only potentially conflict-generative, and, therefore, to be managed. If I had expressed publicly in-the-moment my emotional frustration with this focus group process, what dynamic shifts in parties' collective perceptions might have been empowered in the focus group dialogue? If I had practiced radical empathy and shared my emotional response to this individual participant's story would this have detracted or contributed to the understanding and sharing of others in the group? While, in this instance, I may never know the answers to these questions, such experiences have confirmed a confidence that expressing emotions fosters trust and builds relationships—the bedrocks of any peace practice. People who trust each other and feel connected in mutual relationship will be more likely to develop a collective sense of what Ledearch, almost mystically, calls "the moral imagination." Such a moral imagination is necessary to address wicked problems like systems of inequality and oppression.

SOCIALLY JUST SYSTEMS CHANGE AS THE CRITICAL FOREGROUNDING OF EMOTIONS AND TRAUMA IN CONFLICT

While the skill of reflection-in-action may seem obvious, and at least partially ephemeral, in the practice of conflict intervention, this learned skill is a critical grounding for any sustainable systems change. Trauma and emotions are, in this sense, the most important tools to tap into such long-term outcomes of what we may call inter-communal, or cross-community, peace. Trauma and emotions are a critical process ingredient that leads to desired collective outcomes and can be useful in pushing parties to tolerate, or even acknowledge, identities that are different than their own. Social identity can become a "trap"[42] and thereby stifle competing discourses and flatten the complexity of our multiple social identities. Engaging trauma and emotions mindfully in collective settings is admittedly a gradual approach to systems change, but it may be the only way, short of potentially violent revolution, to create lasting change. Such change is transformation with few associated negative consequences, and emotion and trauma are critical starting points to such work. Such a gradual nonviolent approach, unlike violent revolution, is not only sustainable but also more effective in achieving lasting transformation.[43] Still, even nonviolent activism often falls into the trap of thinking disruption is the only way to achieve lasting systems change. Do not get me wrong, nonviolent disruption certainly has its place in building awareness of an issue, putting the powerful on notice, and fermenting mobilization for quick social change. But devoid of processes that develop trust and emotional connection between conflicting ideologies, or singular identities, even such nonviolent disruptive tactics will have minimal sustainability in achieving lasting systems change, especially as this change relates to social identities and achieving justice for the oppressed.

Take for example the on-going contention over California State Senate Bill 403 (SB 403) as I write this chapter. SB 403 aims to add caste as a protected category, thus prohibiting discrimination on the basis of caste-based ancestry within the state of California.[44] As I write this chapter, activism and counter-activism is ongoing with both supporters and opponents invoking Gandhian-style nonviolent tactics, such as fasting, to achieve their interests and use guilt to push the powerful towards their side. Even with supporters calling for a fast until Governor Gavin Newsom signs the bill into law and opponents fasting to protest the SB 403's progress, these expressions of moral urgency and outrage do little to build trust or relationship between these conflicting parties. Lower-caste friends will say that higher-caste Hindu-right political forces have no desire for trust and relationship with their Dalit communities. Still, these emotional and identity-based responses to this contentious issue do little to narrow the distance between these polarized communities. In such a context, stories, language, discourse, and emotional trauma seem the only avenues to make even the most incremental change in this dynamic; identity is too fraught. In my 2018 book,[45] I argue for narrative storytelling as means to achieving some level of discursive cum social justice shift in Indian anti-caste activism. Here I am widening that initial argument to include the role of emotions and trauma as critical tools for achieving any definition of social justice. Emotionally mindful and trauma-aware storytelling forces conflicting parties to abandon flat affect, complicate conceptions of social identity, and reject disingenuous platitudes of "peace." When confronted (ideally in the same physical shared space) with traumatic stories of caste discrimination, parties shift from their own sense of victimhood to a more interconnected human understanding in which others may also see themselves as victims. Conflicting parties that can publicly tell of their pain and suffering create discursive space to reframe their experiences as survivors, as well as better understand why others may also perceive themselves as victims. Such contact, often missing, is crucial for sustainable change.

Traumatic experience and human emotions, like storytelling narrative, act as foundational implements for effective and sustained social change. But how do we create the contexts for these strategic rhetorical devices to be easily accessed by conflict intervention practitioners? If higher-caste communities have no desire to engage, and indeed harbor socially constructed and learned bigotry towards lower castes, how do we work to bring these separate communities' closer together? I believe the only answer is through telling stories and sharing past emotional traumas. To do this, conflict resolution practitioners must create the spaces and structures (e.g., what Lederach calls "process-structures"[46]) to share emotional suffering and past trauma. So, as conflict resolution practitioners we must develop spaces, processes, and structures where emotional narratives can be voiced and heard. Such process-structures open opportunities for identity divides to be bridged, even as they are complicated to erect and maintain. Over time the creation of open processes to share the emotional pain and stories of the feelings of being discriminated against can and will shift the wider discourse and awareness of those that deny injustice is happening. Again, this is incremental and slow work. It is systems change amidst work to maintain nonviolent systems and structures. It is also important to realize that sometime these systems are violent, yet their immediate destruction would have negative and/or unintended consequences.

Reading the above paragraph, some will say this is wishful thinking in our current context of polarization and identity politics. While theoretically sound, from the perspective of intervention practice the balance between systems change and systems maintenance is much more difficult to weigh, maintain, and achieve. A formative practice experience early in my career, as I taught at the Quaker liberal arts college mentioned at the beginning of this chapter, illustrates well the complexities of constructing a process-structure to deal with emotions and trauma in real world community conflicts. Tensions between systems change and maintenance are also glaringly obvious in this specific context of police and community relations. In the Spring semester of 2015 (my last semester at Guilford College), I was approached by the City of Greensboro Department of Human Relations (now called the Department of Human Rights) about bringing some students from the practice center I directed to help facilitate discussions on police-community relations in the city. Greensboro had just hired a new white Police Chief, after a racially contentious public search process that was punctuated by a feeling in the community that police were not listening to the community's needs. Not involved in the set-up and organization of this community dialogue process, I agreed to mobilize interested students from our conflict practice center and arrived a few minutes early to debrief with organizers prior to the public event, which was held at a local HBCU. My stated goals were to give students opportunity to test their skills in community dialogue as well as to learn a little about the conflict context of their city of residence (which was a new home for many of them). Me, along with six undergraduate students, tasked with facilitating discussion during the second half of the night's agenda, then proceeded to the auditorium for the opening welcome to the community event. As we walked in, we all noticed the uniformed Greensboro police officers that lined the walls of the auditorium. The tension in the room was immediately palpable.

We took our seats near the front as the Director of the Human Relations Department welcomed the community and began to spell out the plan and agenda for the evening. She did not get far before someone from the community blurted out: "why don't the police sit down?" The police, who continued to stand around the three walls which looked towards the front of the auditorium, seemed surprised by this outburst which elicited large hoots and cheers from others in the crowded auditorium. Following attempts to explain why police were in uniform and standing because they were on-duty and that their urge to protect made standing in the back seem to them a reasonable decision, the director then invited the new police chief to deliver a few words of welcome. This explanation and pressing on clearly ruffled many people's feathers but went unacknowledged. Seemingly oblivious to the contentious emotional dynamic in the room, the Chief began to launch into a set of power-point slides with plotted graphs and pie charts showing the decrease in both violent and nonviolent crimes in the city. This was quickly interrupted by community activists frustrated with the perceived slight of their own leaders and the tone-deaf behaviors of the Greensboro police and city officials present (to the crowd they were all the same actor). One man, sitting behind me, rose to his feet and began screaming that the Greensboro Police Department (GPD) was "completely oblivious to community needs!" In his excitement, arms waving, he smacked me in the back of the head and then apologized. Tensions were high and whispering gripes in the crowd began to rumble through the auditorium. Reverend Nelson Johnson, a long-time community activist, minister, and leader of the Beloved Community Center (BCC) then stood up and said: "Thanks chief, you can sit down now!" and proceeded to name the many issues the community had with the Greensboro Police's "rough" handling of community members.

After this impromptu presentation by Reverend Johnson, the Director of the Human Relations Department retook the microphone and explained that this was intended as a kickoff and welcome to the dialogue, not the dialogue itself. She then explained that we would be breaking into more manageable groups and retiring to three different break-out rooms to have community dialogue and discussion. Before we did so she asked me and my six undergraduate students to come up front and be recognized as those that would, in groups of two, facilitate these break-out dialogue sessions. Before the director could finish imploring basic community guidelines for civil discourse, immediately someone from the back of the auditorium shouted: "But they are all WHITE!" The director, herself a person of color, reacted by saying that she hoped people in the audience would give the process a chance and she promptly dismissed the community to split up into one of three dialogue rooms down the hall. Ultimately the dialogue conversation in which my students facilitated were cordial but tense. Still, this opening set of exchanges did not help build the community confidence that was hoped for by the convenors. In turn, the productive potentials of the event were limited and circumscribed from the start.

As I reflect on this night, a few important points are salient in my memory. Firstly, convenors seemed undeterred by the community's emotional responses and worked to manage them, as opposed to working with these emotions. In order to achieve a preconceived sense of their planned goals for the evening, emotions were minimized and brushed aside. The organizers of the event seemed more focused on their hoped-for outcomes (or concrete ideas they believed they could fashion as change) than the in-the-moment creativity and ambiguity that overflowing emotions might provide. Working with, as opposed to managing, emotions is a critical skill in effective conflict practice. I am not insinuating that this is easy, sitting with and stifling the urge to control emotions is no simple task, especially as your own sense of self, ego, safety, and emotional and physiological cues are impacted. In our current context of racial reckoning some might chalk the urge to control and manage up to "white culture,"[47] but more than dominant white culture, or patriarchal bias, subconsciously controlling emotions is baked into human nature. Slowing down the physiological responses to the expression of deep emotions can be challenging. Wilmot and Hocker (2011) argue that emotions "evolved with specific purposes related to human survival."[48] This is an important realization for conflict intervention practitioners as emotions in conflict are anything but irrational; in fact, they may be the most historically rationalized forms of expression known to humans. For the organizers of the event, the strong emotions or anger, fear, and frustration expressed by community members was a problem to be managed and not an opportunity to help build connection and understanding between the community and the police.

City organizers' approach appeared as tone-deaf to past trauma and elicited further negative reactions in community members escalating a conflict spiral that could have been de-escalated instead. An humble acknowledgment of unknowing and in-the-moment ability to change tact would have gone a long way to opening confidence in a community dialogue process. At the same time, police who are not trained in trauma-informed ways, expressed frustration as opposed to empathy. This is a typical response when you perceive your identity is being attacked. Emotions, like language and discourse, can act to position parties in conflict. Failure to notice emotional resonance will elicit similar behavioral responses that a lack of listening will and "when important identity and relationship issues are at stake, emotion is simply part of the picture."[49] So, emotional intelligence (e.g., the capacity to notice and recognize emotions) is a critical skill for all conflict intervention practitioners. Emotions are not even mentioned in many major texts of the field,[50] and if the concept of emotions do appear in the index, it is primarily related to their role in escalation.[51] But can't emotions, rather than being managed as only escalatory, be used to move parties towards resolution (e.g., de-escalation) too? This is reminiscent of the tensions between systems change and systems maintenance. Emotions can be positive and negative, but like radical activists discounting systems maintenance, conflict resolution practitioners managing emotions, can be a slippery slope that leads to worse outcomes. Assuming that emotions are only a deficit to peaceful intervention gives credence to the "oppression story." There are contexts when emotions do need to be managed, but I would argue this dialogue on police and community relations was not one of those contexts. Intervention practitioners must do more than "penetrate emotional barriers."[52] They must activate emotional borders to reframe and reset parties' perception of the other to allow opportunities for empathy and empowerment. This is why emotions are a critical fulcrum for the work of balancing systems maintenance and systems change, as well as, for being a trauma-aware conflict practitioner.

CONCLUSIONS AND THINKING TOWARDS A TOOLBOX FOR TRAUMA-INFORMED CONFLICT INTERVENTION

This chapter discusses balancing social justice and systems maintenance in conflict intervention practice. It argues that these goals are interconnected, not polar opposites, and that effective and lasting change requires aligning reactive and proactive approaches to change and emotional memories and traumas. Individual identity concerns often make complimentary approaches to social justice and systems change seem opposed or at odds with each other. True systems and structural change represent a gradual process-structure, requiring ongoing creative innovation, not one-time fixes. Practitioners need a sense of the "moral imagination" and both critical reflection and reflection-in-action to effectively intervene and transform protracted conflicts involving social justice. Unlike the traditional blue-collar workers' toolbox that includes physical tools, a series of skills and honed clinical practices are needed to balance gradual transformation of unjust systems and the calling out of unjust contexts. Calling out injustice is important, but so is "calling in"[53] a diverse set of ideas and identities to achieve effective social change. Trauma and emotions are critical for grounding such long-term systems change, they are not distractions at cross-purposes with such goals. The final full chapter focuses on further developing, applying, and articulating the concrete tools critically needed to respond to emotions and trauma constructively. A creative reflective conflict practice that is trauma-aware and emotionally mindful provides the fortitude for the change those that are marginalized and traumatized yearn to see.

NOTES

1. For an interesting take on the importance of patience in the modern world see: Uday Mehta, "Impatience and Modern Society." *Social Research: An International Quarterly* 90, no. 3 (Fall 2023): 459–78.

2. Shon Meckfessel argues that what he calls a "disruptive deficit" (16) leads many activists to shun nonviolence and see the alternatives to creating change as either "silence or violence" (18). Shon Meckfessel, *Nonviolence Ain't What It Used to Be: Unarmed Insurrection and the Rhetoric of Resistance* (Chico, CA: AK Press, 2016).

3. See: Sydney Tarrow *Power in Movement: social movements and contentious politics*, second edition (Cambridge, UK: Cambridge University Press, 1998); Charles Tilly, *The Contentious French* (Cambridge, MA: Harvard University Press, 1988).

4. Horst W. J. Rittel and Melvin M. Webber. "Dilemmas in a General Theory of Planning," *Policy Sciences* 4, no. 2 (June 1973): 155–69.

5. One must note here that most successful social reformers were indeed under thirty years of age when they engaged in activist leadership and resistance activities. Think for example of Malcom X, Martin Luther King, or B. R. Ambedkar, all respected leaders in their communities before the age of thirty.

6. See: Erica Chenowith and Maria Stephan, *Why Civil Resistance Works: The Strategic Logic of Nonviolent Conflict* (New York: Columbia University Press, 2012).

7. Mara Schoeny and Wallace Warfield, "Reconnecting Systems Maintenance with Social Justice: A Critical Role for Conflict Resolution," *Negotiation Journal* (July 2000): 263.

8. Donella Meadows, *Thinking in Systems* (White Junction, VT: Chelsea Green Publishing, 2008), 19.

9. If we take the emotion of anger as an example, often anger and frustration exacerbates processes of identity solidification and "othering." For more on the dynamic processes of in-group and out-group identity formation and theoretical complexities of defining "othering," see Sherif (1956), Billig, and Tajfel (1973), and Akbulut and Razum (2022). Muzafer Sherif, "Experiments in Group Conflict." *Scientific American* 195, no. 5 (1956): 54–59. http://www.jstor.org/stable/24941808; M. Billig and H. Tajfel, "Social categorization and similarity in intergroup behaviour." *European Journal of Social Psychology* 3 (1973): 27–52; and N. Akbulut and O. Razum, "Why Othering should be considered in research on health inequalities: Theoretical perspectives and research needs." *SSM—Population Health* 20 (2022): 101286. https://doi.org/10.1016/j.ssmph.2022.101286.

10. Rittel and Weber, "Dilemmas in a General Theory of Planning," op. cit., 160.

11. Ibid., 61 (emphasis added).

12. Austin Choi-Fitzpatrick, Douglas Irvin-Erickson, and Ernesto Verdeja, eds., *Wicked Problems: The Ethics of Action for Peace, Rights, and Justice* (New York: Oxford University Press, 2022), 11.

13. See Donald Schon (1983), op. cit.

14. Davis Anderson Hooker and Shelia Bedi, "Re-defining Justice and Creating Pathways for Healing: The Limits of the US Legal System and the Promise

of Politicised Healing as a Model for Redressing Racialised Harm," *Journal of Transdisciplinary Peace Praxis* 3, no. 1 (February 2021): 36.

15. Hooker and Bedi, 2021, op. cit., 36.

16. Thenmozhi Soundararajan, *The Trauma of Caste: A Dalit Feminist Meditation on Survivorship, Healing, and Abolition* (Berkeley, CA: North Atlantic Books, 2022), 5.

17. Isabel Wilkerson, *Caste: The Origins of Our Discontent* (New York: Random House, 2020), 18.

18. Ibid.

19. Sara Cobb, *Speaking of Violence*, 2013, op. cit., 32. See also: T. C. Boas, "Conceptualizing Continuity and Change." *Journal of Theoretical Politics* 19, no. 1 (2007): 33–54.

20. John Paul Lederach, *The Moral Imagination: The Art and Soul of Building Peace* (New York: Oxford University Press, 2010), 5.

21. Barry Johnson (1996) defines polarities as "sets of opposites which can't function well independently" (xviii). He continues: "Because the two sides of a polarity are interdependent, you cannot choose one 'solution' and neglect the other" (xviii). Barry Johnson, *Polarity Management: Identifying and Managing Unsolvable Problems* (Amherst, MA: HRD Press, 1996).

22. John Paul Lederach, *The Moral Imagination: The Art and Soul of Building Peace* (New York: Oxford University Press, 2010).

23. Ibid., 73.

24. Mara Schoeny and Wallace Warfield (July 2000), 263, op. cit.

25. Johnson (1996) is, again, informative here. He uses the analogy of the difference between catching and ball and juggling balls to illustrate the difference between problems to be solved and polarities to be managed. Barry Johnson, *Polarity Management*, op. cit., 87.

26. Ashley Bohrer, "How Is It to be Done?: Dilemmas of Prefigurative and Harm-Reduction Approaches to Social Movement Work," in *Wicked Problems: The Ethics for Action in Peace, Rights, and Justice*, edited by Austin Chio-Fitzpatrick, Douglas Irving-Erickson, and Ernesto Verdeja (New York: Oxford University Press, 2022), 73–83.

27. Mihn Dang, "The Paradox of Survivor Leadership," in *Wicked Problems: The Ethics for Action in Peace, Rights, and Justice*, edited by Austin Chio-Fitzpatrick, Douglas Irving-Erickson, and Ernesto Verdeja (New York: Oxford University Press, 2022), 87–96.

28. Robert Bush and Joseph Folger, *The Promise of Mediation: The Transformative Approach to Conflict* (San Francisco: Jossey-Bass, 2005), 9.

29. C. Argyris and D. Schon, *Theory in Practice: Increasing Professional Effectiveness* (San Francisco: Jossey Bass, 1974).

30. Robert Bush and Joseph Folger, *The Promise of Mediation*, op. cit., 9–17.

31. Ibid., 17.

32. Ibid., 9.

33. Ibid., 11.

34. Ibid., 13.

35. Ibid., 16.

36. Ibid., 17.

37. See: I. W. Zartman, *Ripe for Resolution: Conflict and Intervention in Africa* (New York: Oxford University Press, 1989).

38. See Rinker and Lawler (2018), op. cit.

39. Martin Luther King, Jr. likely articulated this emotion-filled argument against a gradual approach to change better than anyone else in his April 1963 "Letter from a Birmingham Jail." In that short piece he writes in one example-filled excessively long sentence: ". . . when you suddenly find your tongue twisted and your speech stammering as you seek to explain to your six year old daughter why she can't go to the public amusement park that has just been advertised on television, and see tears welling up in her eyes when she is told that Funtown is closed to colored children, and see ominous clouds of inferiority beginning to form in her little mental sky, and see her beginning to distort her personality by developing an unconscious bitterness toward white people; . . . then you will understand why we find it difficult to wait." Found at: https://www.africa.upenn.edu/Articles_Gen/Letter_Birmingham.html, accessed September 4, 2023.

40. Richard Jenkins, *Social Identity*, Third Edition (New York: Routledge, 2008), 5.

41. See Donald Schon (1983), op. cit.

42. Yascha Mounk, *The Identity Trap: A Story of Ideas and Power in Our Time* (New York: Penguin Press, 2023).

43. See: Erica Chenowith and Maria Stephan, *Why Civil Resistance Works: The Strategic Logic of Nonviolent Conflict* (New York: Columbia University Press, 2012).

44. Amy Qin, *"California Could Become the First State to Ban Caste Bias as Prejudices Linger,"* New York Times, Sunday, September 10, 2023, https://www.nytimes.com/2023/09/08/us/california-caste-discrimination.html#:~:text=Caste%20Bias%3A%20California's%20State%20Legislature,debate%20among%20South%20Asian%20immigrants, accessed September 10, 2023.

45. Jeremy Rinker, *Identity, Rights, and Awareness: Anti-Caste Activism in India and the Awakening of Justice through Discursive Practices* (Lanham, MD: Lexington Books, 2018).

46. Lederach (2005), *Little Book of Conflict Transformation*, op. cit.

47. For some discussion of the idea of white culture, see: Mona Chalabi, "What Is White Culture Exactly? This Is What the Stats Say." *The Guardian*, February 26, 2018, https://www.theguardian.com/world/2018/feb/26/white-culture-statistics-vegetables-alcohol, accessed, February 26, 2023.

48. William Wilmot and Joyce Hocker, *Interpersonal Conflict*, Eighth Edition (New York: McGraw-Hill, 2011), 200.

49. Ibid., 199.

50. See the various editions of Ramsbotham, Woodhouse, and Miall for example. Oliver Ramsbotham, Tom Woodhouse, and Hugh Miall, *Contemporary Conflict Resolution* (Malden, MA: Polity, 2011).

51. See, for example, Louis Kreisberg, *Constructive Conflicts: From Escalation to Resolution* (New York, NY: Rowman & Littlefield, 1998).

52. Louis Kreisberg, *Constructive Conflicts,* ibid., 226.

53. See the work of Loretta Ross outlined in Jessica Bennett, "What if Instead of Calling People Out, We Called Them In?: Prof. Loretta J. Ross is combatting cancel culture with a popular class at Smith College," *New York Times,* November 19, 2020.

5

BUILDING A TOOLBOX FOR TRAUMA-INFORMED CONFLICT PRACTICE

This final chapter relies on the metaphor of a blue-collar worker's toolbox. This is a metaphor likely familiar to trained mediators. Like a plumber or carpenter, to ply their trade, mediators require a set of tools to work effectively. Rather than a pipe wrench (plumber) or a hammer (carpenter), mediators need practical knowledge about conflict (basic needs theory, relative deprivation theory, etc.), practice skills (reframing, active listening, etc.), and abilities or competencies (cultural, communicative, reflective empathy, etc.) to effectively transform social conflicts. These sets of knowledge, skills, and abilities (KSAs for short) are learned through both study of conflict theory and experience in the practice of conflict resolution interventions. While many of these KSAs might be called "soft skills," this does not diminish the fact that they require diligent practice and honing to be deployed efficiently and effectively. Also inherent in these KSAs is an emotional intelligence and awareness of the deep individual and collective impacts of trauma. This chapter aims to bring together all the tools and guideposts we have identified in the preceding chapters and build on the metaphor of a mediator's toolbox to outline an emotionally mindful and trauma-informed set of practices for conflict resolution practitioners. Armed with this outline or framework, conflict resolution practitioners will be better prepared to be trauma-aware and emotionally mindful. Of course, the map is not the territory, but having access to a metaphorical toolbox, conflict practitioners are more likely to slow down conflict processes and approach transformation from a place of emotional intelligence and trauma consciousness.

Part summary and part organizing framework, this chapter articulates a trauma-informed and emotionally mindful toolbox for working with and intervening in social conflict. The astute reader will realize that I have used the terms "outline," "framework," "toolbox," and "map" interchangeably. This is intentional, as the trauma-informed and emotionally aware conflict practitioner is like a field general assessing multiple resources to reach desired aims—in this case nothing short of conflict transformation. Less concerned with rational actors and managing interests, this trauma-informed toolbox instead focuses attention on emotions and responding to emotional feedback and conflict dynamics. By identifying narrative-based access points to approach trauma in conflict processes, I hope to develop a sense of praxis-based consistency for the trauma-informed and emotionally mindful conflict practitioner. Admittedly this is a tall order given trauma's heterogeneous individual sequalae and the cultural and contextual variability of social conflict. I will begin by summarizing many of the tools discussed in earlier chapters. This will be followed by a trauma-informed framework for intervention, which will be applied to a final historical conflict narrative, which is still evolving today, in the book's Afterword. Being trauma-informed and emotionally mindful are interrelated, yet distinct, methodologies of practice. To be trauma-informed, a practitioner must be emotionally aware and mindful, but it is possible to be emotionally aware and not trauma-informed. In some sense then these ideas are distinct, but there is a large degree to which they are mutually inclusive and overlapping methodologies of practice; imagine a Venn diagram in which two circles of emotionally mindful and trauma-informed practice are mostly overlapping, with minimal area of difference (see figure 5.1 below). While I have lumped these two methodologies of practice together throughout the book, in this final chapter I will tease them apart, aiming to further improve conflict practice. In highlighting the limited areas of divergence between these methodologies of practice, we strengthen our capacity to not only listen and be proximate to suffering but expand our capacity for resilience. Before we build upon this toolbox we must first summarize and clarify what tools have been introduced throughout the book.

Overlapping Methodologies of Practice

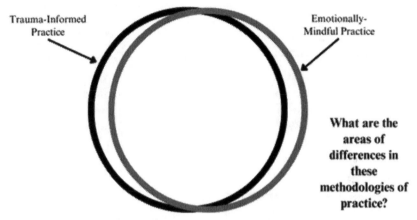

Trauma-Informed Practice

Emotionally-Mindful Practice

What are the areas of differences in these methodologies of practice?

Figure 5.1   Venn Diagram of the Overlapping Methodologies of Practice.

WHAT TOOLS HAVE THUS FAR BEEN IDENTIFIED?

From the very start of this book, I have argued that emotions "are the foundation of reason."[1] This means that rational choice frameworks must acknowledge emotions, not ignore them. Embracing a trauma-informed approach means not being afraid of emotions and being ready and willing to use emotions to help set (and most possibly solve) the destructive problems associated with social conflict. This represents the first tool for our proverbial toolbox: a problem setting mindset which does not worry about rushing towards problem solving. This means painstakingly listening to collective historical trauma and getting proximate to the suffering of conflict parties. And it means complete trust in conflict resolution processes without preconceived notions as to conflict outcomes. This sort of mindset or proclivity is a primary step (or tool) in a process of developing an intervention role as a narrative therapist cum conflict resolution practitioner.

> Rather than "systems," we think about "culture" or "society." Instead of seeing ourselves as mechanics who are working to fix a broken machine or ecologists who are trying to understand and influence complex eco-systems, we experience ourselves as interested people—perhaps with an anthropological or biographical or journalistic bent—who are skilled at asking questions to bring forth the knowledge and experience that is carried in the stories of the people we work with.[2]

Such work of narrative therapy cum trauma-aware and emotionally mindful conflict intervention requires cultural competency, context awareness, and humility. It also requires critical thinking and an inquisitive attitude of deep Socratic open-ended questioning. Further, underlying such work is a belief that trauma is not simply a problem to be overcome but also a source of growth and opportunity (what Tedeschi, 2018 calls post-traumatic growth).[3] Again, the words of narrative therapists Freedman and Combs (1996) challenge conflict practitioners to rethink trauma stories as deficits and reset problems as opportunities as opposed to problems in need of quick solutions. "Problems develop when people internalize conversations that restrain them to a narrow description of self. These stories are experienced as oppressive because they limit the perception of available choices."[4] Our goal as trauma-informed and emotionally aware conflict intervenors is to open opportunities for organic and collective change. Think of the refugee from war that feels unsafe even outside the war zone and refuses to go outside of their home for fear of being collateral damage, even as there is no war raging outside. The work of emotional mindful and trauma-aware practitioners is largely about providing conflict parties with "options for mutual gain."[5] This is done by trusting a conflict cum therapeutic process and having faith that deep emotions and painful sharing will ultimately lead to better places. This is what Elise Boulding called "the 200-year present."[6] Change in this sense is not achieved quickly, but rather over a span of generations. As we discussed in earlier chapters trusting this type of approach which faces history often involves resisting your own desire for comfort in controlling/managing emotional expression and allowing the discomfort and sense of loss of control in emotional outbursts to work themselves out. While this can feel destabilizing to conflict practitioners trained in rational interest-based negotiation, it also opens opportunities for radical breakthroughs in protracted social conflicts.

Of course, the trauma aware and emotionally mindful conflict practitioner must be open to listening, reading, and carefully analyzing victim narratives. Paying close attention to the meanings underlying atrocity stories and understanding victimhood psychology is central to both these methodologies of practice. Understanding victimhood psychology, victims' stories, and the awareness of the universality of victimhood makes the uncertainty and ambiguity brought out by trauma stories more manageable. Such self-reflective and discourse analysis skills do "not excuse the actions of others; it simply places these actions in a larger context, helping us access the deeper dynamics perpetuating conflict."[7] For practitioners, keen on being emotionally aware and trauma-informed, it is clear they must work to understand narrative structures, narrative agency, and conflict parties' social positioning. Developing the role of a narrative therapist cum conflict resolution practitioner requires not just "soft skills" like radical empathy, but analytical skills to read narrative meaning in complex cultural and discursive context. This is both a political and clinical role; one that views conflict as a social ailment that needs long-term treatment rather than quick resolution. Changing dynamics of social conflict demand our attention and embrace our emotions, not simply attempts to limit or manage emotions we perceive as negative or difficult. While such work is more effective when done by those proximate to the suffering, it can be done by outsiders that have cultural and contextual competence and a dose of humility. In some sense, tools like deep listening and reframing are transferable to contexts one is less familiar with, but "insider partials"[8] do have distinct advantages as trauma-informed and emotionally aware practitioners in many contexts. Those with insider knowledge and lived experience of a social conflict and its dynamics have unique political understandings of power and the workings of systems.[9] Outsiders to a conflict must work to get "up to speed" on the political and discursive contexts of the situation as well as have a keen ability to avoid "narrow characterizations"[10] of identities or events. In some sense, the training and preparation for this work entails an anthropological ability to "go native" and develop an insider understanding of a conflict context, but this is far from a universal or transferable skill set. To be what Ruth Behar calls a "vulnerable observer"[11] requires an ability for reflexivity that allows a practitioner to reach towards the virtue of equanimity. Still, developing an emotional valence that navigates insider and outsider social positions, while certainly a balancing act, is a learnable and necessary skill set for conflict practitioners. While it takes cognitive training to be hyper-aware of your own responses to stress and emotions, as well as others' sense of vulnerability, this competency is critical in conflict practitioners. Etic versus emic as well as internal versus external awareness are primary skills of a good listener, researcher, and action scientist. An ability to remain impartial and not wed to any identity position, through challenging in the midst of atrocity, trauma, and/ or human suffering, requires constant vigilance and self-reflection on the part of conflict intervenors. "In any conflict, if we consider ourselves solely as victims, we cannot discover our contribution to the conflict or our power to make a positive contribution."[12]

I would describe this complex balancing act that conflict intervention professionals must navigate as an ability for embodied awareness amidst trauma and traumatic emotions. When that pit in your stomach tells you to avoid, manage, or distract, that is when practitioners must embody reflective awareness. This involves not just cognitive training to be hyper aware of the self, but reflexivity to one's own responses to stress, atrocity stories, and especially negative emotions. Emotion, as felt experience and not rational thinking, is both subjective and objective reality. As practitioners, our expression of emotions, as well as our own responses to them, must hold space to balance both realities. Rational and emotional sentiments are both open to constructive criticism, but being trauma-aware involves being particularly mindful that constructive criticism of emotions will often land with conflict parties in non-rational, or even unintended, ways. Being explicit and intentional in our responses to emotional outbursts of conflict parties helps empower these parties to "mean effectively."[13] This is political in that it assists low-power parties in building self-esteem and self-respect. It is clinical in that it facilitates conflict parties in understanding their own roles in meaning making and conflict dynamics. In some ways these dual purposes are mutually intertwined. The embodied awareness of trauma-informed and emotionally aware conflict resolution practitioners embraces the ambiguity and irony of the present moment and uses it, along with critical moments in social conflict to leverage prosocial conflict transformation.

This all sounds so simple in writing and theory, but indeed is much more complicated in practice. An adaptive-reactive mindset and instantiation of the values of comity, nonviolence, and fairness are easily professed, but more difficult to achieve in practice. Relatedly, virtues of justice, equanimity, and benevolence are themselves practice ideals in continual need of being made real through concrete action. In western traditions we rationalize the practice of these virtues, but in eastern traditions we can see how these critical human virtues arise as a combination of both rational and emotional development. Sallie Queen has noted this in her attempts to define the modern global movement of socially engaged Buddhism. She writes: "Engaged Buddhist ethics also do not privilege the intellect over emotions in the ethical domain. On the contrary, it is central to Engaged Buddhist ethics that we develop emotionally as much as intellectually."[14] This is complex psycho-social terrain, and this makes developing a pat and simple toolbox or practitioners' guide for social conflict so difficult; a moving target for individuals with unique psychologies in complex society. This meeting of rational theory and emotional practice is to some extent ineffable. This socially engaged praxis of actualizing benevolence, justice, and/or equanimity takes social and emotional intelligence gained through experience. It requires a move from mere knowledge to wisdom.

Here, I am reminded of the three phases briefly outlined earlier in chapter 3 of this book. While deceivingly simple, these phases were underscored as a sort of in-the-moment guide to applying trauma-aware and emotionally mindful responses to violent conflict episodes. If conflict resolution practitioners continually cycle through these phases throughout their conflict interventions, their practice will wax towards trauma-informed approaches and emotional awareness. This sounds idyllic or mystical, but trauma-informed and emotionally aware practice is not fully effable as a simple linear process or straightforward guide. With time and practice we come closer to the ideal. Like the phases of the moon, practitioners must cycle through phases that are never the same, or replicable, as context and dynamics of any conflict situation is different as well as constantly changing and one's own psychological state is in constant flux. By self-reflecting on what you are feeling as a traumatized event is retold (phase one) practitioners process how they uniquely and individually embody the trauma. Such self-reflection allows the practitioner to slow down the socially constructed desire to express sympathy and manage emotions and instead re-direct compassion and radical empathy towards others (phase two). Buddhists call this Metta bhavana or cultivating loving-kindness towards other sentient beings. In my experience, when one practices this cultivation of loving kindness or radical empathy (through meditation or just the simple practice of being present and exhibiting a demeanor of equanimity in conflict practice), it opens opportunities to live the core values of comity, nonviolence, and fairness and actualizes the virtues of justice and fairness discussed above (phase three). When my own father died in January 2015, I experienced the power of others practicing Metta bhavana for me. I was leading a meditation retreat with a colleague when I was notified by my brother of his passing. When the community (sangha) of the retreat center became aware of this news they began a collective meditation to gift me loving kindness. I cannot tell you how much that

practice of Metta bhavana impacted my own grieving process. The collective expression of loving kindness has real effects. The third phase
often comes as an epiphany, not as a planned, or intentional, practice. If
the first two of these simple phases are done well and with intentionality,
then phase three can effectively engage with irony and ambiguity and,
often, births creative epiphanies for dynamic shifts in social conflict. It is
cycling through these three phases that opens the creative potential for
systems-level activism and places change and systems maintenance on
an even playing field. Although my father's death was not an example
of social conflict, the collective loving kindness I felt and experienced
did remind me of his life that was exemplar of values and virtues of
comity and justice. His passing, in one sense, opened a sense of ambiguity in realizing this and simultaneously realizing my loss. While such
epiphanies are the goal of trauma-informed and emotionally mindful
conflict practice, conflict practitioners often miss the cues and opportunities inherent in cycling through these phases. I do not use my father's
death as an example to praise or paint him in a perfect light, but rather
to illustrate how these phases can lead to growth from trauma. Furthermore, training in these phases is difficult, and like training in meditation,
such conflict resolution training requires constant practice, reflection on
one's own trauma and conflict experiences, and vigilance. Not linear,
such trauma-informed and emotionally mindful conflict practice is an
iterative practice of acting, observing, and reflecting in an on-going cir-
cular process (for a visual representation of this, see figure 5.2 below).

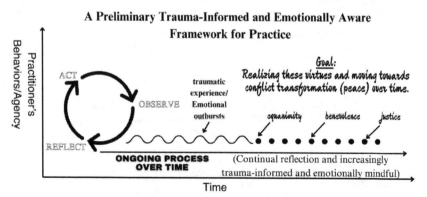

Figure 5.2 Framework for Trauma-Informed and Emotionally Aware Conflict
Practice.

WHAT TOOLS NEED FURTHER DEVELOPMENT?

While these tools I have described sound powerful theoretically, their implementation in practice is often lacking due to dominant norms of social interaction and historical/cultural socialization around emotions and trauma. Safe space and structure are needed for such tool's full expression and development, but often in the context of social conflict such space and structure are not available and/or are wanting. Setting the problem in a way that does not disregard, or shut out, the possibility of emotions seems to be step one. A healthy fear, or dread, of emotions is normal human nature, but conflict resolution practitioners must steal the courage to move past this fear or dread and proactively engage emotions as neither good nor bad, but rather simply present. This is easier said than done in many cultures and indeed requires a consistent practice to achieve. Different cultures read emotions and trauma in different socially constructed ways. Norms about emotional expression vary widely and lack of attention to this can escalate social conflict when such social constructions are unknown to either of the conflict parties. As Kevin Avurch has argued, "Culture is not the cause of conflict, rather it is the lens through which conflict is refracted."[15] For practitioners, this signals that we must be attentive to cultural competency while simultaneously appreciating and validating emotions. This can be further complicated by the fact that trauma, in some cultures, is understood as taboo and/or disruptive to social harmony. At times, culturally competent trauma-informed and emotionally aware approaches can seem at cross purposes, and it requires an aptitude for uncertainty and ambiguity while navigating such uneven terrain. Changing language away from taboo terms like "trauma" and talking about "stress" can also help communicate across cultural perceptions.

Trauma-informed and emotionally mindful conflict practice, though not intended to be therapeutic, is in many ways mirrored by the processes of cognitive behavior therapy (CBT). "In a nutshell, the cognitive model proposes that dysfunctional thinking (which influences client's mood and behavior) is common to all psychological disturbances."[16] The CBT model of therapy is then based on helping people to evaluate their thinking to be able to affect a "decrease in negative emotions and maladaptive behavior."[17] The similarities to Buddhist ideas of right mindfulness, wisdom, and action must be noted here. In Buddhist teaching, the five skandhas (aggregates) when clung to are the cause of all human suffering. These five skandhas of form (matter), sensation (feeling), perception (awareness), mental formations (volition), and consciousness (discernment) must be understood as ultimately unreal and as necessary to throw off, or blow out (nirvana), to become a Buddha (enlightened one). Whether re-evaluating your thinking (as in CBT) or throwing off the five skandhas (as in Buddhist practices of attainment) these practices require ongoing vigilance and adherence to a set of practice processes. Adepts of either tradition (Buddhism or trauma-aware and emotionally mindful conflict practice) must be constantly attentive and the use of tools (or what Buddhists' call upaya—skillful means) to practice and attain extremely difficult to achieve ideal states. In a sense then, striving to be an emotionally aware and trauma-informed practitioner is an ongoing and never-ending practice toward achieving an ideal state, like a Buddhist adept's striving toward nirvana or King Arthur's quest for the holy grail. This is not to assign moral righteousness or make a religious argument for the practices I am describing, but rather to draw an analytical comparison to the complexity, vigilance, and dedication required to achieve the ideal of trauma-informed and emotionally aware conflict practice. The more I write about trauma-aware and emotionally mindful conflict practice, the more I understand that it is an ever-developing practice journey like a quest. Practitioners strive to realize emotionally-aware and trauma-informed dynamics and outcomes; these dynamics and outcomes are not a forgone conclusion even for emotionally intelligent and trauma-centered practitioners. Contexts change and cultural cues can be missed, but constant attention to the emotional expressions and traumatic impacts of story on conflict parties is an ever-evolving practice. As such, I am continually reminded of my inadequacy in being the guide, or expert, to processes that are in some sense never completely accessible. Not wanting to emulate Cervantes' Don Quixote[18] I, therefore, proceed lightly and with the recognition that developing tools and frameworks to assist is an important, and simultaneously inadequate, contribution to growing an emotionally mindful and trauma-informed conflict practice.

Obviously, these conflict knowledge, skills, and activities (KSAs) can be extremely challenging, especially in cultures where norms of equality, and virtues of justice and benevolence, do not match practitioners' own lived experience. Challenging clients to disrupt unhelpful thinking as a therapist, or cultivate loving kindness as a Buddhist practitioner, is like assisting conflict parties to both be mindful and embody their emotions—it takes vigilant commitment, self-reflection, and constant attention and perseverance. Of course, such processes in conflict are conditioned by socially constructed cultures and identities not fully in practitioners' control. And with these cultures and identities comes differing conceptions of "power distance."[19] If we stay grounded in the everyday social-psychological context of conflict parties we can move towards a peace with justice, but it is keeping our eyes on this ever-changing conflict context that is the key tool that requires our attention and continual development. I have tried to develop a visual framework for further articulating this dynamic process in figure 5.2 below. In a previous book in this ACR practitioner guide series, Julie Macfarlane and Bernie Mayer argue that conflicts that address mediators' memories of trauma can be extremely difficult. They write: "But in the end, determination, courage, and the audacity to speak truth to power were the irreducible requirements to go forward. No professional discipline has a monopoly on this."[20] Like any professional discipline, trauma-informed and emotionally aware conflict practice requires ethical commitments to virtues of equanimity, justice, and benevolence, as well as the values of those on the bottom of hierarchies.

A PRELIMINARY FRAMEWORK FOR INCLUSIVE, TRAUMA-INFORMED, AND EMOTIONALLY MINDFUL PEACE PRACTICE

While complex and dynamic, trying to capture what I would term inclusive, trauma-informed, and emotionally mindful conflict practice, is no easy task. The representation in figure 5.2 above visualizes the complex and dynamic reality of engaging social conflict mindful of the past emotional and traumatic experiences of conflict parties. It is not a static, or universal representation, but an attempt to further explain the dynamic realities of an emotionally mindful and trauma-aware conflict practice that is an inclusive invitation towards sustainable social change in conflict situations and dynamics.

In figure 5.2 above, the conflict transformation practitioner starts with action, observation, and reflection of their own behaviors and social agency. This is a continual and iterative process, internal to the framework, which the practitioner repeatedly cycles through as an ongoing practice throughout an intervention. Like the three phases of reflection discussed above, about how we as practitioners embody trauma, cultivate loving kindness and radical empathy, and realize their core values and virtues, this process of action, observation, and reflection leads conflict practitioners towards realizing the human virtues of equanimity, benevolence, and ultimately, justice. But, of course, this leading towards is not a linear and pre-ordained reality (which is represented by the wavy line of peaks and valleys of traumatic experience and emotional outbursts). In this sense this iterative process of acting, observing, and reflecting acts as what John Paul Lederach calls a platform for transformation.[21] Being emotionally aware and trauma-informed in turn reinforces the human values of equanimity, benevolence, and justice; the trauma-informed and emotionally aware practice is self-reinforcing, the more your practice the more developed the practice becomes. The above framework is reflexive, or what Lederach has called "responsive"[22] to others, and, in an elemental sense, it is an attempt to "remystify practice."[23] While theoretical and difficult to visualize in practice, this framework may most clearly be illustrated through application to a specific conflict context. Of course, as contexts change the simplicity of the framework can and will adapt and evolve based on practitioners' own reflections, embodiment of trauma, and immersion in a conflict's specific emotional context. Realizing this, the above framework is an applied one and, thus, application may go farther in explaining it than general description. I invite readers to adapt this fluid model and apply it to their own contexts.

To illustrate this framework for inclusive and trauma-informed peace practice, I want to return to the specifics of the story that I first alluded to in chapter 4, about the social exclusion and social boycott experienced by a Dalit (formerly untouchable) family constructing a new home in eastern Maharashtra. In again returning to Indian caste conflict to apply this framework, I am implicitly endorsing the argument that Isabel Wilkerson (2020) makes when she writes: "Race in the United States, is the visible agent of the unseen force of caste. Caste is the bones, race the skin."[24] Caste conflict in this sense is not somehow divorced from the American experience, rather the hierarchies of domination and discrimination it enlivens are active and present although largely described via the grammar of race and racism. Despite my own process frustrations around this respondent's story taking over the focus group facilitation that I was leading, narrating the specifics of his story can also assist in illustrating and developing culturally competent, inclusive, and trauma-informed intervention practices. In short, it can help us articulate the trauma-centered framework and toolbox I hope to empower through writing this book. Stories like these are never delivered devoid of emotion, my apologies in advance if the emotion does not come fully through in the writing.

SACHIN'S STORY

While residing in the small village of Jalgaon, in the eastern Indian state of Maharashtra, Sachin's family faced casteist reprisals when they began to build their new house in the area. Having purchased the land in a new housing colony that was mostly inhabited by high caste brahmins, Sachin and his family soon realized they were the only Mahars (one of the largest Dalit sub-castes in Maharashtra) in the housing colony. Sachin recounts: "It quickly became clear they did not like us living among them and one of our neighbors even harassed us while we were building by shouting 'you cannot live here!'"[25] Once when he passed a neighbor on the street Sachin heard him say: "build your home somewhere else."[26] At this time, Sachin was still in the 12th form and he accompanied his father to the police station to file a police complaint (known in India as an FIR—first incidence report) about the casteist slurs that neighbors were "hurling"[27] at them. The police did write the complaint on a blank piece of paper which was not stamped or official, but later they tore up that paper when the high caste neighbors complained to the police. Coming from the same community as many of the police officers, these neighbors had used their connections to stop any case from being filed, a regular occurrence in a polity where familiarity and patronage are king. Sachin and his family had broken no laws, but rather the norms of caste. The police even told Sachin's family not to register any complaint against these people as they were powerful.

Upsetting the power dynamic in such a village locale was, and is, a serious breach of norm, often punishable by violent enforcement of the norm. During the entire building process and first years of living in the house, the family was mentally tormented by their neighbors, and the family couldn't sleep at night as they felt hopeless. Besides rocks being thrown at their house, no direct violence occurred. Still, despite the mental harassment, they remained adamant on not leaving the house they had worked so hard to construct. Neighbors used to throw their garbage in front of the house and yell casteist slurs when the family members were walking down the very street they lived on. On the few occasions that they threw stones in the direction of the house, other neighbors just laughed instead of helping or intervening. The trauma and mental anguish of all this had an impact on the family's health, especially Sachin's mother who is now schizophrenic and his father who became paralyzed two years after the initial incidents. By the time the family's health issues started building up, they had realized that there were no avenues for help from neighbors, police, or the health system. The structures of modern Indian society were closed to such complaints and recourse to any type of justice was lacking. To this day Sachin blames his mother's mental illness and his father's poor health, and early passing, on the social exclusion and discrimination from neighbors that they faced by building their house in that colony. While the family eventually moved away from that area, the lasting sense of victimhood, trauma, and pain never left them. In his recounting this painful story Sachin himself appeared visibly shaken and tired. Even among Dalit activists, such stories elicit anger and raw emotions.

Even though justice in this example will likely remain elusive, the virtues of equanimity and benevolence can be regained as a sort of step towards reconciliation. As a conflict transformation professional in such a context, even if achieving real justice is no longer possible, steps towards developing a sense of justice can, and should, be actively celebrated and achieved. Encouraging ongoing action, observing, and reflection (see the left side of figure 5.2 above) the emotional resonance of past traumatic events and atrocity stories can still help parties make meaning and mean effective. The failure to voice such stories keeps the trauma and emotions bottled in a container with the potential to develop destructive outcomes. This clearly illustrates the need for transformative platforms. By this I am suggesting that creating new actions that observe and reflect on the past traumas can move parties to develop new and pro-social meanings about past traumas. Bottling-up talk, observation, and reflection of past trauma and emotions limits the possibility of growth and movement towards developing the virtues of equanimity, benevolence, and justice in a conflict situation and fore-closes avenues for realizing positive peace. Engaging in such an iterative and continual process of developing or encouraging conflict parties' own actions, observing and reflecting without forgetting the past pain and trauma is the work of trauma-informed and emotionally mindful conflict practice. Below I try to further draw the connections between Sachin's experience and the toolbox or framework of trauma-informed and emotionally mindful conflict practice I have outlined above. This is not to suggest that all traumas can result in post-traumatic growth,[28] but rather that, in applying the tools and framework that I have been suggesting, over time, one can move towards justice, even if never able to completely achieve it.

APPLYING A TOOLBOX AND FRAMEWORK OF TRAUMA-INFORMED AND EMOTIONALLY MINDFUL CONFLICT PRACTICE

Initially, and most obviously, as a conflict practitioner there is a need to be as proximate as possible to Sachin's suffering. This includes not only listening, but also expressing empathy without confusing this empathetic response with a socially constructed desire to comfort and manage Sachin's negative emotions. In the focus group discussion, like others I have facilitated, stories like Sachin's have a collective resonance and impact. Raw emotions and traumatic memories must have space for "outlet or absorption"[29] and practitioners, like other focus group participants, become the outlet for the expression of such strong emotions. How such a group responds to (e.g., how they absorb) these emotional stories of trauma histories, impacts the storytelling and builds or reinforces the social identity of both the storyteller and his/her listeners. The sociologist Harold Blumer called this anti-positivist approach to understanding what constitutes and constructs society "social interactionism."[30] It is this dynamic construction of social reality that trauma-informed and emotionally aware conflict practitioners are constantly mediating in practice. Stories aim at making meaning from past events, not just trying to understand the causes but also the lasting effects. "Storytelling is the central part of the [reconciliation] process, not only for victims reconstructing the story, but also for persons representing the aggressor group."[31]

Although no members of the oppressor group were present to hear Sachin's story in the moment, the need to expose higher caste identities to such stories is paramount to sustainable social change. Sachin's narrating the private health challenges of his parents and family, although socially and culturally taboo, is also a critical driver of lasting shifts in the symbolic interactionism that creates and maintains social systems and structures. As Joseph Montville has cogently argued: "the challenge in dealing with victimhood psychology is that of reviving the mourning process, which has been suspended as a result of traumatic experience, and help it move towards completion."[32] While "reviving the mourning process" may seem counter-intuitive in contexts of past violence, the trauma-aware and emotionally mindful conflict practitioner realizes the potential shifts in thinking such stories can have when brought into lived social reality. The ideas of completion (Montville) and absorption (Erikson) importantly connect individual psychological states and emotions to collective social realities and structures. Stories like Sachin's have a transformative ability to change not only the dynamic of a small group, but if deployed strategically and effectively by social justice movement activists, to change larger systems and structures. Stories are themselves important actors in conflict and can have important individual and social impacts. In arguing for "narrative's ambiguity" as a "political resource" Francesca Polletta argues that "we expect to have to interpret stories. We expect their meaning to be both larger than the events they relate and allusive."[33] Reconnecting this analysis of Sachin's story to the framework presented in figure 5.2 above, it becomes evident that it is a story or narrative, that helps practitioners' cycle through the iterative process of acting, observing, and reflecting as they move conflict contexts closer towards the virtues of equanimity, benevolence, and justice. To again quote Lederach: "stories create a holistic approach to thinking and understanding in which people are invited to mingle with the characters as a device of interacting with their own realities."[34]

My own feeling of needing to create equity among focus group participants and provide equal time for participants to speak got in the way of fostering a trauma-informed and emotionally mindful space, or platform, for change. My research needs got in the way of listening fully to Sachin's story. This tendency to manage one's own facilitative expectations must be overcome in favor of a transformative mindset, or what Erik Erikson has described as "to think in traumatological terms."[35] Sachin, during our focus group dialogue, narrated many other painful stories, many about securing rental housing as a low-caste person. How we as facilitators and mediators steer parties away from initially important identities as victims, and associated victimhood psychology, and move them towards identities as survivors of trauma with social agency is integral to sustainable conflict resolution. Stories of trauma and expressions of emotions are critical drivers in these resolution and transformation processes. Failure to attend to them, I believe, is the primary reason for failed peace settlements. The trauma-informed and emotionally mindful conflict intervention practitioner is aware of these past traumas and attentive to emotional shifts. Although, at times, slow moving processes, such as trauma-aware and emotionally mindful processes are key to sustainable change. Such practitioners are also not afraid to probe trauma and emotions for their prosocial opportunities.

CONCLUSIONS: TOWARD THE BUILT TOOLBOX

Shifting our enculturated mindset from the idea that emotions are only conflict generative, and/or the antithesis of reason will not be easy and is a generational project, Boulding's 200-year present. This fact does not stop us from building our own trauma-informed and emotionally aware toolbox for conflict practice. In doing so, we must also realize that each intervenor's toolbox with be unique to them, and each intervenor will rely on their individual self-reflexive strengths in conflict intervention and communicative style. Like the practice of any science or art, personal habits like discipline and honest self-reflection are foundations for conflict intervention success. Aspiration and intent do not always correlate with an ability to help conflict parties mean effectively and/or use meaning effectively for social change. Actualizing peace and non-violence, as we know, does not develop through aspiration, but rather action. Still, trauma-aware and emotionally mindful conflict practitioners are like artists that must first find their voice before effectively using it to create change. A built toolbox takes time, discernment, and individual self-reflection as well as deliberate and disciplined attention to both emotional communication and the traumatic background or canvas. The metaphor of the plumber here shifts to one of painter working on a blank canvas. The built toolbox has tools unique to each artist and their univocal voice.

Being proximate to suffering is not enough, one must also reflect on the meaning gained from this proximity. Time, space, and structure are foundational to effective transformative interventions in social conflict. While the KSAs of trauma-informed practice and emotionally mindful practice most certainly overlap, what is unique in these methodologies of practice is, in part at least, defined by what individual practitioners bring with them to their practice. Being trauma-informed can mean that you are being mindful of conflict parties' emotions, but it can also mean holding in your own emotional responses as an intervenor. This takes what Audrey Lorde called "radical self-care."[36] This is the complex element of art in these methodologies of practice, knowing when your emotional response can be tapped for resolutionary effect. Like the traditional liberal arts methodologies, practitioners must emphasize rational and deliberative thinking in the face of expressions of trauma and emotions while simultaneously not allowing either logic or emotions to completely drive one's thinking. This is a delicate balance—remember at the beginning of the book how I talked about Occam's razor! This practice reminds me of one of my favorite films, *The Razors Edge*.[37] Building our metaphorical trauma-aware and emotionally mindful toolbox requires constant vigilance and practice; we do not reach full expertise in such a methodology, but we strive towards it.

Recently my own University has gone through an extremely contentious process of academic portfolio review involving the discontinuation of full academic disciplines on our campus. As university administrators have asked angry students, and professors threatened with losing their jobs, to remain "civil" in public forums, the level of frustration has grown, and conflict groups have formed. Faculty colleagues have continually reminded administrators that it is possible to respond with reason and emotion simultaneously. We can hold that space as humans, but amidst conflict, often emotions and collective historical trauma become weaponized and conceived as separate from rational and civil discourse. The real and imagined borders that form between conflict groups escalates the rhetoric and further alienates those that appear to be reacting emotionally to issues rather than in a rational manner. This binary between emotional and rational thought is unfortunate and is an expression of the common bias of privileging rationality over emotion, which is socially constructed. The socially constructed binary and bias is, of course, possible to change, even if it will take deliberative actions over time. Still, the emotional resonance of the current academic review process on my university will have lasting impacts on faculty morale and student confidence in the institution. Intervening in this contentious context will require listening to both emotional and reasoned arguments about ways forward as a collective. Even if these individual and social processes of emotion and logic are interconnected, they are often assumed to be separate and separatable. To achieve a collective sense of mission and identity, such emotional resonance and past trauma must be discussed in public. A built toolbox requires acknowledgment of past trauma and emotions and, a willingness to share, to be useful.

For contentious conflict and socially constructed borders to come down, practitioners must hone their own inner voice in order to know themselves. Such self-reflective awareness is a prerequisite to any intervention response. There must be a collective majority that acknowledges past harm and trauma. And finally, there must be a willingness to sit with messy emotional expressions of the past harm. To not shy away from the messy emotions of conflict is, in itself, a skill that requires much practice. One could say that emotionally mindful and trauma-aware conflict practice is thus not simply a set of knowledge, skills, and abilities (KSAs) that a trained and well-seasoned practitioner hones and perfects, but also a ready context for the embrace of trauma and emotions in the collective. In a sense, William Zartman's concept of "ripeness"[38] in conflict intervention is important here. When a culture of acknowledgment of past wrongs is coupled with practitioners' self-reflective skills, situational awareness, and embodiment, a conflict context is ripe for emotionally aware and trauma-informed intervention. What Edward Azar called "protracted social conflict (PSCs)"[39] represents the ideal context for deploying an emotionally aware and trauma-informed toolbox. Elsewhere I have written about how past collective trauma is an important driver of PSCs.[40] In PSCs, conflict stories have evolved, and conflict discourse has hardened over time to socially construct distinct identity-based conflict groups. Deploying a trauma-informed and emotionally aware toolbox, or framework, is critical to effective and lasting change in these contexts. Problem setting and asset-based thinking is central to changing a conflict narrative and its hardened discourse. Changing a conflict narrative can, in turn of course, have an impact on the wider discourse about the place of trauma and emotions in social practice. Trauma-informed and emotionally aware conflict practice can itself create transformative effect on a more macro level of culture and society; the practice can shift discourse about the role of emotional reasoning and intelligence, as well as the lasting impacts of collective trauma, on a culture of society. Seeing trauma as an opportunity, and not just a hinderance, moves us closer to collective coexistence and peace. I hope this book has given you some tools and guides to this important work. I believe that peaceful futures depend on us shifting our mindset towards an embrace of trauma and emotions to support our overreliance on data and rationality.

NOTES

1. Van der Kolk, *The Body Keeps Score*, 2014, op. cit., 64.
2. Freedman and Combs, *Narrative Therapy*, 1996, op. cit., 18.
3. Richard G. Tedeschi, *Posttraumatic Growth: Theory, Research and Applications* (New York, NY: Routledge, 2018), op. cit.
4. Freedman and Combs, *Narrative Therapy*, 1996, op. cit., 48.
5. Ury, Fisher, and Patton, *Getting to Yes*, 2011, op. cit., 31.
6. See: https://longnow.org/ideas/elise-boulding-on-the-200-year-present/, accessed February 13, 2024. See also: Elise Boulding, *Building a Global Civic Culture: Education for an Interdependent World, The John Dewey Lecture* (New York: Teachers College Press, 1988).
7. Sara Cobb, Sarah Federman, and Alison Castel, eds. *Introduction to Conflict Resolution: Discourses and Dynamics* (New York: Rowman & Littlefield, 2020), 588.
8. John Paul Lederach, *Preparing for Peace*, 1995, op. cit.
9. Incidentally, Lederach, citing Adam Curle (1971), also calls this the approach "the long view of conflict." See: John Paul Lederach, *Preparing for Peace*, 1995, op. cit., 12.
10. Cobb, Federman, and Castel, eds. *Introduction to Conflict Resolutions* (New York: Rowman and Littlefield, 2020). As they articulate in their extensive introduction to part III of the book, "Epoch Three: Transboundary Conflicts, 2001–Present," "Narrow characterizations do not allow for alternative constructions of 'Us' and 'Them' and, therefore, provide the conditions for war and preclude any path to peace" (591).
11. Ruth Behar, *The Vulnerable Observer*, 1996, op. cit.
12. Cobb, Federman, and Castel, eds. *Introduction to Conflict Resolution*, op. cit., 588.
13. Francesca Polletta, *It Was Like a Fever*, op. cit., xii.
14. Sallie Queen, *Being Benevolent: The Social Ethics of Engaged Buddhism* (Honolulu: University of Hawaii Press, 2005), 67.
15. Kevin Avruch, *Culture and Conflict Resolution* (Washington, DC: United States Institute of Peace Press, 1998), 30.
16. Judith S. Beck, *Cognitive Behavior Therapy: Basics and Beyond*, Third Edition (New York: Guilford Press, 2021), 4.
17. Beck, *Cognitive Behavior Therapy*, 2021, op. cit., 4.
18. See: Miguel De Cervantes Saavedra, *Don Quixote* (New York: Penguin Classics, 2023 [1605]).
19. Geert Hofstede, Gert Jan Hofstede, and Michael Minkov, *Cultures and Organizations: Software of the Mind, Intercultural Cooperation and Its Importance for Survival*, Third edition (New York: McGraw-Hill, 2010), 61. In this work Hofstede et. al. defines power distance as "the extent to which the less

powerful members of institutions and organizations within a country expect and accept that power is distributed unequally. . . . Power distance is thus described based on the value system of the less powerful members. [This is rather than being] explained from the behavior of the more powerful members. . . ." (61).

20. Julie Macfarlane and Bernie Mayer, "When Mediator's Sue," in *More Justice, More Peace: When Peacemakers Are Advocates*, edited by Susanne Terry (Lanham, MD: Rowman and Littlefield, 2020), 245.

21. J.P. Lederach, *The Little of Conflict Transformation*, 2005, op. cit., 41 (Figure 4: Transformational platforms).

22. See J.P. Lederach, "Conflict Transformation," on https://www.beyondi ntractability.org/essay/transformation, accessed January 29, 2024. In this essay, Lederach writes: "Transformation requires recognition of the other and some degree of responsiveness, not just recalcitrance or coercion."

23. For more on this idea of remystifying practice, see: J. P. Lederach, R. Neufeldt, and H. Culbertson, *The Reflective Peacebuilding Toolkit: A Planning, Monitoring, and Learning Toolkit* (The Joan B. Kroc International Institute for Peace Studies, University of Notre Dame and Catholic Relief Services, Southeast East Asia Regional Office, 2007), 4–5, https://pulte.nd.edu/assets/172927 /reflective_peacebuilding_a_planning_monitoring_and_learning_toolkit.pdf, accessed January 29, 2024.

24. Isabel Wilkerson, *Caste: The Origins of Our Discontents* (New York: Random House, 2020), 19.

25. Personal interview with Dalit activist, Sachin, April 2023. I have used only his first name to protect privacy.

26. Personal interview with Dalit activist, Sachin, April 2023.

27. Personal interview with Dalit activist, Sachin, April 2023.

28. The idea of post-traumatic growth was first identified in the mid-1990s by Tedeshi and Calhoun (1995). Outlining principles of traumatic growth, Tedeschi and Calhoun develop a model of growth that outlines processes of schema change and emotional support of others to shift the initial response of distress after trauma towards secondary responses that manage distress and support schema and cognitive behavior change. See: Richard G. Tedeschi, and Lawrence G. Calhoun, *Trauma & Transformation: Growing in the Aftermath of Suffering* (Thousand Oaks, CA: Sage Publications, Inc., 1995), 89.

29. Erik Erikson, *Gandhi's Truth: On the Origins of Militant Nonviolence* (New York: W.W. Norton & Company, 1969), 98.

30. Harold Blumer, *Symbolic Interactionism: Perspective and Method* (Berkeley, CA: University of California Press, 1986).

31. Joseph Montville, "Justice and the Burdens of History," in *Reconciliation, Justice, and Coexistence*, edited by M. Abu Nimer (Lanham, MD: Lexington Books, 2001), 133.

32. Joseph Montville, "Justice and the Burdens of History," 2001, op. cit., 133.

33. Francesca Polletta, *It Was Like a Fever*, 2006, op. cit., xvii–ix.

34. John Paul Lederach, *Preparing for Peace*, 1995, op. cit., 82.

35. Erik Erikson, *Gandhi's Truth*, 1969, op. cit., 98.

36. Audrey Lorde, *A Burst of Light and Other Essays* (Garden City, NY: Dover Publications, 2024).

37. John Byrum, *The Razor's Edge: The Story of One Man's Search for Himself* (Columbia Pictures, 1984). This film is an adaptation of a 1944 novel by W. Somerset Maugham.

38. I. William Zartman, "The Strategy of Preventive Diplomacy in Third World Conflicts," in *Managing US-Soviet Rivalry*, edited by Alexander George (Boston: Westview Press, 1983) See also: https://www.beyondintractability.org /essay/ripeness by William Zartman, accessed February 13, 2024.

39. Edward Azar, "The theory of protracted social conflict and the challenge of transforming conflict situations," in *Conflict Processes and the Breakdown of International Systems*, edited by D. A. Zinnes (Denver, CO: Graduate School of International Systems, University of Denver, 1984), 81–99.

40. J. Rinker and J. Lawler, "Trauma as a collective disease and root cause of protracted social conflict." *Peace and Conflict: Journal of Peace Psychology* 24, no. 2 (2018): 150–64, accessed http://dx.doi.org/10.1037/pac0000311.

AFTERWORD

Traumatic Story as Developing Practices of Resistance *and* Resilience to Socially Constructed Borders

A s I am completing the writing of this practitioners' guide, I am teaching a new graduate-level course I created called "Borders, Partitions, and Other Generative Conflict Narratives" at my university. This has afforded me a new angle from which to think about trauma-aware and emotionally mindful conflict practice in the context of borders (physical and constructed social identities) and their connection to ongoing processes of decolonization. Many from partitioned India would like to put history behind them and act as if the violence of partition was only a result of British colonial rule. While colonial history is an important variable in the South Asian partition experience, it is not simply either colonization or decolonization that explains this history and lasting collective trauma that stems from the birth of the world's largest democracy. Social hierarchies, built over millennia, cannot be fully understood by histories of colonial occupation. Still, triggering events and "chosen traumas"[1] are important touchstones for trauma-informed and emotionally mindful conflict intervention processes. Failure to take these past events into account leaves open opportunities for identity groups to use them to mobilize resistance to change and/or the creation of exclusive identities. Desire to avoid them for fear of communal resurgence is ill conceived and though it may seem to keep the peace may be more potentially problematic for the realization of long-term peace and reconciliation.

Much has been written about decolonization since the killing of George Floyd in May 2020 during the height of the coronavirus pandemic. The destabilizing shifts in thinking and practice that this time-period unfastened led many to question the assumed foundations of our knowledge and practice in many occupations and fields of study. In the field of peace and conflict studies there were renewed calls for decolonization processes because of the context of awakening in the summer of 2020.[2] While the discipline of Peace and Conflict Studies has always centered on justice, and, at least, given lip-service to processes that de-center hierarchies and historical genealogies of power, much work on decolonization of the discipline remains to be done. I hope this guide has provided a trauma-informed lens to assist in this ongoing process. Decolonization processes take time and vigilant commitment. I see trauma-informed and emotionally mindful conflict practice as a key means of productively forwarding this decolonization process, and like the decolonization of countries like India, changing to a trauma-informed and emotionally mindful mindset takes time and expends collective social and emotional capital over generations.

Borders provide an understanding of the spatiality of division and difference, but also a lens through which to assess and explain the historical behaviors of conflict parties over time. A lens that explores the world through borders is, in other words, responsive to both time and space. This temporality and spatiality represent a foundation for the type of practice I have been arguing for in this practitioner's guide. Borders imply a placed-based and context-specific focus, as well as an appreciation of the emotional impacts of memory and time on "human security." Such a spatial and temporal focus is required in both decolonization and trauma-aware conflict practices. Challenging us to be emotionally mindful at every moment, these practices are heavy and laden with traps and snares. In returning one last time to the socio-political context of modern India, the final story I want to tell in this afterword is a story of the evolution of narrative identities over time and their ongoing traumatic legacy within the borders of the Indian polity. While the reader may wonder why my examples in this guide so often return to India, I believe it is through modern India that we can see so many of the complexities of diversity and inclusion playing out in real time and space, often and unfortunately with deadly consequences. India's diversity surpasses even that of the United States. The centuries-long story of the Babri Masjid in Ayodhya, Uttar Pradesh is a history of continual erasure and construction of identity, citizenship, and nationalist borders, or boundaries, between people. I tell it briefly here as a contemporary conflict context illustrative of the power of emotions and trauma in conflict generation and perpetuation. It is, of course, not the only contemporary context in which historical trauma clearly manifests in contemporary violence, but it provides a clear articulation of the dire need for the trauma-informed and emotionally mindful conflict practices outlined in this practitioners' guide.

No doubt that the killing of George Floyd, or the controversy over confederate statues in the United States, could act as similar illustrations of the importance of these conflict transformation practices, but due to sheer population numbers the death toll and consequences of communalism sparked by Ayodhya seems of another scale altogether. As readers in the United States are more familiar with these more local contemporary contexts, I ask, as I take you back to contemporary India one last time, that you keep these local contexts close at hand. I take the reader to India as I think its contemporary context lays bare what Isabelle Wilkerson calls "the bones"[3] of systems of hierarchy and domination at work around the world, including here in the United States. These systems of oppression are critical borders to interrogate, and the social hierarchies these systems create are universal, although they manifest differently in different locales. Revivalist histories exist around the world, but it is in overcoming these systems of oppression in which the true work of decolonization lies. I engage these complex hierarchies via India, as to me this is the oldest and clearest expression of these socially constructed hierarchies and, thus, represents the most direct and effective context of oppression from which to break such conflict generative borders. While for Americans, India conjures images of Gandhian nonviolence and pluralistic peace, the reality on the ground is much different. Hindu-Muslim communalism, and caste hierarchies, are not only a past context of collective trauma, but these socially constructed identity borders and hierarchies are alive and violently active in contemporary India's national mindset. Social actors in India use these past traumas to call for the revival of past assumed glories of a society, often by focusing on distant historical "chosen traumas."[4] The centuries-long controversy over the Babri Masjid illustrates well the evolution and hardening of majoritarian othering narratives across both time and the space of the subcontinent. It also shows us a way forward towards peace and reconciliation if we are not afraid to engage both trauma and emotions.

BEING EMOTIONALLY MINDFUL AND TRANSFORMING COLLECTIVE HISTORICAL TRAUMA: THE BABRI MASJID CONTROVERSY

On December 6, 1992, a large Hindu mob converged on a fourteenth century mosque named the Babri Masjid in the Northern Indian State of Uttar Pradesh and pulled it apart brick by brick with crude handheld implements and their bare hands. This was not the opening salvo of this conflict, nor was it the culmination or victory of Hindus over Muslims in India, even if this is how it felt to many elated Hindu nationalists. The conflict and "transgenerational transmission"[5] of the trauma of this context, dates to, at least, 1528, when Mir Baqi, a military commander of the Mughal emperor Babur, first constructed the Babri Masjid (mosque). At some point well after construction, local Hindus, upset at Mughal (Muslim) rule, colonization, and domination in India began to clamor that this mosque had been built on the historic site of the birth of the Hindu god Ram. The only existent evidence as to when this argument was first made comes in the British colonial era. Despite accounts in the ancient epic Sanskrit literature of the *Ramayana* that Ayodhya was the birthplace of the Hindu lord Ram, the first accounts of the claim that the Babri Masjid was the exact birthplace site of Ram in Ayodhya surfaced only in 1858.[6]

Regardless of any historical evidence of Ram's earthly biography, the story that the exact spot of his birth was the location of the Babri Masjid took hold in the late 1800s as nationalist sentiments grew in support of expelling the new colonial rulers, the British Raj. Time and context matter greatly in the development of this story; frustrations over British colonial rule morphed with chosen traumas of past Mughal rule of the Indian subcontinent, merging to develop a confluence of Hindu majoritarian sense of historical slight. As calls to free India from the British Raj intensified, calls for liberating the Babri Masjid from previous Muslim colonizers also grew. This period represents an important revival and reinvention of Hindu religious identity. Aspiring nationalism and a desire to see Hinduism returned to an assumed ancient greatness became a confluence with anti-British and anti-Muslim sentiment. Thus, the Babri Masjid controversy grew as a chosen trauma for

Hindu majority India; a sort of cause celeb particularly for those that felt Hindus had endured centuries of occupation and "dignity threats"[7] by outside occupiers. Regardless of the veracity of these claims, the emotional transference of multiple traumas to this site is clear. In 1949, soon after India's independence from Britain and simultaneous partition from Pakistan, a local Hindu priest, in the dead of night, placed a Ram idol inside the mosque and claimed divine intervention. From that time forward there has been legal contestation between Hindus and Muslims over the land and control of this contested religious space. Hindu activists from the "Ramjanmabhoomi movement" have argued for Hindu control of the Babri Masjid site—a narrative of contestation that has had more to do with the erasure of past Muslim rule in India than the facts of a historical Ram's birth. The earliest reference to Ayodhya in Valmiki's Ramayana, an epic Sanskrit poem of religious literature, makes reference to the fact that Rama (Ram) rules as King of Ayodhya and soon after the poet Valmiki is asked to "use your discovery to tell Rama's story, and your verses will defeat Time."[8] References to his place of birth do little more than locate it in the city of Ayodhya and archaeological evidence of Ram's true existence is much weaker than the evidence for Jesus Christ. But even if we put aside arguments about whether Ram was an actual person, or fictitious character made into a God, the contested story and sense of dignity violation developed by nationalist Hindu forces in the late 1800s and early 1900s trapped believers into a collective discursive belief that Hindus had too long been subjugated by external rulers, and that Ram Raj—or Rama's perfect kingdom—as an ideal Hindu kingdom of the past, should be rebuilt.

After almost two decades of legal maneuvers from both Hindu and Muslim religious leaders culminated on November 9, 2019, when the Indian Supreme Court ruled unanimously that even though the placing of an idol in 1949 was "an act of desecration" and the 1992 demolition was "illegal," nevertheless the site should be managed by a majoritarian Hindu trust.[9] Like the 1992 destruction of the Babri Masjid, this ruling sparked communal unrest. Although less violent than in 1992, the 2019 ruling established a new chosen trauma for Muslims and marked a triumphant chosen glory for Hindu nationalist forces. Many tensions remain unaddressed. Quoting for the over 900-page Supreme Court judgment:

> For a case replete with references to archaeological foundations, we must remember that it is the law which provides the edifice upon which our

multicultural society rests. At the heart of the Constitution is a commitment to equality upheld and enforced by the rule of law. Under our Constitution, citizens of all faiths, beliefs and creeds seeking divine provenance are both subject to the law and equality before the law. The Constitution does not make a distinction between the faith and belief of one religion and another. All forms of belief, worship and prayer are equal.[10]

Despite the judgment's many calls for upholding India's multicultural society and equality of all faith traditions, the verdict did little to assuage many people's fears of the verdict as the end of India's secular democratic pluralism. To this day communal religious tensions between Hindus and Muslims are high and Ayodhya represents a context of collective trauma for both communities fast in their belief that the Babri Masjid is a sacred site for competing archaeological reasons.

But what does this contestation really have to do with historical trauma? What evidence do we have of the meaning of these stories of indigeneity and competing claims to contested space? Time and context are critical factors that can help us understand the underlying meaning and intentions of these claims of contested space. Going back to the mosque's destruction in 1992 we see that this was done on December 6. This date is not unimportant to several marginalized populations of India as it is the death date of the revered social reformer, Dr. B. R. Ambedkar. Even if the claims of Hindu nationalists and Hindutva (Hindu-right) forces that organized the rally to Ayodhya in December 1992 were aimed at Muslim "others" in a newly envisioned Hindu polity, December 6, as the death date of B. R. Ambedkar, father of Indian's constitution and leader of the former untouchables, signals, to many, a wider Hindu attack on all non-Hindu Indians. Such choice and timing of the Babri Masjid attack is no coincidence, but rather a calculated symbolic move to lump non-Hindu identifying Indians together with all anti-national forces of resistance. It is a move to alienate and make an exclusive claim to Hindu rule and citizenship. Ayodhya symbolically marks the start of majoritarian rule in a previously secular and multicultural Indian democracy. Together Muslims, Ambedkar Dalits, and all those considered outside the Hindu fold, can then be exposed as non-citizens, alien invaders, and not deserving of the rights and responsibilities of state citizenship. In short, the visible attack on the Barbi Masjid, and the pogroms against Muslims that followed, were only an outward expression of more implicit and symbolic attacks on lower caste and other undesirable marginals in newly majoritarian and exclusivist Hindu Indian society.

Low-castes and Dalits were the target of an invisible attack in this context, one might, indeed, label this what Cobb (2013) calls "narrative violence."[11] Calling for, and engaging in, the destruction of the Babri Masjid on December 6 is an attempt to erase the history of Indian constitutionalism and replace it with Ram devotionalism, which cannot be seen as separate from either Hindutva (national devotionalism to India as a Hindu nation) or furtherance of caste hierarchies enshrined in Hindu scriptures. Religion, hierarchy, and nationalism are all a single thread in this revivalist conflict. Such narrative violence leaves marginalized minorities in a "state of exception,"[12] isolated and living as broken in relation to the public and political sphere. Dalits (broken people) are, therefore, an auxiliary target of the Ayodhya controversy with Muslims being the public face of the other. While Muslims and Hindu's collective historical trauma of Muslim rule of India, are the primary target of Hindutva activism over the Babri Masjid, other marginal communities are sucked into the vortex of this movement as anti-national or lesser citizens. Such narrative violence is both calculated and has been extremely effective in othering India's minorities and foregrounding India's dominant Hindu Brahminical culture as the norm in society. Just like language and norms implicitly support "white culture" in North America, discourse about freeing Ayodhya implicitly further Brahminical Hindu culture and interests in South Asia.

With modern India being ruled by the Hindu-right Bharatiya Janata Party (BJP), resistance to the construction of a Ram temple on the Babri Masjid site has been limited. Fear of violent reprisals have severely limited minorities' freedom to respond. Furthermore, despite Hindu religious leaders arguing that the January 22, 2024, inauguration of the temple and installation of the Ram Lalla idol was not done on an auspicious time based on the Hindu calendar, the January 22 event was not without its own symbolic controversy. That the January 22 date and the 10-day ritual purification period that Narendra Modi, current BJP prime minister of India, preformed in preparation for the Ram temple inauguration fell between India's constitution day (November 26) and republic day (January 26), a traditionally auspicious, though secular period in the modern Indian polity's calendar, was also no coincidence. This context was not lost on Dalit anti-caste activists and other minority groups. This period between the adoption of the Indian constitution

(November 26) and the commemoration of the constitution's adoption and official transition to an Indian constitutional republic (January 26) is an auspicious and celebratory time for Ambedkar Buddhists and other Ambedkar followers, who value B. R. Ambedkar as the father of the Indian constitution. The choice of this period was strategic and political, placing the BJP as the heir apparent to the culmination of a Ram Raj (conceived of as an ancient period of peaceful Hindu rule of India as described in the epic Sanskrit literature of the *Ramayana*). For left-leaning Indians of all stripes, the construction of a Ram temple on the site of the Babri Masjid signals the end of multicultural democracy; for right-leaning Hindus it signals the resilience and solidification of Hindu return to power in the Indian subcontinent after years of humiliating colonization and foreign rule. Even though the temple construction is incomplete, and the temple is only projected to open to the public in August 2024, Modi and the BJP pressed on with this symbolic message as an inauguration of not only the temple but also Modi's 2024 campaign for reelection as India's prime minister.

What can this convoluted story of the attack on India's democratic foundations and history of religious pluralism tell us about trauma-informed and emotionally mindful conflict practice? What does such a politically charged story of historical revival and patronage tell us as practitioners eager to understand historical trauma and build resilience? For one, it is yet another example of how stories, or narratives, matter greatly. Narratives create subject positions which can act to create and define imagined borders between socially constructed identities. Narrative, or stories, regardless of historical fact, mobilize identity groups to fight, sometimes violently, for social and cultural change. Whether these identities are socially avowed, ascribed, or achieved matters little in the face of the power of effectively deployed narratives. Powerful forces can strategically ascribe identity through well deployed narratives and revivalist renderings of history, as in the case in Modi's use of the narrative of the creation of the Ayodhya Ram temple. This narrative rallied Hindu-centric forces in great preparation of the temple inauguration. BJP mobilization called for the entire nation to preform collectively purification rituals, along with Prime Minister Modi, in preparation for the temple inauguration. Many Indians raised the Hindu flag outside their homes and preformed the ten-day purification rituals alongside their prime minister. Narendra Modi, as the instantiation of Lord Ram on earth, then consecrated the temple on January 22,

2024. While Chinese history is replete with stories of the emperor being imbued with the divine right to lead, known as the mandate of heaven, India, until recently, had no similar religious tradition. Chinese historical accounts of the mandate of heaven expose an unquestioned certainty in the emperor's divinity. Placing Narendra Modi as divine ruler or Godhead has less historical precedent but is equally a political move to affirm power in an historical third term as Prime Minister. While the implications for secular democracy in India remain to be known, this consecration of the Ram temple in Ayodhya and its disregard for any residual sense of collective historical trauma seems clear. Symbolically and intentionally the Ayodhya story fulfills deeply held majoritarian goals and elides minorities' collective historical traumas. The result is a place where emotions are not allowed, and trauma is ignored; "a place that defies narrative itself."[13] For conflict resolution practitioners such a place is central to the work of trauma-informed and emotionally mindful conflict transformation. This place is necessary to visit if lasting peace is desired.

Resistance and resilience in the face of ignored historical trauma and outbursts of emotional expression requires firm footing and the bravery to speak truth to power. As conflict resolution practitioners this means challenging victims as much as it means resisting oppressors. Narrative constructions require collective acceptance of subject positions as both victims and perpetrators. Therefore, the stories that foreground the ambiguity of hierarchy and conflict in victim narratives are important tools in the work of trauma-informed and emotionally aware conflict practice. Resilience entails retelling stories to make meaning that helps minoritized parties to mean effectively. Resistance is calling in historical traumas to contest historical reconstructions aimed at maintaining elite or dominant interests. This is not a calling out of bad actors, but a calling in to alternative narratives of political elites. This is contested political terrain for sure, but to sit outside this terrain is to cede your voice to the interest of powerful forces that are sometimes in the majority and sometime just the loudest. One need not look too far to see this dynamic at play politically in the modern culture wars in the United States. Current U.S. government gridlock over immigration policy is tied up in comparable narratives of exclusive conceptions of nationalism and citizenship. Beyond American exceptionalism these jingoistic narratives, left unchecked, do immense work of polarization. In such a context the loudest narrative of evil by others victimizing American citizens is deployed to masterful effect. Resistance and resilience to such victim narratives must be grounded in clearly articulating past trauma and foregrounding emotional awareness about the harm these traumas have caused. Progressives have struggled to fashion such effective narratives. Failure to engage on the level of trauma and emotion leaves space for collective historical traumas to grow and metastasize like a cancer in society. Trauma-informed and emotionally aware conflict practice are a bulwark against the spread of collective historical violence and its attenuate anti-social destruction.

KNOWING CONTEXT, SPACE, AND TIME: PRACTICING TRAUMA-AWARE AND EMOTIONALLY MINDFUL INTERVENTION

So, back to how to guide practitioners on the effective response to the politics of fear and victimization. As I argued in chapter 1, expanded identity awareness opens new avenues for resisting dominate powers in society. Challenges to victimization narratives require close analytical reflection of received narrative tropes, cultural meanings, and situational context, as well as an understanding of, and ability to challenge, received dominant narratives. This work is not for the faint of heart; it requires humility and a willingness to be vulnerable. It is also true that if I had a straightforward and foolproof method for how to engage with the politics of victimization and fear, I would be a well-paid political consultant instead of an academic practitioner writing this guide. While we are all both victims and perpetrators in a complex cosmic dance, we can and must look past simple rationality and punitive responses to deal with injustice. We must explore emotional reactions to real trauma to develop the space and resilience to reverse the long durée of collective historical trauma and transform protracted conflict. Past traumas live in the body and stories told about them "are rarely the total control of speakers; this is particularly obvious when considering that 'told' narratives live beyond any immediate interaction because they circulate and reverberate in social networks."[14] Given this inability to completely control the evolution of narrative careful response to victimization and fear is critical for practitioners. Self-reflection, moral leadership, and mindful alignment of virtues and values is necessary to deal with this narrative ambiguity and variability.

The trauma-informed practitioner must be attentive to how our ideal types solidify and reify social positions, limit reflexivity, and challenge individual agency in conflict. Such attentive awareness is the first step to being emotionally mindful and trauma-informed. It does not mean that victims' stories are irrelevant, but rather that they must be understood within specific space, context, and time. Victim narratives matter greatly, and they must be privileged in ways that do not mask intention or attempt to merely solve problems. Trauma informed and emotionally mindful practitioners must set the problem by not over-privileging victims at the expense of perpetrators—this is how cycles of violence are maintained and perpetuate (remember the STAR snail model, figure I.1, introduced in the book's introduction). Reflectively setting the problem, as opposed to rushing to solve the problem, requires a newfound acceptance of emotions as important drivers of reason and rational choice. It also requires a willingness to sit with evil, to not dehumanize it, and to not psychologically displace it. It is too easy as conflict intervention practitioners to displace the trauma and psychological suffering of conflict parties by reverting to rational interests or mistaking individual traumas experience as collective acceptance of past narratives. Pumla Gobodo-Madikizela calls this process the "psychological mechanism . . . [of] . . . splitting"[15] as she describes her interviews with Eugene De Kock, South Africans' expression of the "prime evil" of police extrajudicial murder of black South Africans during the apartheid regime. By being proximate to suffering trauma-informed and emotionally mindful conflict practitioners can, and must, invoke psychological reflexivity and self-reflection as they work to resist evil, build resilience, and not shy away from moral groundings in justice. As I have said, this is a fraught social, psychological, and political space, and working through it takes time. Unfortunately, our dominant conceptions of practice do not always allow the time for this important work. "Time is money" as the capitalist in the United States oft say. But any good work does not get done with speed. Deliberate change requires deliberative and often time-consuming thought, reflection, and engagement. No silver bullet can be given to handle such deeply personal, emotional, and traumatic episodes of conflict, but humble awareness and radical empathy that all have experienced various levels of harm is an important beginning of lasting conflict intervention. Mindfulness is in one sense having spatial, temporal, and contextual awareness of conflict parties

lived experience. Such mindful awareness is at the root of the practices
I have been trying to foreground in the *Practitioners' Guide to Trauma-
Informed and Emotionally Mindful Conflict Practice.*

PARTING PEACE DOTS (NOT BULLET POINTS)

A quaker friend often talks of peace dots as opposed to bullet points
when he articulates a list. This is an important reminder of the power of
words, not even fully formed stories, to construct our collective reality
and perceptions of the world. Taking note of the martial language we use
in many walks of life can illuminate how we collectively see the world
from the vantage point of a particular culture. We often speak in the
idiom of war by saying things like: "attacking an issue" or "getting in the
trenches" of a difficult problem. These are examples of war-centered language that can be hard to root out of our cultural assumptions about conflict, war, and conflict resolution. If we want to develop a more peaceful
world, resisting martial language is one form of personal resistance and
resilience. Quaker religious tradition has fostered this in their collective
emphasis on the use of language, consensus, and discernment in their
spiritual process. As with any change, a trauma-informed, and emotionally mindful shift of conflict practice certainly starts with words. So, I end
this guide with a few peace dots (not bullet points) aimed at reminding
readers of some key takeaways from this practitioner's guide. The following list may not be exhaustive, but it is aimed at being appreciative:[16]

- Social actors can simultaneously think rationally and emotionally;
- Emotions and trauma are heavy and difficult to handle in conflict
  practice, but this does not mean practitioners should shy away
  from them;
- Fear is an emotional response to stimuli and, if embraced, as opposed
  to avoided, holds great potential for individual and collective change;
- Effective change agents move towards the most difficult subjects,
  not away from them;
- In an assets-based approach trauma is not a problem to be overcome, but an opportunity to grow and change;
- Dichotomies of victim and perpetrator are rarely useful in conflict
  transformation and should be approach with reflexive skepticism;

- Trauma-informed and emotionally mindful conflict practice is a gerund—e.g., the work is always in process of being done, yet never complete;
- Trauma and emotions are always local, context specific, and have both individual and collective impacts;
- Story (narrative) provides the space and structure to be able to voice grievance and, if used effectively by conflict intervention practitioners, to fashion nonviolent ways to help parties mean effectively;
- If conflict parties mean effectively then others should better understand their positions and interests in conflict;
- Like story, silence is a form of action; as nonviolent practitioners of conflict transformation, we cannot remain silent to injustice or violence, and we can use silence to underscore ambiguity and moments of irony; and
- Collective historical trauma is always an actor in conflict, it may not always make itself apparent, but it is there.

Though far from exhaustive, I hope the above peace dots leave the reader with a sense of the spaces of access to trauma-informed and emotionally mindful conflict transformation practices. Trauma-informed and emotionally mindful practices are creative forms of resistance to unequal power asymmetries. Reminiscent of what former U.S. Representative John Lewis called "good trouble,"[17] these practices are done by what Bayard Rustin called "angelic troublemakers."[18] Given the depth and breadth of trauma in the world, we can get overwhelmed. My goals herein have been not to overwhelm, but rather to point to sustainable change of focus in conflict intervention practice. Focus on the hopeful human growth possibilities that trauma affords, if it is effectively embraced, is not an attempt to see the world with only rose-colored glasses. Rather, it expresses an intentional desire to take an appreciative inquiry approach[19] to complex social change. While the book is not about eradicating trauma, it is about addressing, using, and handling it. I hope, now that readers have come to the end of this guide, they have a better sense of how to heal collective historical trauma one village at a time through narrative practices of empowerment, reflection, and local proximity.

NOTES

1. Vamik Volkan, *Bloodlines*, 1997, op. cit., 48.

2. See Polly Walker's short article in the summer 2020 issue of the *Peace Chronicle* magazine of the Peace and Justice Studies Association. Polly Walker, "Decolonizing Peace Studies: Moving toward Settler Responsibilities for Colonialism" (Summer 2020), found at: https://www.peacejusticestudies.org/chronicle/decolonizing-peace-studies-moving-toward-settler-responsibilities-for-colonialism/, accessed January 21, 2024. Also see: Lisa Schirch's "Decolonizing Peacebuilding: A Way Forward out of Crisis," Toda Peace Institute, Policy Brief 130, June 2020, found at: https://toda.org/assets/files/resources/policy-briefs/t-pb-130_decolonising-peacebuilding_schirch.pdf, accessed January 21, 2024.

3. Isabelle Wilkerson, *Caste: The Origin of Our Discontents*, op. cit., 19. Note that Wilkerson sees caste as the bones, while race is simply the skin of these hierarchies of oppression.

4. Vamik Volkan, *Bloodlines*, 1997, op. cit., 48.

5. Ibid., 43.

6. See: https://www.thehindu.com/news/national/a-timeline-of-the-ram-janmabhoomi-movement-1858-2024/article67730189.ece, accessed February 1, 2024.

7. Donna Hicks, *Dignity: Its Essential Role in Resolving Conflicts* (New Haven: Yale University Press, 2011), 12. Hicks writes: "Dignity threats call up a reaction from our ancient emotion center as if our lives were on the line even when they are not" (12).

8. William Buck, *Ramayana* (Berkeley: University of California Press, 1976), 8.

9. See: https://www.indiatoday.in/india-today-insight/story/from-the-india-today-archives-2019-how-supreme-court-finely-balanced-its-ram-temple-verdict-2491253-2024-01-20, accessed January 28, 2024.

10. Ibid.

11. Sara Cobb, *Speaking of Violence* (2013), op. cit., 27.

12. Agamben, *Homo Sacer: Sovereign Power and Bare Life*. 1st edition (Stanford, CA: Stanford University Press, 1998). Cited in Sara Cobb, *Speaking of Violence* (2013), op. cit., 27.

13. Sara Cobb, *Speaking of Violence* (2013), op. cit., 27.

14. Ibid., 23.

15. Pumla Gobodo-Madikizela, *A Human Being Died That Night: A South African Story of Forgiveness* (New York: Houghton Mifflin Co., 2003), 41.

16. For more on Appreciative Inquiry, a life-giving force for social change, see: Jane Watkins, Bernard Mohr, and Ralph Kelly, *Appreciative Inquiry: Change at the Speed of Imagination*, 2nd edition (New York: Pfeiffer Publishing,

2011). See also: https://www.taosinstitute.net/resources/appreciative-inquiry, accessed February 12, 2024.

17. See: Dawn Porter, *John Lewis: Good Trouble* (1 hour and 36 minute Documentary, 2020) available on Amazon Prime: https://www.amazon.com/John -Lewis-Good-Trouble/dp/B089M54WFD, accessed February 14, 2024.

18. After returning from a conference in India in 1948, Bayard Rustin wrote, "We need, in every community, a group of angelic troublemakers." Though oft credited with this phrase I was unable to find the primary text in which Rustin writes this, but much has been written on this idea. See: https://www.pbs.org /wnet/african-americans-many-rivers-to-cross/history/100-amazing-facts/who -designed-the-march-on-washington/, accessed February 14, 2024, and A. Terrance Wiley, *Angelic Troublemakers: Religion and Anarchism in America* (New York: Bloomsbury, 2014) for more on this idea.

19. See n. 16 above. Rather than a deficit-based approach that focuses on depreciation, appreciative inquiry focuses on an assets-based approach focused on appreciating what works.

INDEX

Ambedkar, B.R., 25n40, 45, 50, 52,
  75-76, 83, 91n34, 97, 110-13, 132,
  143n5, 174, 176
anti-caste activism/t, 20, 100, 125,
  132, 175

Buddhism, 34, 36-37, 75-76, 152, 156
caste: atrocity, 20, 43, 65, 71-76,
  91n35, 110, 112; marginalization,
  20, 32, 100, 102; reservations,
  18, 47; system, 5, 14, 18-19, 29,
  43-44, 77-78, 80-84, 101, 110-11,
  124-26, 171; trauma, 14, 49, 53,
  64, 72, 76, 101, 116-17n32, 125,
  132

conflict: ambiguity, in, 78, 95-97,
  99, 103, 105, 107, 111-14, 132,
  140, 152, 154; management, 2-3,
  6; nested, 70-71, 77, 84; practice,
  3, 7, 9, 16, 35, 39, 43, 54, 64-65,

79, 87, 96, 114, 128-29, 139, 147,
  152-53; resolution, 1-5, 7, 9-10,
  13, 32-33, 38-39, 42-44, 54-55,
  57n28, 62, 64-67, 70-71, 75,
  78-80, 84-87, 97-97, 106-8, 110,
  112-13, 123-24, 127-31, 135, 138,
  141, 147, 149, 151-55, 162, 177,
  180; theory, 3, 5, 9, 35, 39, 43, 64,
  79-80, 96, 114, 125, 128, 132, 152;
  transformation, 19, 21, 23n18, 29,
  33-35, 38-39, 55-56n10, 80, 86-87,
  97, 103, 110, 112, 128-31, 148,
  152, 157, 160, 171, 177, 180-81

Dalit, 13, 16-17, 19-20, 25n40,
  34, 43, 45-48, 51-53, 64, 72-76,
  90-91n34, 97-103, 112, 137,
  158-60, 174-75
DEI. See diversity, equity, and
  inclusion
diversity, equity, and inclusion, 170

emotional awareness, 53-54, 62, 69, 81, 84, 100, 113, 151-53, 156, 165, 178

emotions: conflict, in, 2, 5, 7-10, 13, 17-18, 21, 29, 31-35, 47-48, 70, 84, 99, 109, 131-32, 135, 141, 157, 160, 163-65; intelligence, and, 7, 44, 62, 69, 78, 84, 113, 125, 135, 147, 153, 165

Floyd, George, 14, 83, 85-86, 101, 112, 170-71

hierarchy, 14, 46, 81-82, 98, 111, 116n28, 126, 131, 171, 175, 177

irony, 20, 59n70, 96-97, 99-107, 109, 111-14, 152, 154, 181

justice: identity, and, 38-39, 109; memory, and, 31, 97; politics/power, and, 30, 45, 105, 109, 117n45, 138, 176, 178

Lederach, John Paul, 23n18, 34, 44, 66, 70, 77-78, 86, 127, 138, 158, 162

mean effectively, to, 97-98, 101, 109, 135, 152, 163, 177, 181

mediation, 2-4, 8-9, 24n27, 95, 105, 130-31

micro-aggressions, 44, 46-47, 100, 105, 109, 117n47

mindfulness: Buddhist, 72, 75-76, 152-53, 155-56; emotional, 66, 69, 77, 105, 113, 179

moral imagination/stance, 78-79, 86, 107, 116n23, 127-29, 136, 142

narrative: agency, 5, 34, 38-39, 43, 47, 53-54, 65, 99-100, 109-10,

126, 151; ambiguity, 21, 27n69, 39, 42, 96-97, 99-100, 102-4, 109, 150, 162, 177-78, 181; analysis, 38, 150, 162; ellipsis, 39, 102

Occam's razor, 114, 123, 132, 164
overlapping methodologies, 148-50, 163-64

paradigm shift, 4, 6-7, 34
peacebuilding, 5-6, 8-9, 18, 21, 23n18, 31, 62, 64, 77-78, 107, 110, 123, 128; trauma-informed, 5, 18, 21, 62, 78
peace systems, 34, 40, 56n20, 125
Peace and Conflict Studies (PCS), discipline of, 2-4, 6-9, 13, 21, 40-42, 57n28, 63-64, 84, 89n20, 121, 123, 170, 185
positivist, 3, 7, 21, 33, 38, 161
post-traumatic growth (PTG), 13, 150, 161, 167n28
practitioners' toolbox, 142, 147-48, 153, 161, 163-65
proximate, 5, 44, 77, 86, 148-49, 151, 161, 163, 179

race, 1, 4, 20, 30, 51, 61, 72, 78, 80-81, 83, 92-93n51, 116-17n32, 126, 158, 182n3
racial caste, 80-84
radical empathy, 84, 86-87, 96, 99, 109-10, 113, 115n4, 151, 153, 158
rasa (Sanskrit term), 3-4, 7, 20
reconciliation, 8-9, 16, 55-56n10, 78-80, 83-84, 108, 160-61, 170, 172
reflection, 2, 12, 32, 44, 46, 66, 80, 88n9, 97, 102, 109, 113-14, 122, 128, 133-34, 136, 142, 151, 153-54, 157-58, 160, 163, 178-79, 181
reflexivity, 54, 67, 69, 71, 88n9, 131-32, 151-52, 179

resistance/resilience, 4–5, 7, 13, 20, 30, 33–34, 43–44, 47, 53, 71–72, 76, 86, 96, 101, 103, 109–10, 122–23, 169, 174–75, 177–78, 180–81

Schon, Donald, 3, 6, 31, 79–80, 88n9, 109, 134
social emotional learning (SEL), 3, 66, 89–90n23, 90n24
Strategies for Trauma Awareness and resilience (STAR), 12, 14–15, 64, 179
systems thinking, 26n55, 124

trauma: awareness, 12–13, 15, 38, 44, 54, 71, 76, 84, 96, 105, 113, 152, 156, 178; chosen, 47, 96, 99, 169, 171–73; collective historical, 8–9, 13–14, 17, 25n43, 32, 35, 47, 65, 72, 85, 96, 101, 104, 106, 126, 131, 149, 164, 171–73, 175, 177–78, 181; individual, 7, 9, 13, 15, 32–33, 104–6, 131, 148, 179, 181; sequalae, viii, 15, 32–33,

73, 77, 100, 104, 106, 131, 148; vicarious, 77
trauma-informed: intervention, 1–2, 6, 13, 18, 35, 61, 64–66, 78, 124, 142, 148, 153, 158, 163, 165

Vermula, Rohit, 99–104, 109–10, 112, 116–17n32
victimhood: identity, 17–19, 29, 31, 34–35, 37, 80, 86; narratives, 18, 34–35, 37–38, 43, 54, 86, 112, 150; psychology, 17–21, 35, 47, 53–54, 84, 87, 110, 112, 150, 161–62
violence: direct/personal, 40–43, 159; narrative, 40–43, 55–56n10, 116n23, 126, 175; structural/cultural, 30, 40–43, 71, 80
vulnerability, 31, 34, 48, 53, 86, 151

World Conference Against Racism, Racial Discrimination, Xenophobia, and Related Intolerance (WCAR), 19–20
wicked problem, 123–27, 136

ABOUT THE AUTHOR

Jeremy A. Rinker is an Associate Professor at the University of North Carolina Greensboro (UNCG) where his research has long focused on South Asian communities, untouchability, human rights, and narrative meaning-making in movements for social justice. His works emphasize the skills and practices of nonviolent conflict transformation in justice advocacy and identity formation. He is the author/editor of two books: *Identity, Rights, and Awareness: Anti-Caste Activism in India and the Awakening of Justice through Discursive Practices* (Lanham, MD: Lexington Books, 2018) and *Realizing Nonviolent Resilience: Neoliberalism, Societal Trauma, and Marginalized Voice* (New York: Peter Lang, 2020) He is also currently the Editor-in-Chief of the *Journal of Transdisciplinary Peace Praxis* (*JTPP*). He was previously a Fulbright-Nehru Grantee in India (2013 and 2023) and a Peace Corps volunteer in Kazakhstan (1995–1997). Since the Fall of 2023, Dr. Rinker is Co-chair of UNCG's Department of Peace and Conflict Studies. Jeremy's full biography can be found here: https://www.uncg.edu/employees/jeremy-rinker/.